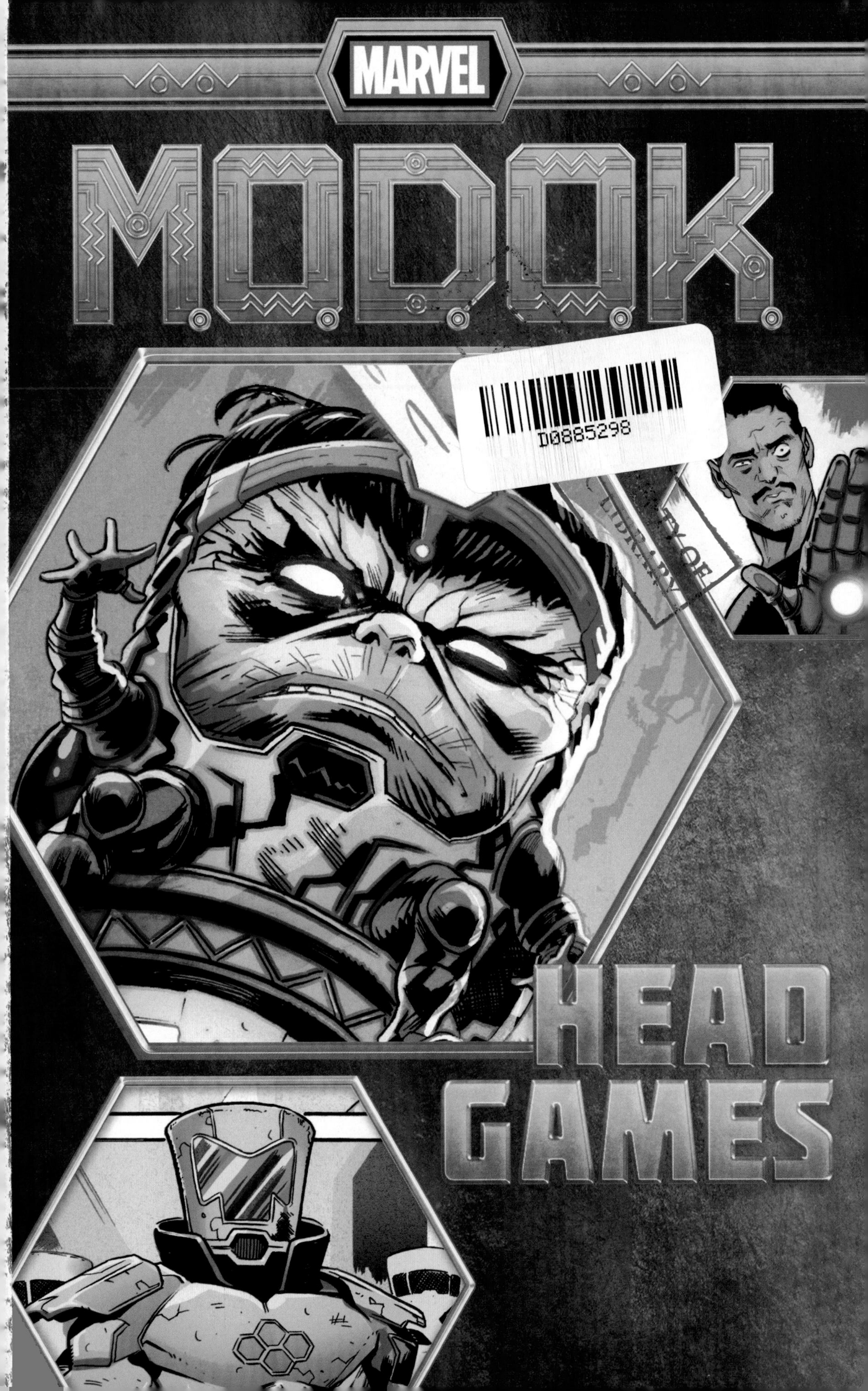
MARVEL
M.O.D.O.K.
HEAD GAMES

...average technician for Advanced Idea Mechanics (A.K.A. A.I.M., an organization of brilliant and morally questionable ... dedicated to amassing power via technological means), George Tarleton ascended beyond puny human limitations on his ...hanks to a series of horrific experiments on him via the Cosmic Cube. The process not only mutated him into a massive-...eing, but also granted him superhuman intelligence and incredible psionic powers--and drove him mad in the process!

Now George has assumed control of A.I.M. under his new identity:

MARVEL

M.O.D.O.K.

HEAD GAMES

JORDAN BLUM & PATTON OSWALT
WRITERS

...OTT HEPBURN — ARTIST
CARLOS LOPEZ — COLORIST
VC's TRAVIS LANHAM — LETTERER

CULLY HAMNER WITH **MIKE SPICER** (#2), **TAMRA BONVILLAIN** (#3) & **CHRIS O'HALLORAN** (#4)
COVER ART

...NALISE BISSA & LAUREN AMARO — ASSISTANT EDITORS
JORDAN D. WHITE — EDITOR
C.B. CEBULSKI — EDITOR IN CHIEF

M.O.D.O.K. CREATED BY **STAN LEE & JACK KIRBY**

JENNIFER GRÜNWALD COLLECTION EDITOR
DANIEL KIRCHHOFFER ASSISTANT EDITOR
MAIA LOY ASSISTANT MANAGING EDITOR
LISA MONTALBANO ASSISTANT MANAGING EDITOR
JEFF YOUNGQUIST VP PRODUCTION & SPECIAL PROJECTS
ADAM DEL RE BOOK DESIGNER
DAVID GABRIEL SVP PRINT, SALES & MARKETING
C.B. CEBULSKI EDITOR IN CHIEF

...EAD GAMES. Contains material originally published in magazine form as M.O.D.O.K.: HEAD GAMES (2020) #1-4, M.O.D.O.K: REIGN DELAY ONE-SHOT (2009) and FALL OF THE HULKS: MODOK DIGITAL (2010). First printing 2021. ISBN 978-1-302-... ...shed by MARVEL WORLDWIDE, INC., a subsidiary of MARVEL ENTERTAINMENT, LLC. OFFICE OF PUBLICATION: 1290 Avenue of the Americas, New York, NY 10104. © 2021 MARVEL No similarity between any of the names, characters, persons, ...ons in this magazine with those of any living or dead person or institution is intended, and any such similarity which may exist is purely coincidental. **Printed in Canada.** KEVIN FEIGE, Chief Creative Officer; DAN BUCKLEY, President, Marvel ... JOE QUESADA, EVP & Creative Director; DAVID BOGART, Associate Publisher & SVP of Talent Affairs; TOM BREVOORT, VP, Executive Editor; NICK LOWE, Executive Editor, VP of Content, Digital Publishing; DAVID GABRIEL, VP of Print & Digital ...F YOUNGQUIST, VP of Production & Special Projects; ALEX MORALES, Director of Publishing Operations; DAN EDINGTON, Managing Editor; RICKEY PURDIN, Director of Talent Relations; JENNIFER GRÜNWALD, Senior Editor, Special Projects; ..., Production Manager; STAN LEE, Chairman Emeritus. For information regarding advertising in Marvel Comics or on Marvel.com, please contact Vit DeBellis, Custom Solutions & Integrated Advertising Manager, at vdebellis@marvel.com. For ...ption inquiries, please call 888-511-5480. **Manufactured between 5/7/2021 and 6/8/2021 by SOLISCO PRINTERS, SCOTT, QC, CANADA.**

3 2 1

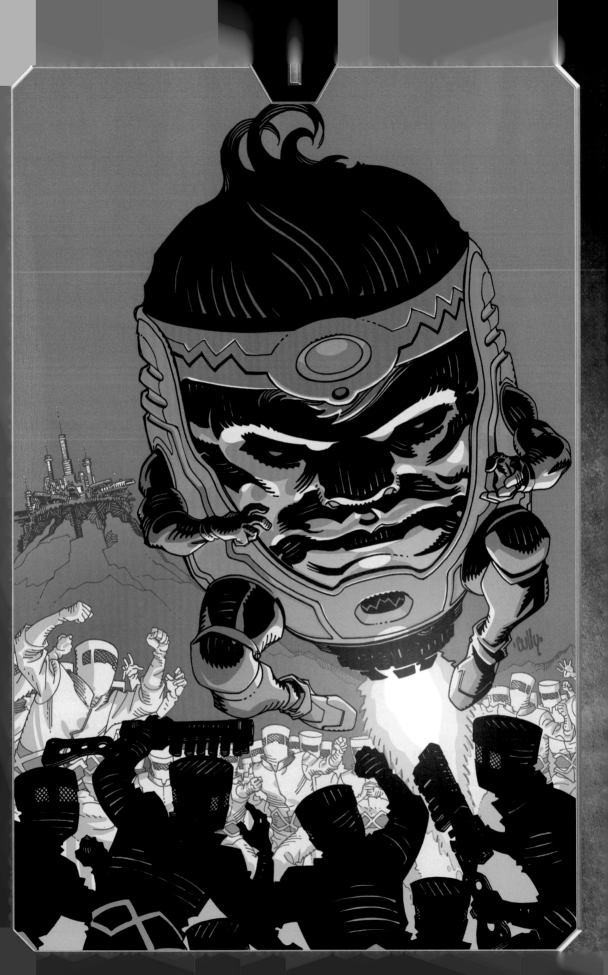

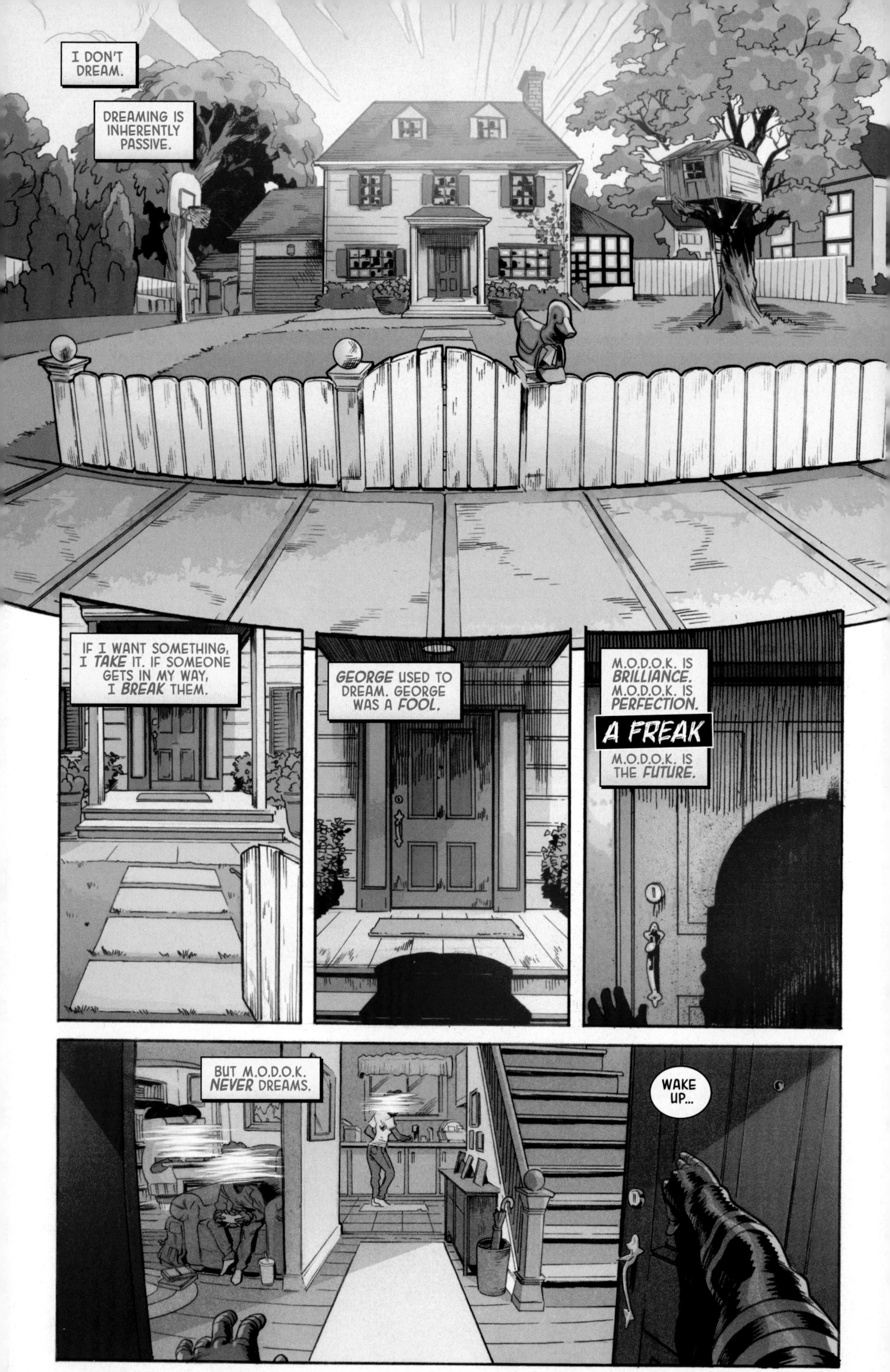
I DON'T DREAM.
DREAMING IS INHERENTLY PASSIVE.
IF I WANT SOMETHING, I TAKE IT. IF SOMEONE GETS IN MY WAY, I BREAK THEM.
GEORGE USED TO DREAM. GEORGE WAS A FOOL.
M.O.D.O.K. IS BRILLIANCE. M.O.D.O.K. IS PERFECTION.
A FREAK
M.O.D.O.K. IS THE FUTURE.
BUT M.O.D.O.K. NEVER DREAMS.
WAKE UP...

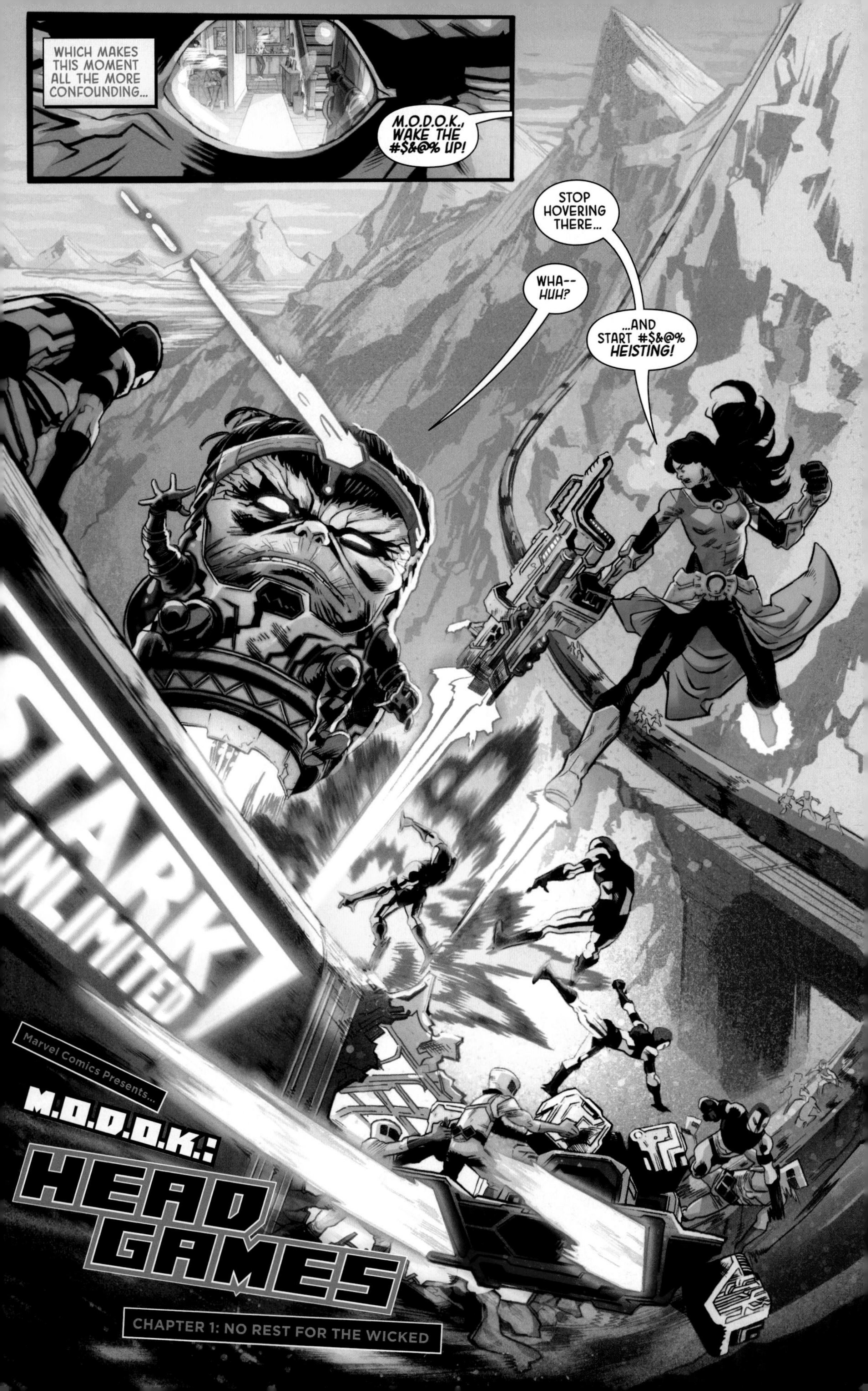
WHICH MAKES THIS MOMENT ALL THE MORE CONFOUNDING...
M.O.D.O.K., WAKE THE #$&@% UP!
STOP HOVERING THERE...
WHA-- HUH?
...AND START #$&@% HEISTING!
STARK UNLIMITED
Marvel Comics Presents...
M.O.D.O.K.:
HEAD GAMES
CHAPTER 1: NO REST FOR THE WICKED

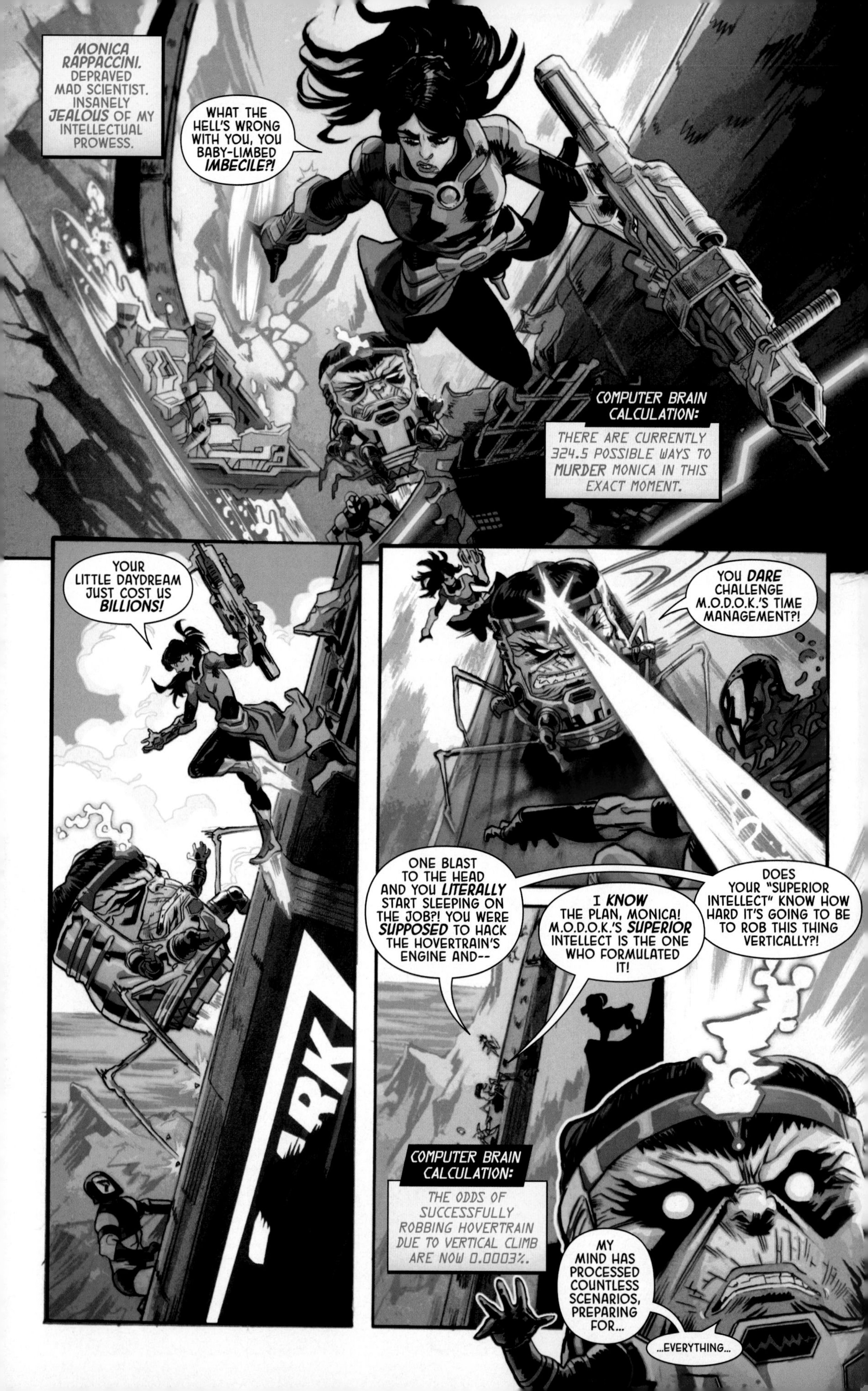
MONICA RAPPACCINI. DEPRAVED MAD SCIENTIST. INSANELY JEALOUS OF MY INTELLECTUAL PROWESS.
WHAT THE HELL'S WRONG WITH YOU, YOU BABY-LIMBED IMBECILE?!
COMPUTER BRAIN CALCULATION:
THERE ARE CURRENTLY 324.5 POSSIBLE WAYS TO MURDER MONICA IN THIS EXACT MOMENT.
YOUR LITTLE DAYDREAM JUST COST US BILLIONS!
YOU DARE CHALLENGE M.O.D.O.K.'S TIME MANAGEMENT?!
ONE BLAST TO THE HEAD AND YOU LITERALLY START SLEEPING ON THE JOB?! YOU WERE SUPPOSED TO HACK THE HOVERTRAIN'S ENGINE AND--
I KNOW THE PLAN, MONICA! M.O.D.O.K.'S SUPERIOR INTELLECT IS THE ONE WHO FORMULATED IT!
DOES YOUR "SUPERIOR INTELLECT" KNOW HOW HARD IT'S GOING TO BE TO ROB THIS THING VERTICALLY?!
COMPUTER BRAIN CALCULATION:
THE ODDS OF SUCCESSFULLY ROBBING HOVERTRAIN DUE TO VERTICAL CLIMB ARE NOW 0.0003%.
MY MIND HAS PROCESSED COUNTLESS SCENARIOS, PREPARING FOR...
...EVERYTHING...

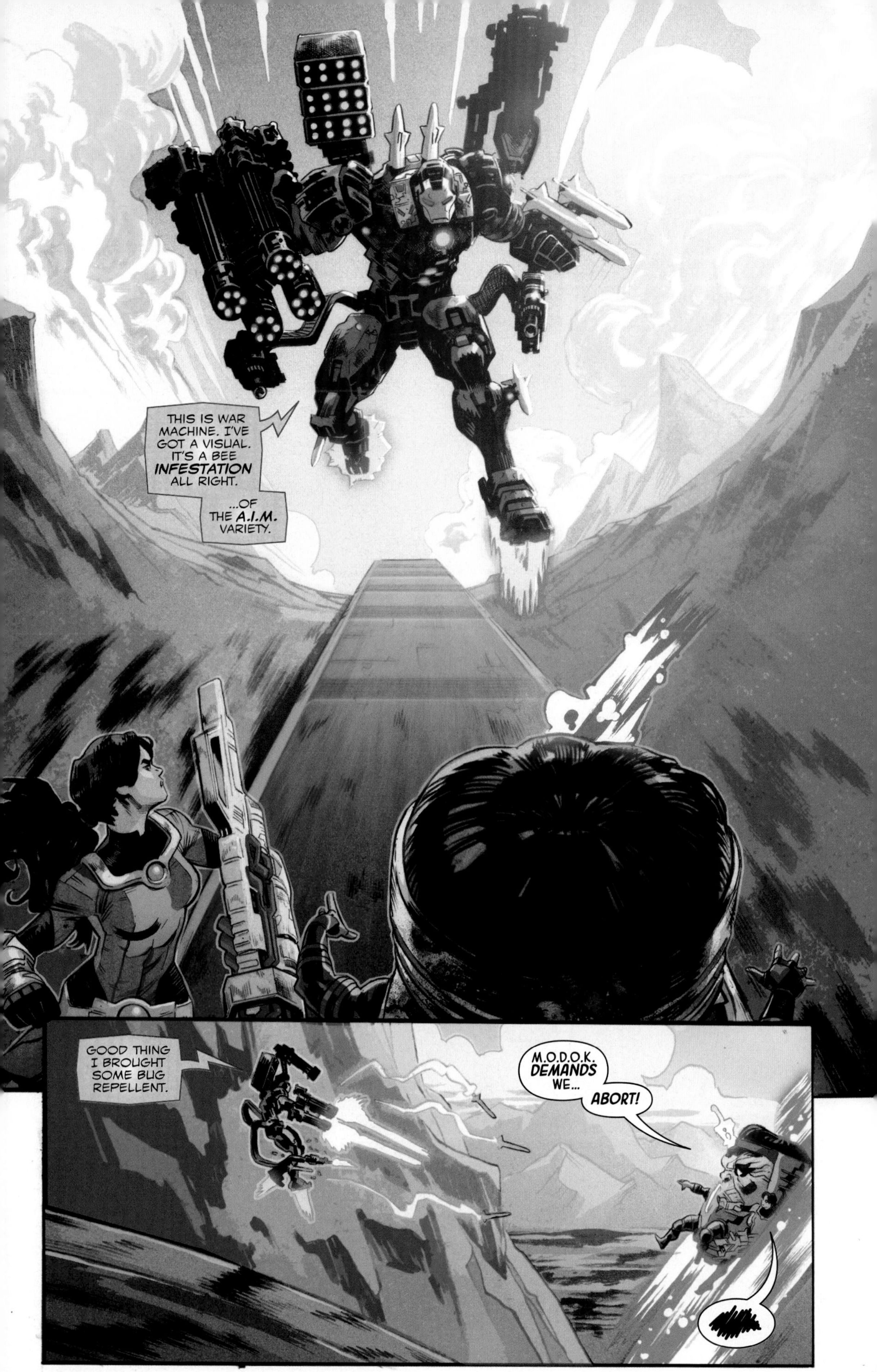
THIS IS WAR MACHINE. I'VE GOT A VISUAL. IT'S A BEE INFESTATION ALL RIGHT.
...OF THE A.I.M. VARIETY.
GOOD THING I BROUGHT SOME BUG REPELLENT.
M.O.D.O.K. DEMANDS WE... ABORT!

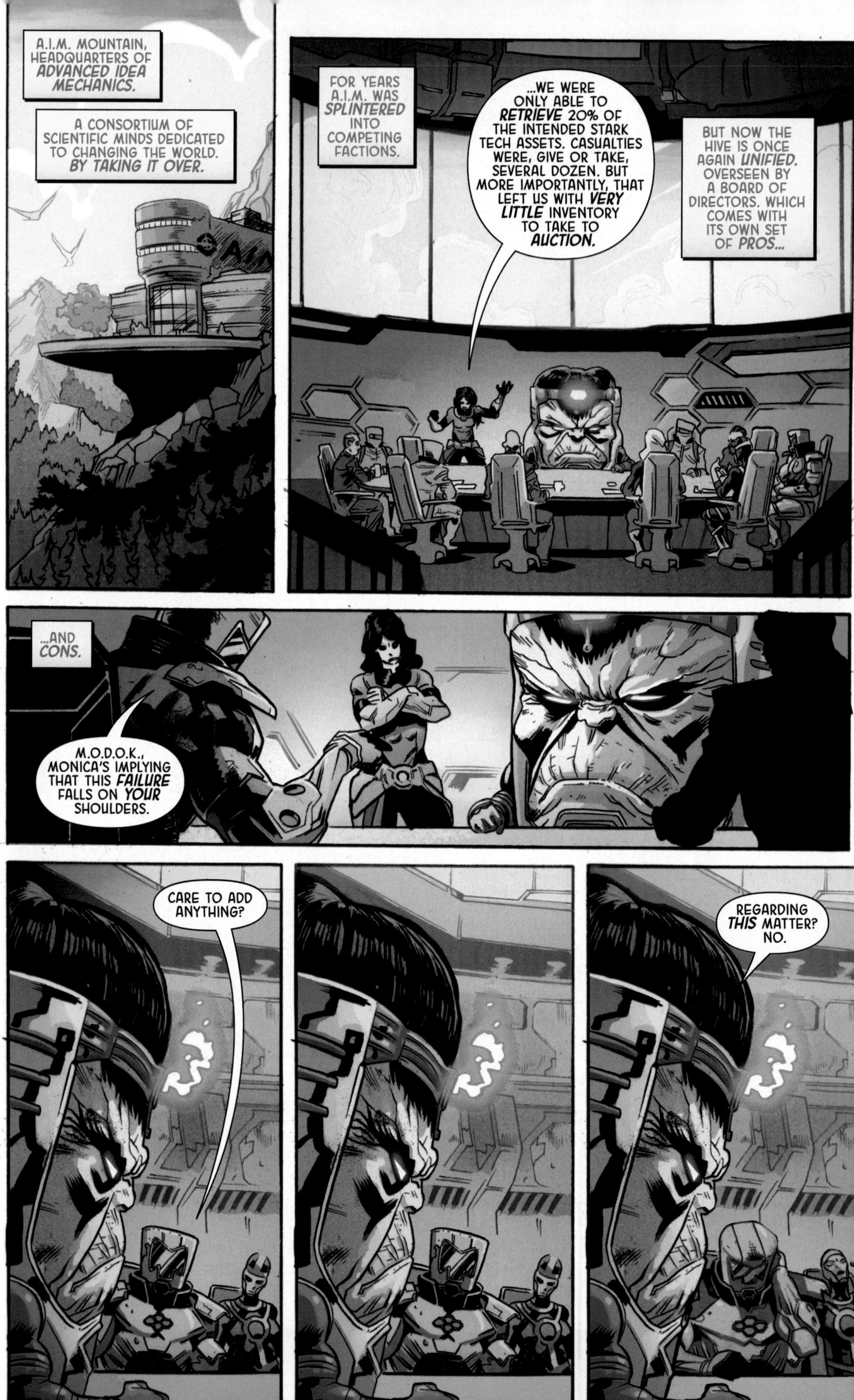
A.I.M. MOUNTAIN, HEADQUARTERS OF ADVANCED IDEA MECHANICS.
A CONSORTIUM OF SCIENTIFIC MINDS DEDICATED TO CHANGING THE WORLD. BY TAKING IT OVER.
FOR YEARS A.I.M. WAS SPLINTERED INTO COMPETING FACTIONS.
...WE WERE ONLY ABLE TO RETRIEVE 20% OF THE INTENDED STARK TECH ASSETS. CASUALTIES WERE, GIVE OR TAKE, SEVERAL DOZEN. BUT MORE IMPORTANTLY, THAT LEFT US WITH VERY LITTLE INVENTORY TO TAKE TO AUCTION.
BUT NOW THE HIVE IS ONCE AGAIN UNIFIED. OVERSEEN BY A BOARD OF DIRECTORS. WHICH COMES WITH ITS OWN SET OF PROS...
...AND CONS.
M.O.D.O.K., MONICA'S IMPLYING THAT THIS FAILURE FALLS ON YOUR SHOULDERS.
CARE TO ADD ANYTHING?
REGARDING THIS MATTER? NO.

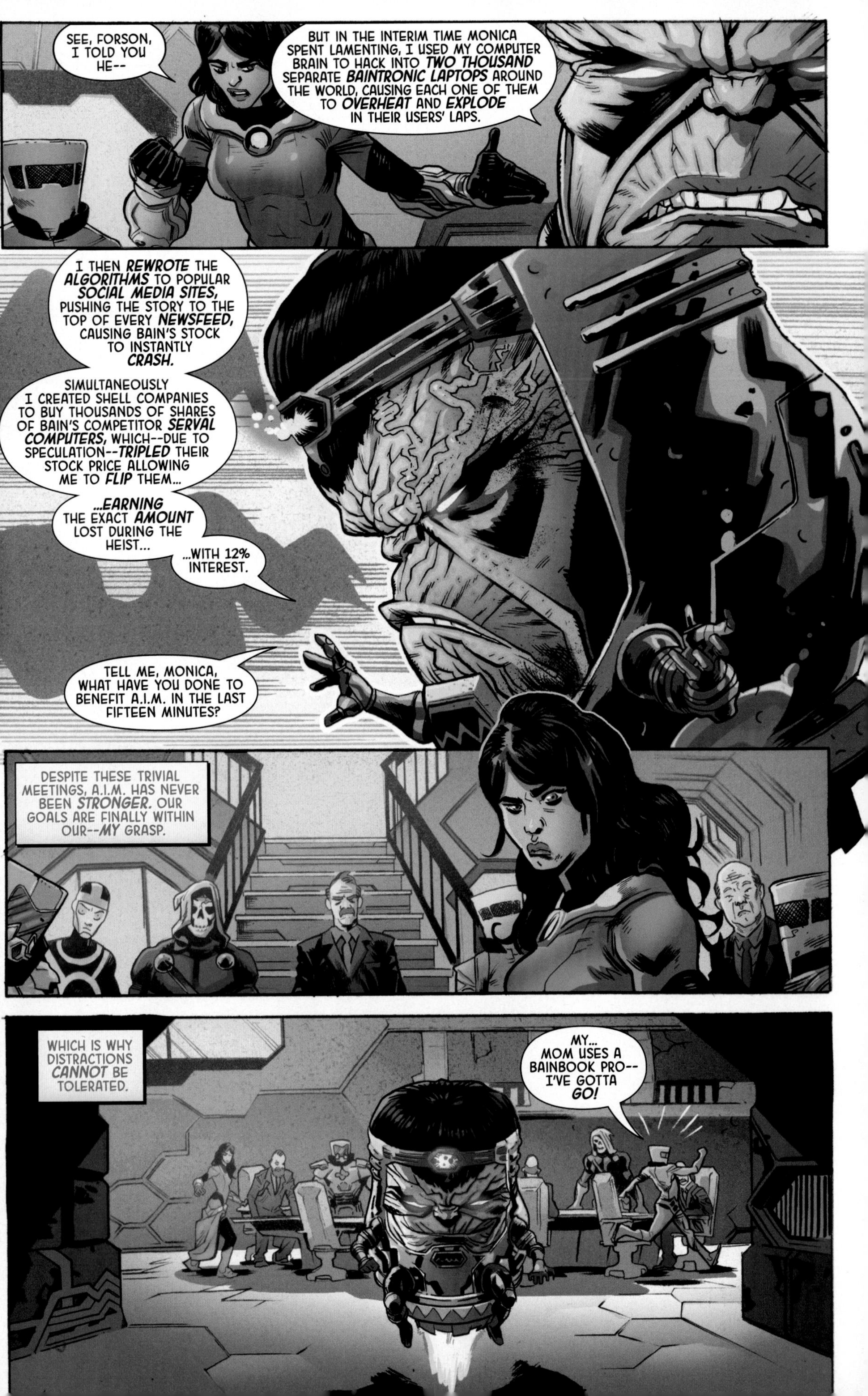

SEE, FORSON, I TOLD YOU HE--
BUT IN THE INTERIM TIME MONICA SPENT LAMENTING, I USED MY COMPUTER BRAIN TO HACK INTO TWO THOUSAND SEPARATE BAINTRONIC LAPTOPS AROUND THE WORLD, CAUSING EACH ONE OF THEM TO OVERHEAT AND EXPLODE IN THEIR USERS' LAPS.
I THEN REWROTE THE ALGORITHMS TO POPULAR SOCIAL MEDIA SITES, PUSHING THE STORY TO THE TOP OF EVERY NEWSFEED, CAUSING BAIN'S STOCK TO INSTANTLY CRASH.
SIMULTANEOUSLY I CREATED SHELL COMPANIES TO BUY THOUSANDS OF SHARES OF BAIN'S COMPETITOR SERVAL COMPUTERS, WHICH--DUE TO SPECULATION--TRIPLED THEIR STOCK PRICE ALLOWING ME TO FLIP THEM...
...EARNING THE EXACT AMOUNT LOST DURING THE HEIST...
...WITH 12% INTEREST.
TELL ME, MONICA, WHAT HAVE YOU DONE TO BENEFIT A.I.M. IN THE LAST FIFTEEN MINUTES?
DESPITE THESE TRIVIAL MEETINGS, A.I.M. HAS NEVER BEEN STRONGER. OUR GOALS ARE FINALLY WITHIN OUR--MY GRASP.
WHICH IS WHY DISTRACTIONS CANNOT BE TOLERATED.
MY... MOM USES A BAINBOOK PRO-- I'VE GOTTA GO!

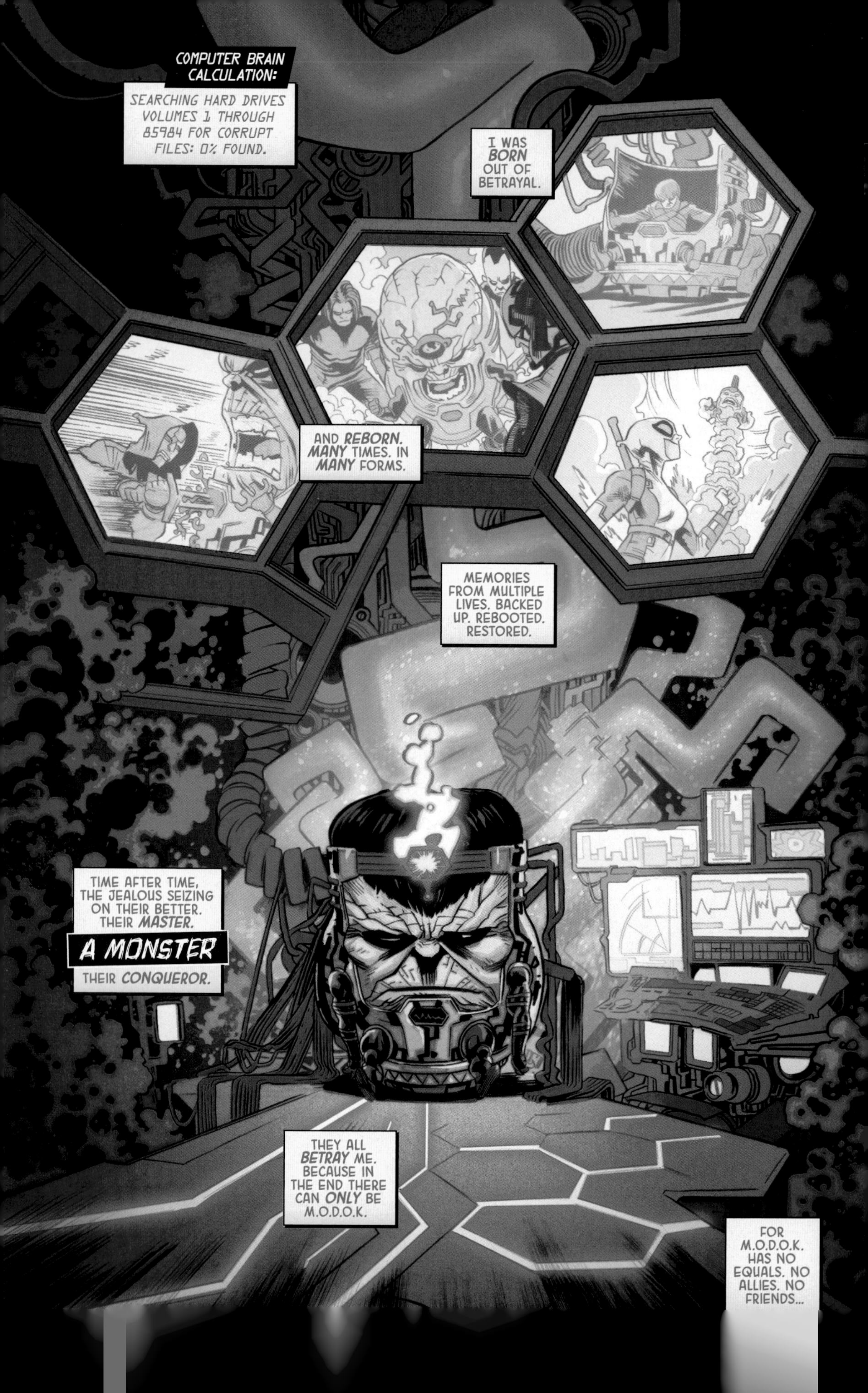
COMPUTER BRAIN CALCULATION:
SEARCHING HARD DRIVES VOLUMES 1 THROUGH 85984 FOR CORRUPT FILES: 0% FOUND.
I WAS BORN OUT OF BETRAYAL.
AND REBORN. MANY TIMES. IN MANY FORMS.
MEMORIES FROM MULTIPLE LIVES. BACKED UP. REBOOTED. RESTORED.
TIME AFTER TIME, THE JEALOUS SEIZING ON THEIR BETTER. THEIR MASTER.
A MONSTER
THEIR CONQUEROR.
THEY ALL BETRAY ME. BECAUSE IN THE END THERE CAN ONLY BE M.O.D.O.K.
FOR M.O.D.O.K. HAS NO EQUALS. NO ALLIES. NO FRIENDS...

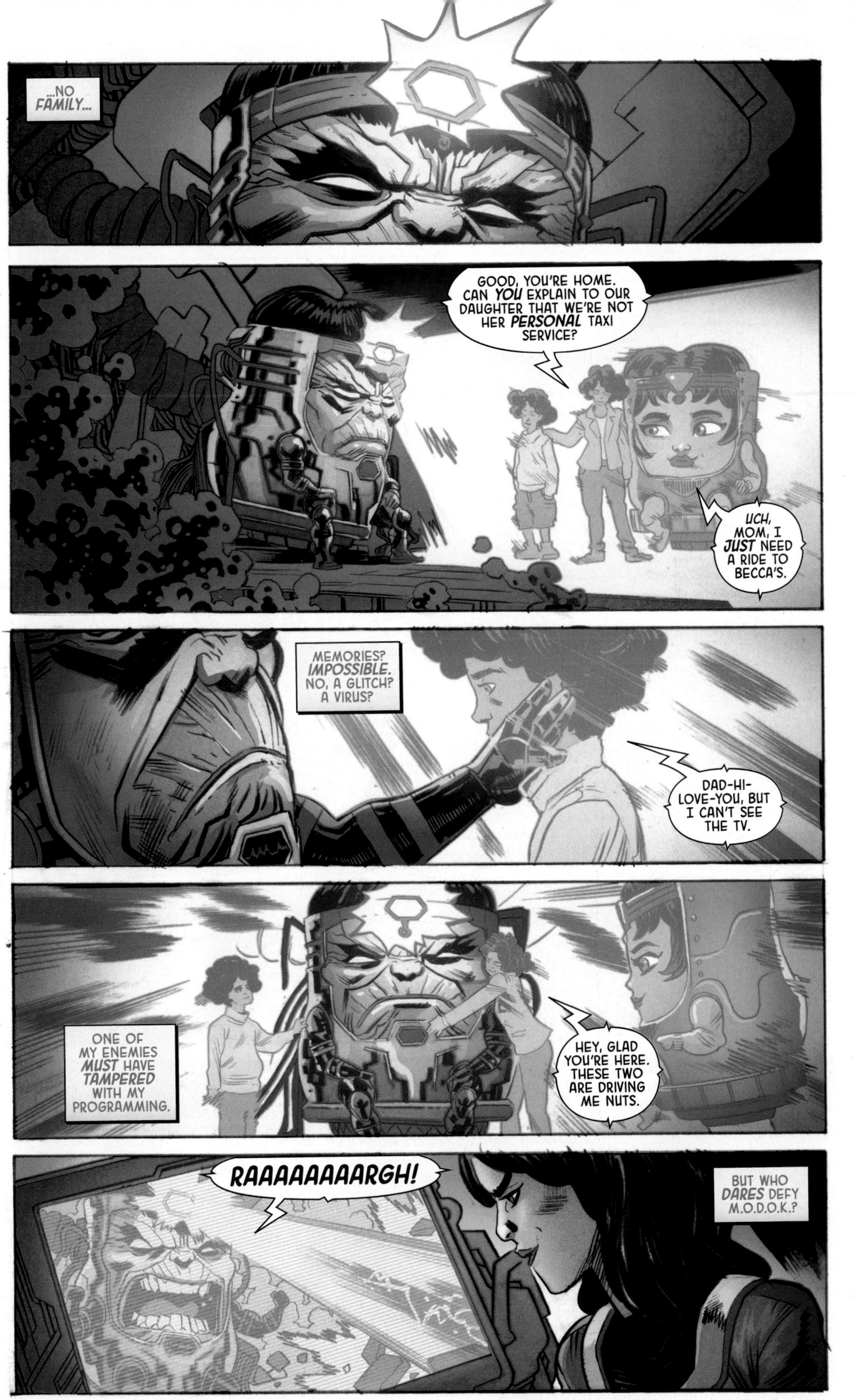
...NO FAMILY...
GOOD, YOU'RE HOME. CAN YOU EXPLAIN TO OUR DAUGHTER THAT WE'RE NOT HER PERSONAL TAXI SERVICE?
UCH, MOM, I JUST NEED A RIDE TO BECCA'S.
MEMORIES? IMPOSSIBLE. NO, A GLITCH? A VIRUS?
DAD-HI-LOVE-YOU, BUT I CAN'T SEE THE TV.
ONE OF MY ENEMIES MUST HAVE TAMPERED WITH MY PROGRAMMING.
HEY, GLAD YOU'RE HERE. THESE TWO ARE DRIVING ME NUTS.
RAAAAAAAARGH!
BUT WHO DARES DEFY M.O.D.O.K.?

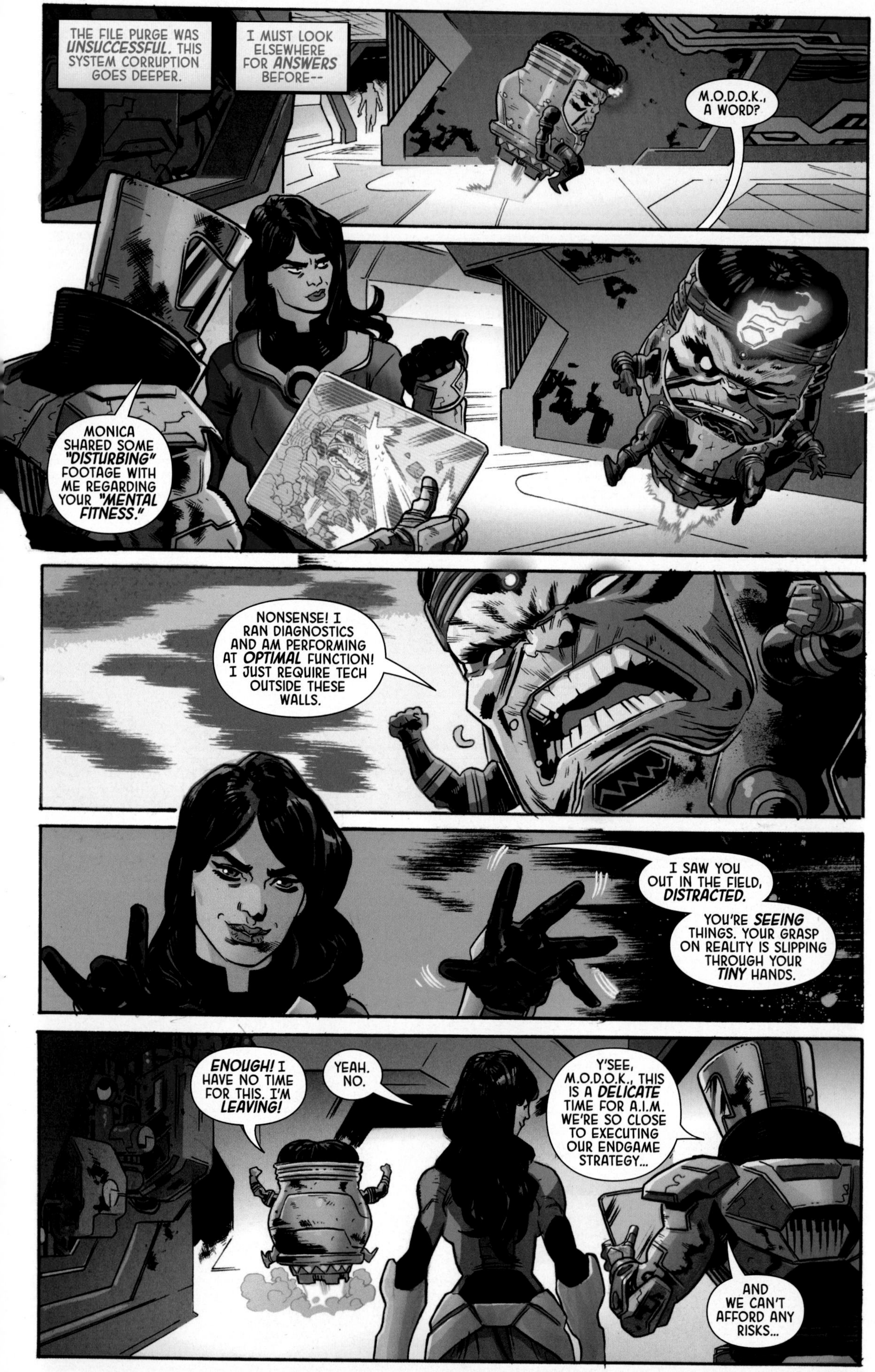
THE FILE PURGE WAS UNSUCCESSFUL. THIS SYSTEM CORRUPTION GOES DEEPER.
I MUST LOOK ELSEWHERE FOR ANSWERS BEFORE--
M.O.D.O.K., A WORD?
MONICA SHARED SOME "DISTURBING" FOOTAGE WITH ME REGARDING YOUR "MENTAL FITNESS."
NONSENSE! I RAN DIAGNOSTICS AND AM PERFORMING AT OPTIMAL FUNCTION! I JUST REQUIRE TECH OUTSIDE THESE WALLS.
I SAW YOU OUT IN THE FIELD, DISTRACTED.
YOU'RE SEEING THINGS. YOUR GRASP ON REALITY IS SLIPPING THROUGH YOUR TINY HANDS.
ENOUGH! I HAVE NO TIME FOR THIS. I'M LEAVING!
YEAH. NO.
Y'SEE, M.O.D.O.K., THIS IS A DELICATE TIME FOR A.I.M. WE'RE SO CLOSE TO EXECUTING OUR ENDGAME STRATEGY...
AND WE CAN'T AFFORD ANY RISKS...

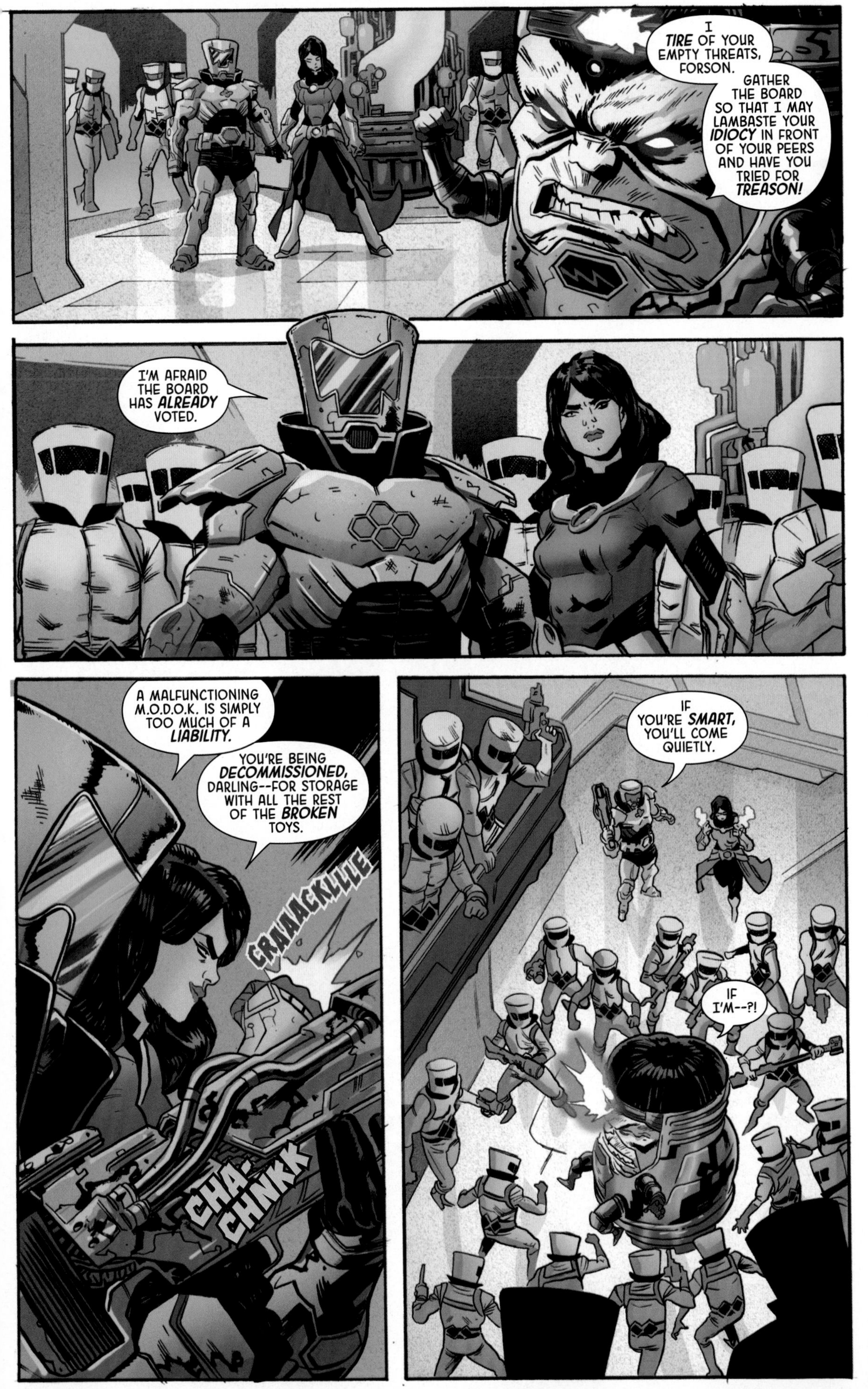
I TIRE OF YOUR EMPTY THREATS, FORSON.
GATHER THE BOARD SO THAT I MAY LAMBASTE YOUR IDIOCY IN FRONT OF YOUR PEERS AND HAVE YOU TRIED FOR TREASON!
I'M AFRAID THE BOARD HAS ALREADY VOTED.
A MALFUNCTIONING M.O.D.O.K. IS SIMPLY TOO MUCH OF A LIABILITY.
YOU'RE BEING DECOMMISSIONED, DARLING--FOR STORAGE WITH ALL THE REST OF THE BROKEN TOYS.
CRAAACKLLLE
CHA-CHNKK
IF YOU'RE SMART, YOU'LL COME QUIETLY.
IF I'M--?!

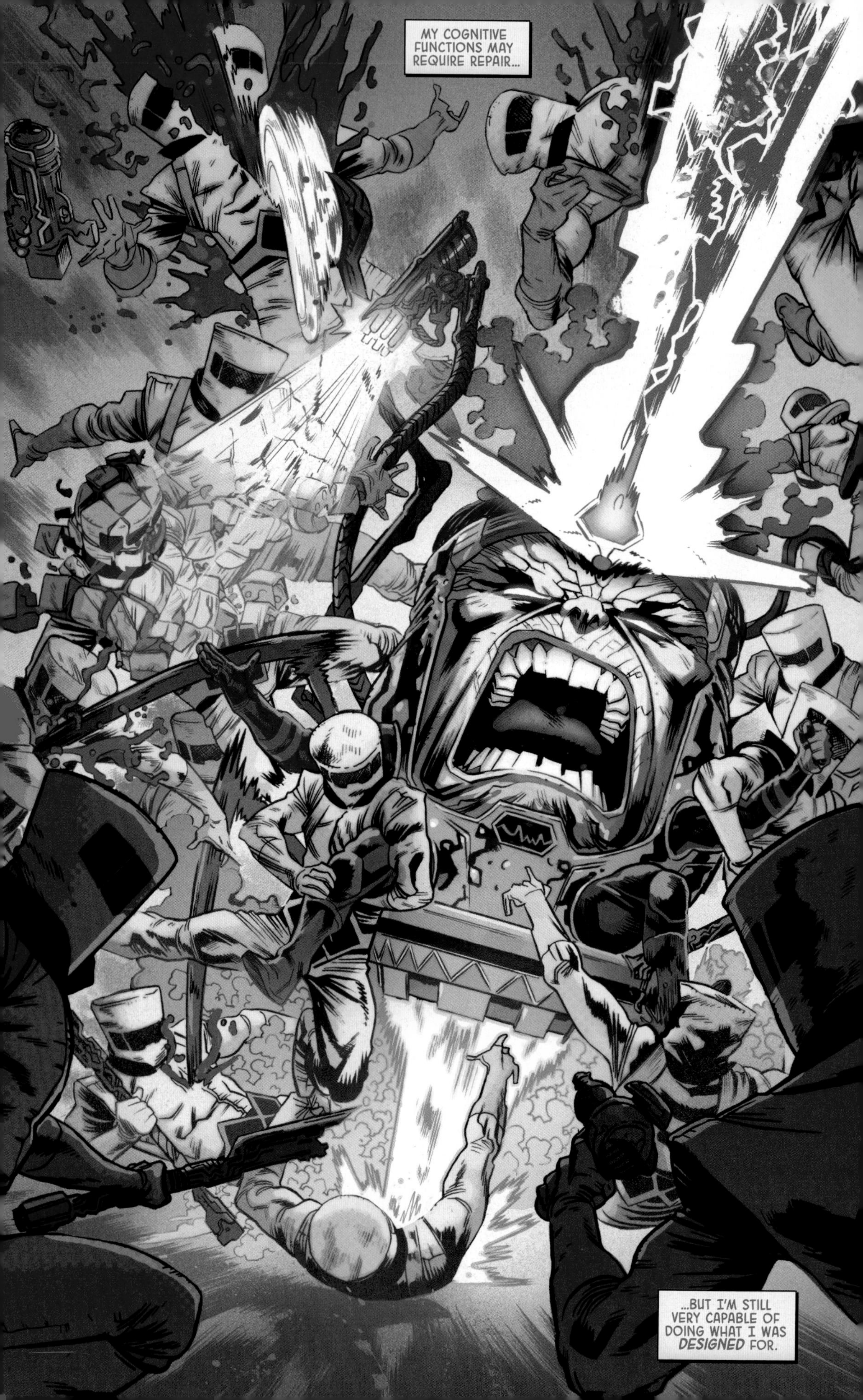
MY COGNITIVE FUNCTIONS MAY REQUIRE REPAIR...
...BUT I'M STILL VERY CAPABLE OF DOING WHAT I WAS DESIGNED FOR.

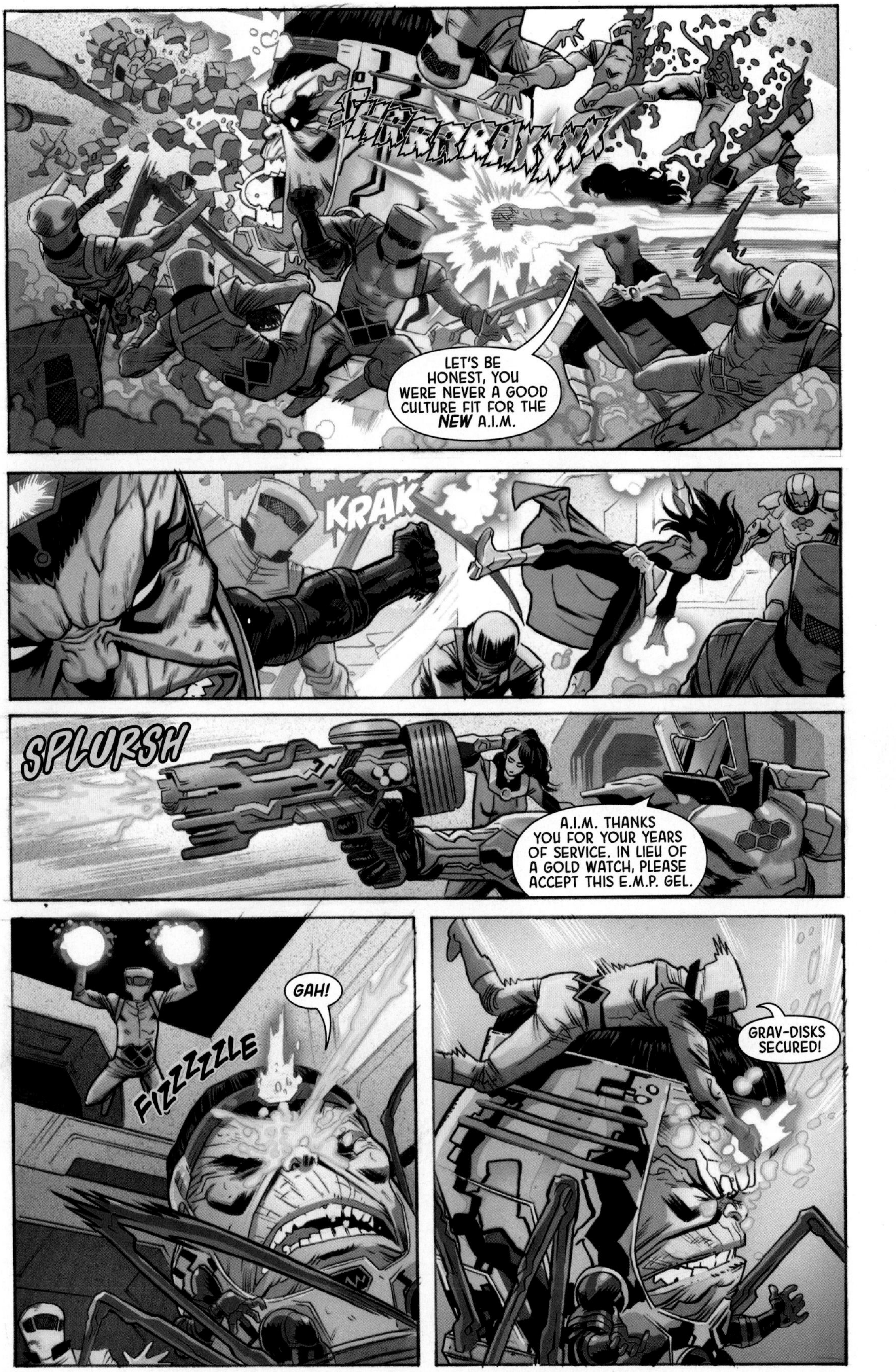
LET'S BE HONEST, YOU WERE NEVER A GOOD CULTURE FIT FOR THE *NEW* A.I.M.
KRAK
SPLURSH
A.I.M. THANKS YOU FOR YOUR YEARS OF SERVICE. IN LIEU OF A GOLD WATCH, PLEASE ACCEPT THIS E.M.P. GEL.
GAH!
FIZZZZZLE
GRAV-DISKS SECURED!

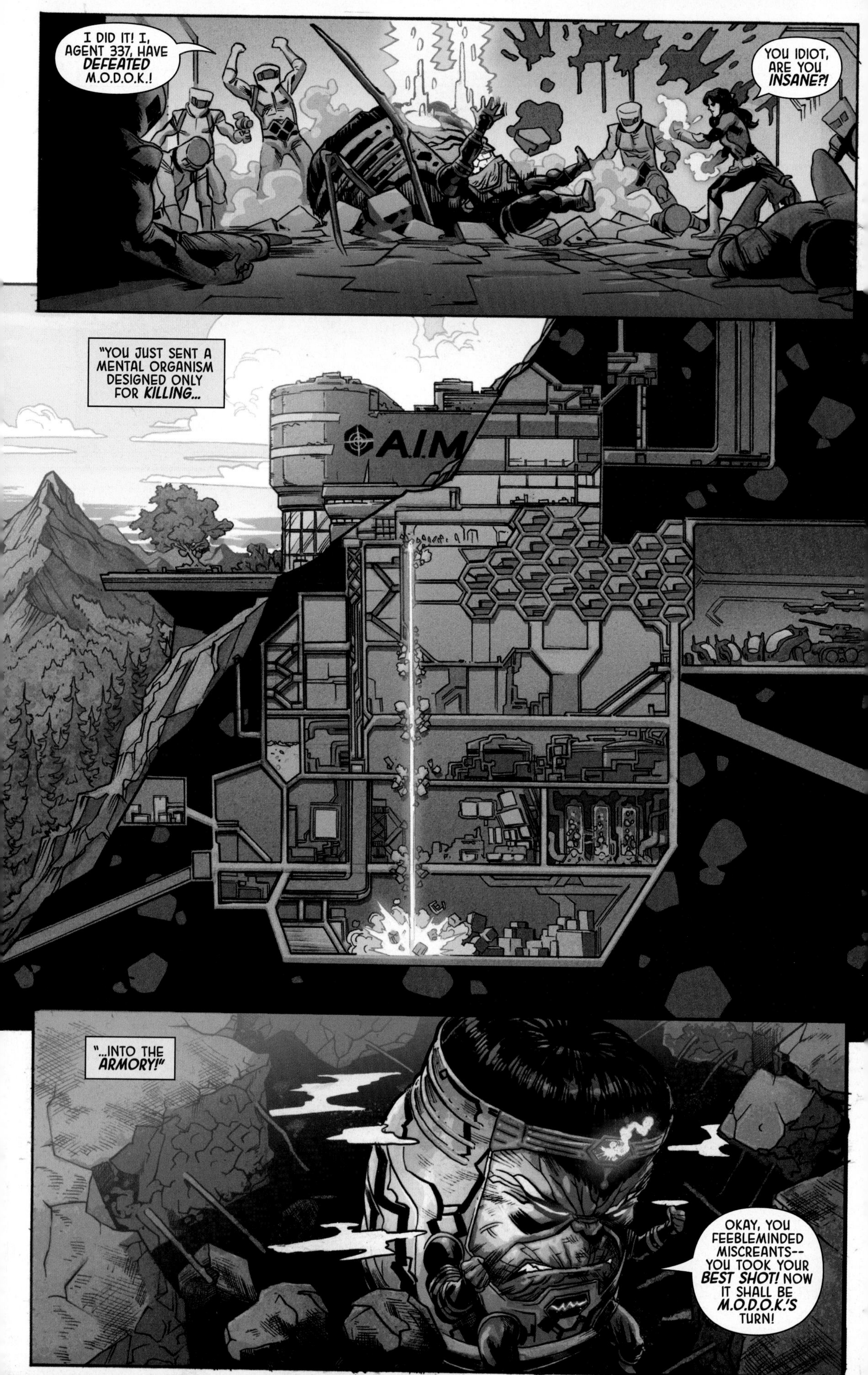
I DID IT! I, AGENT 337, HAVE DEFEATED M.O.D.O.K.!
YOU IDIOT, ARE YOU INSANE?!
"YOU JUST SENT A MENTAL ORGANISM DESIGNED ONLY FOR KILLING...
A.I.M.
"...INTO THE ARMORY!"
OKAY, YOU FEEBLEMINDED MISCREANTS-- YOU TOOK YOUR BEST SHOT! NOW IT SHALL BE M.O.D.O.K.'S TURN!

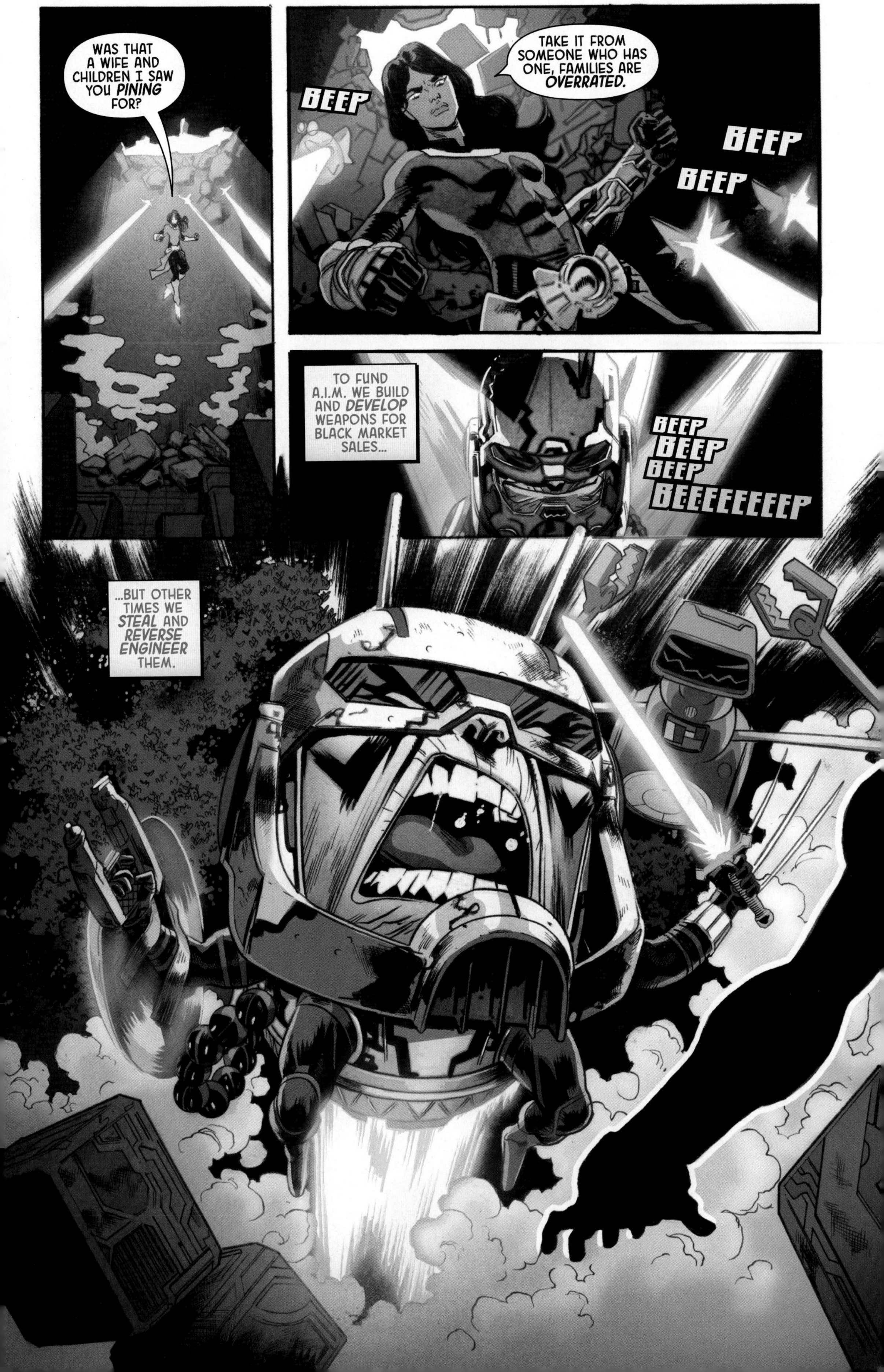
WAS THAT A WIFE AND CHILDREN I SAW YOU PINING FOR?
TAKE IT FROM SOMEONE WHO HAS ONE, FAMILIES ARE OVERRATED.
BEEP
BEEP
BEEP
TO FUND A.I.M. WE BUILD AND DEVELOP WEAPONS FOR BLACK MARKET SALES...
BEEP
BEEP
BEEP
BEEEEEEEEP
...BUT OTHER TIMES WE STEAL AND REVERSE ENGINEER THEM.

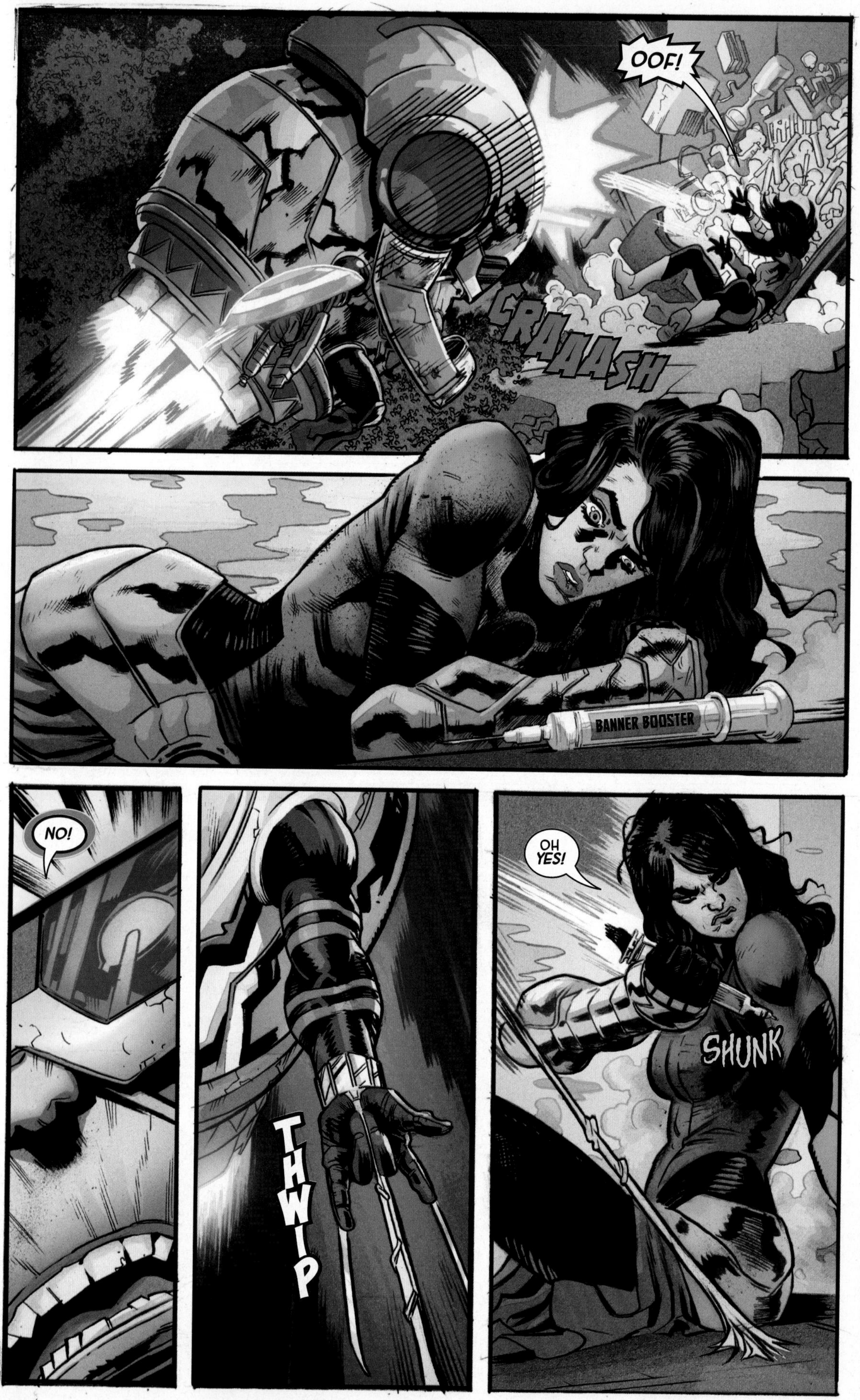
OOF!
CRAAAASH
BANNER BOOSTER
NO!
THWIP
OH YES!
SHUNK

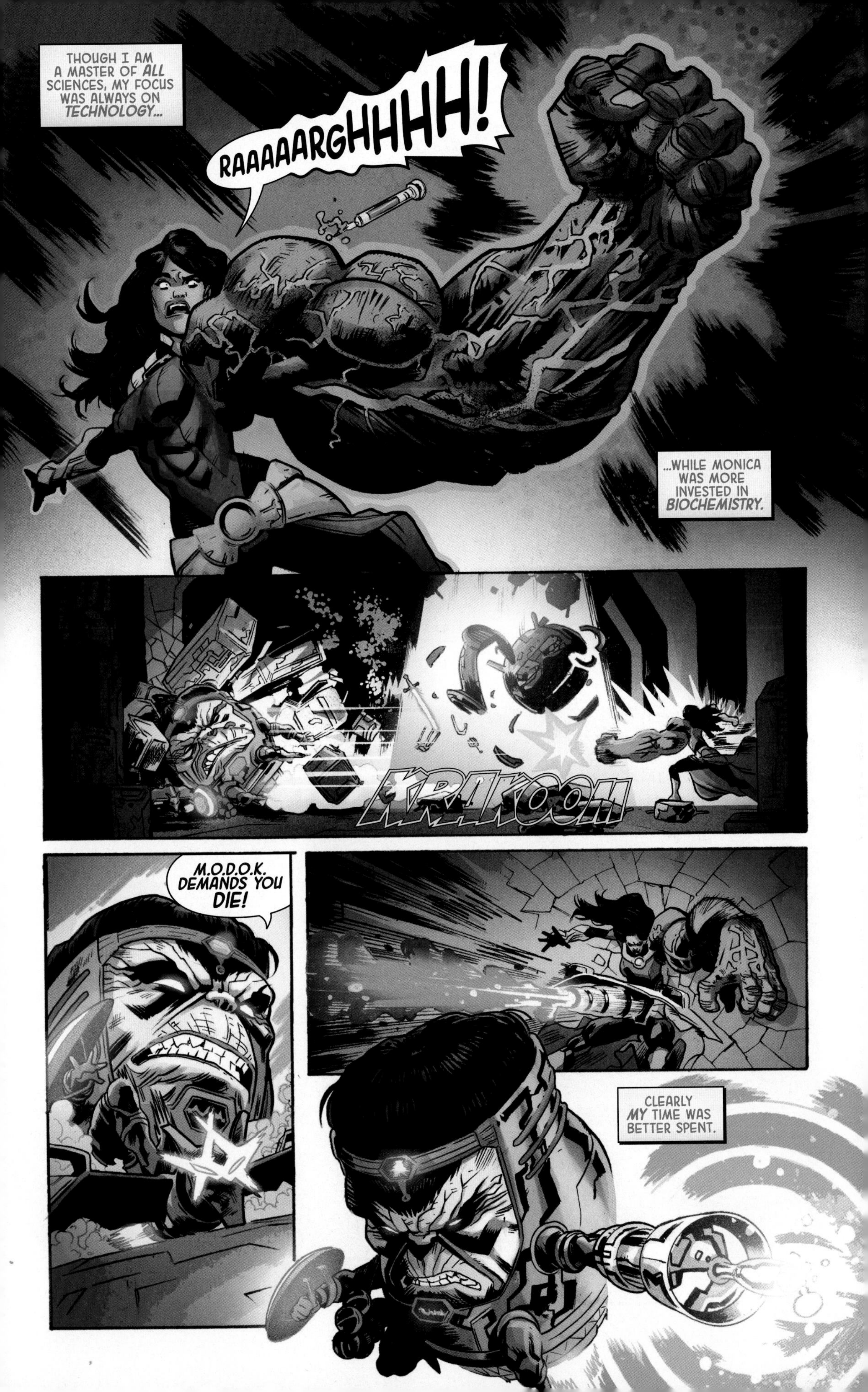
THOUGH I AM A MASTER OF ALL SCIENCES, MY FOCUS WAS ALWAYS ON TECHNOLOGY...
RAAAAARGHHHH!
...WHILE MONICA WAS MORE INVESTED IN BIOCHEMISTRY.
KRAKOOM
M.O.D.O.K. DEMANDS YOU DIE!
CLEARLY MY TIME WAS BETTER SPENT.

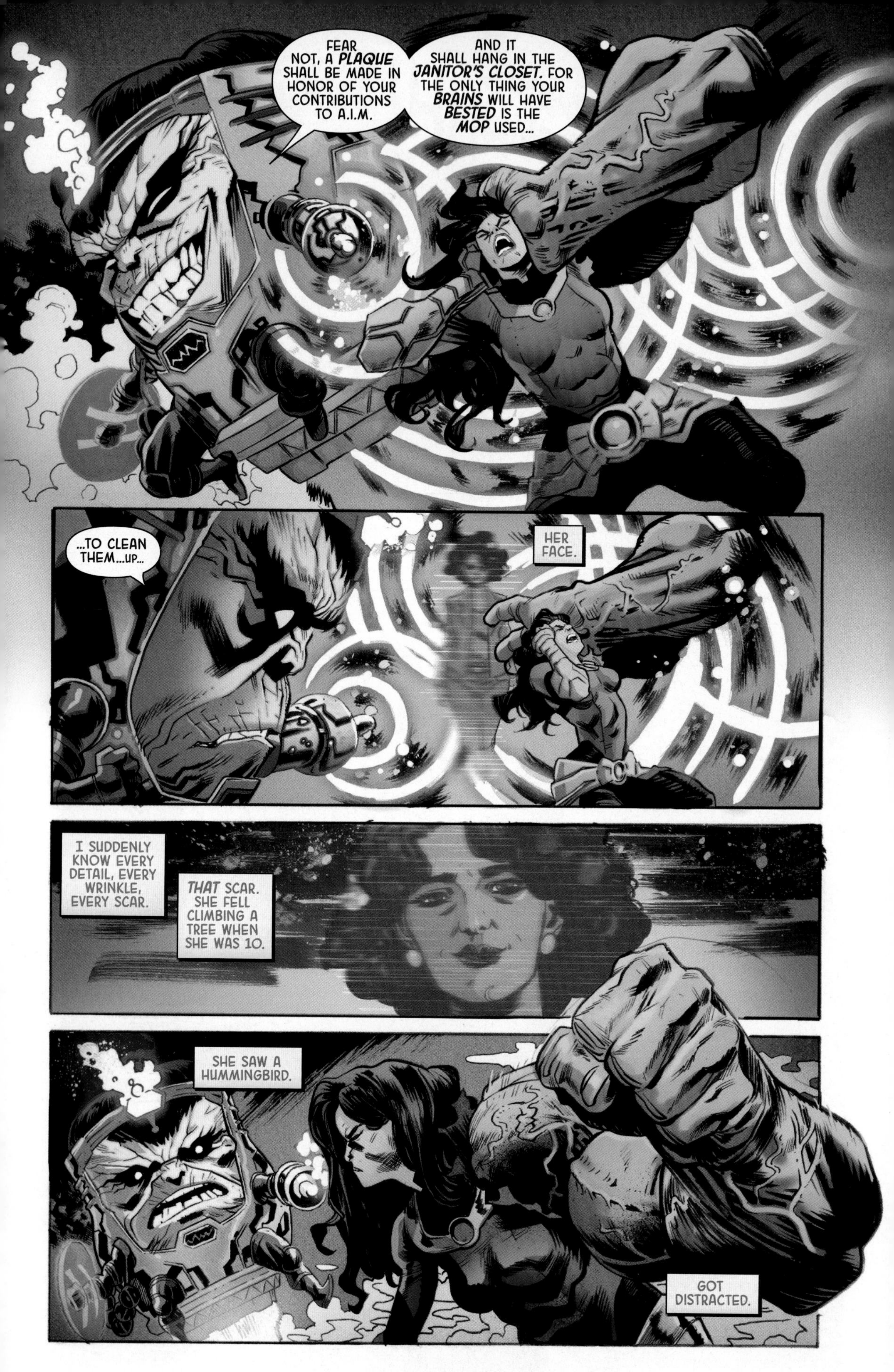
FEAR NOT, A PLAQUE SHALL BE MADE IN HONOR OF YOUR CONTRIBUTIONS TO A.I.M.
AND IT SHALL HANG IN THE JANITOR'S CLOSET. FOR THE ONLY THING YOUR BRAINS WILL HAVE BESTED IS THE MOP USED...
...TO CLEAN THEM...UP...
HER FACE.
I SUDDENLY KNOW EVERY DETAIL, EVERY WRINKLE, EVERY SCAR.
THAT SCAR. SHE FELL CLIMBING A TREE WHEN SHE WAS 10.
SHE SAW A HUMMINGBIRD.
GOT DISTRACTED.

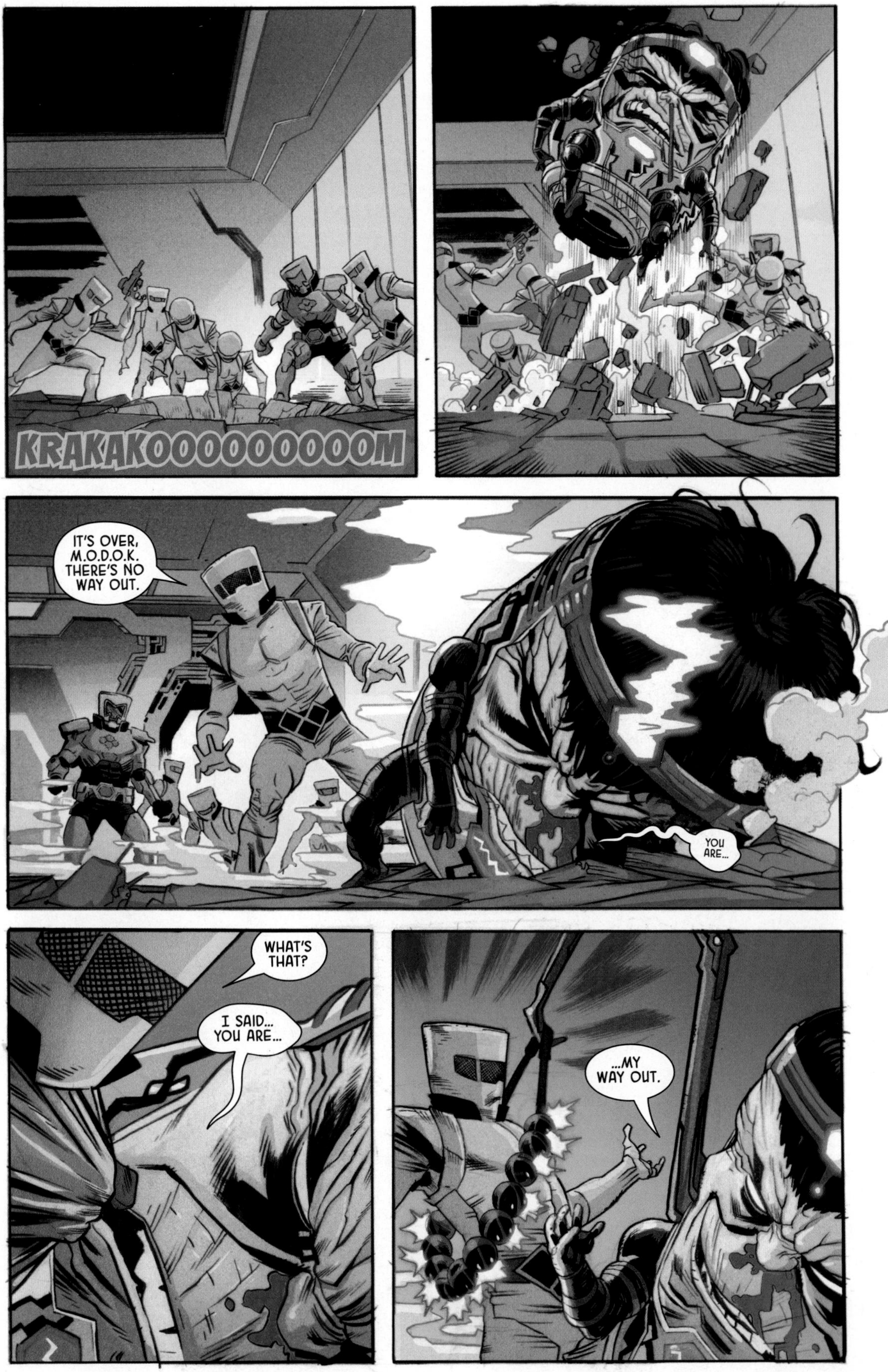
KRAKAKOOOOOOOOOOM
IT'S OVER, M.O.D.O.K. THERE'S NO WAY OUT.
YOU ARE...
WHAT'S THAT?
I SAID... YOU ARE...
...MY WAY OUT.

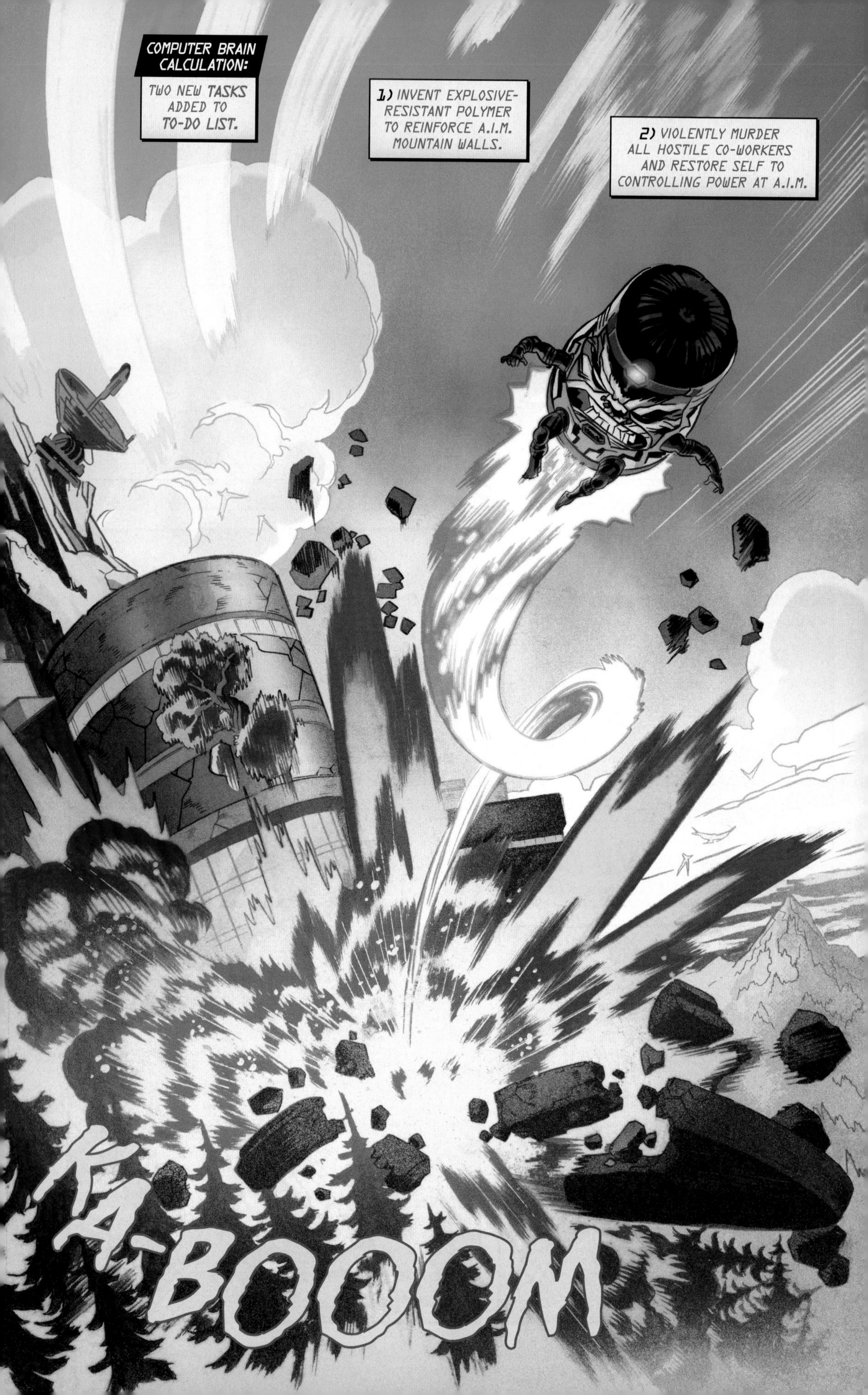
COMPUTER BRAIN CALCULATION:
TWO NEW TASKS ADDED TO TO-DO LIST.
1) INVENT EXPLOSIVE-RESISTANT POLYMER TO REINFORCE A.I.M. MOUNTAIN WALLS.
2) VIOLENTLY MURDER ALL HOSTILE CO-WORKERS AND RESTORE SELF TO CONTROLLING POWER AT A.I.M.
KA-BOOOM

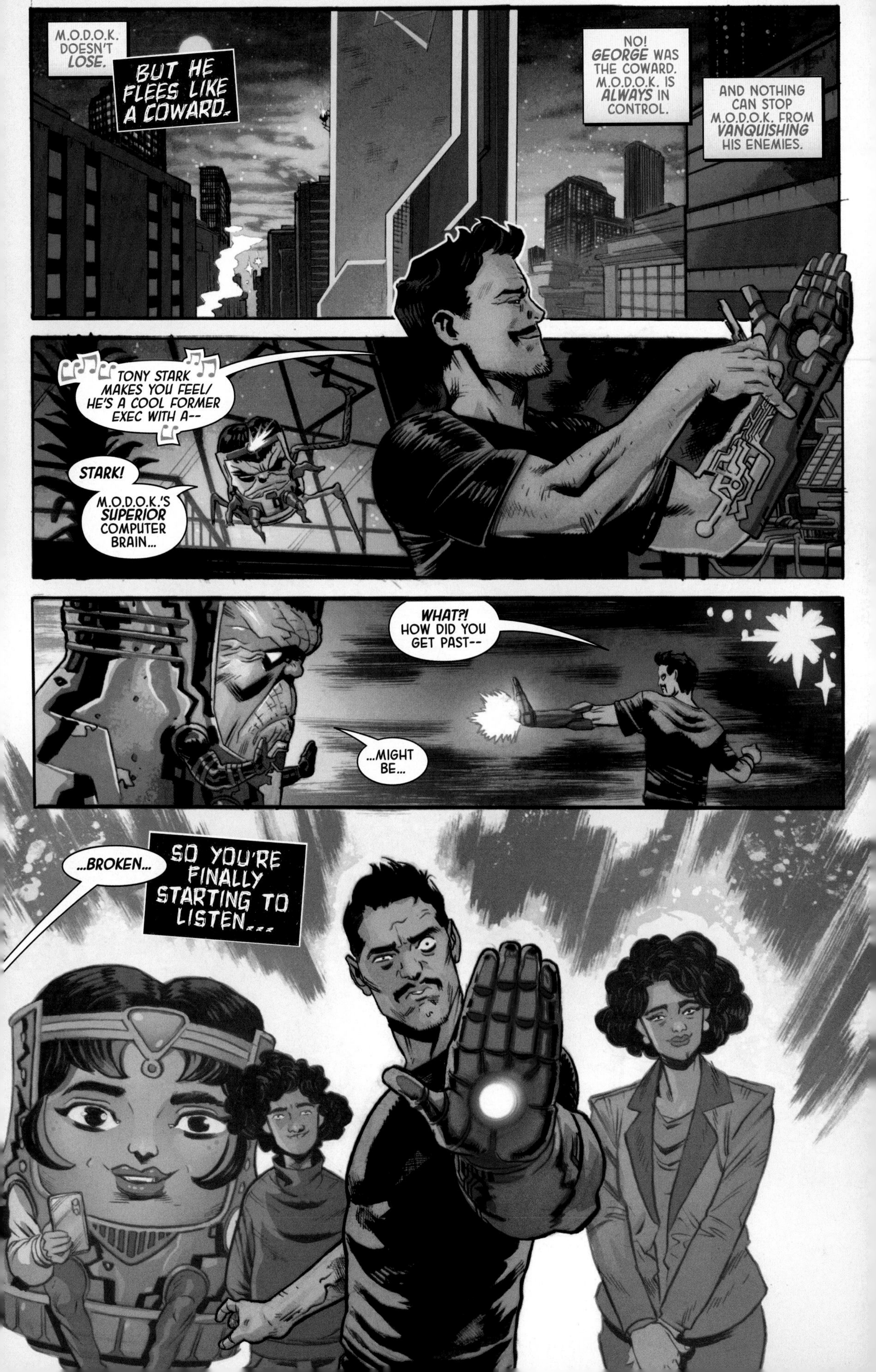
M.O.D.O.K. DOESN'T LOSE.
BUT HE FLEES LIKE A COWARD.
NO! GEORGE WAS THE COWARD. M.O.D.O.K. IS ALWAYS IN CONTROL.
AND NOTHING CAN STOP M.O.D.O.K. FROM VANQUISHING HIS ENEMIES.
TONY STARK MAKES YOU FEEL/ HE'S A COOL FORMER EXEC WITH A--
STARK!
M.O.D.O.K.'S SUPERIOR COMPUTER BRAIN...
WHAT?! HOW DID YOU GET PAST--
...MIGHT BE...
...BROKEN...
SO YOU'RE FINALLY STARTING TO LISTEN...

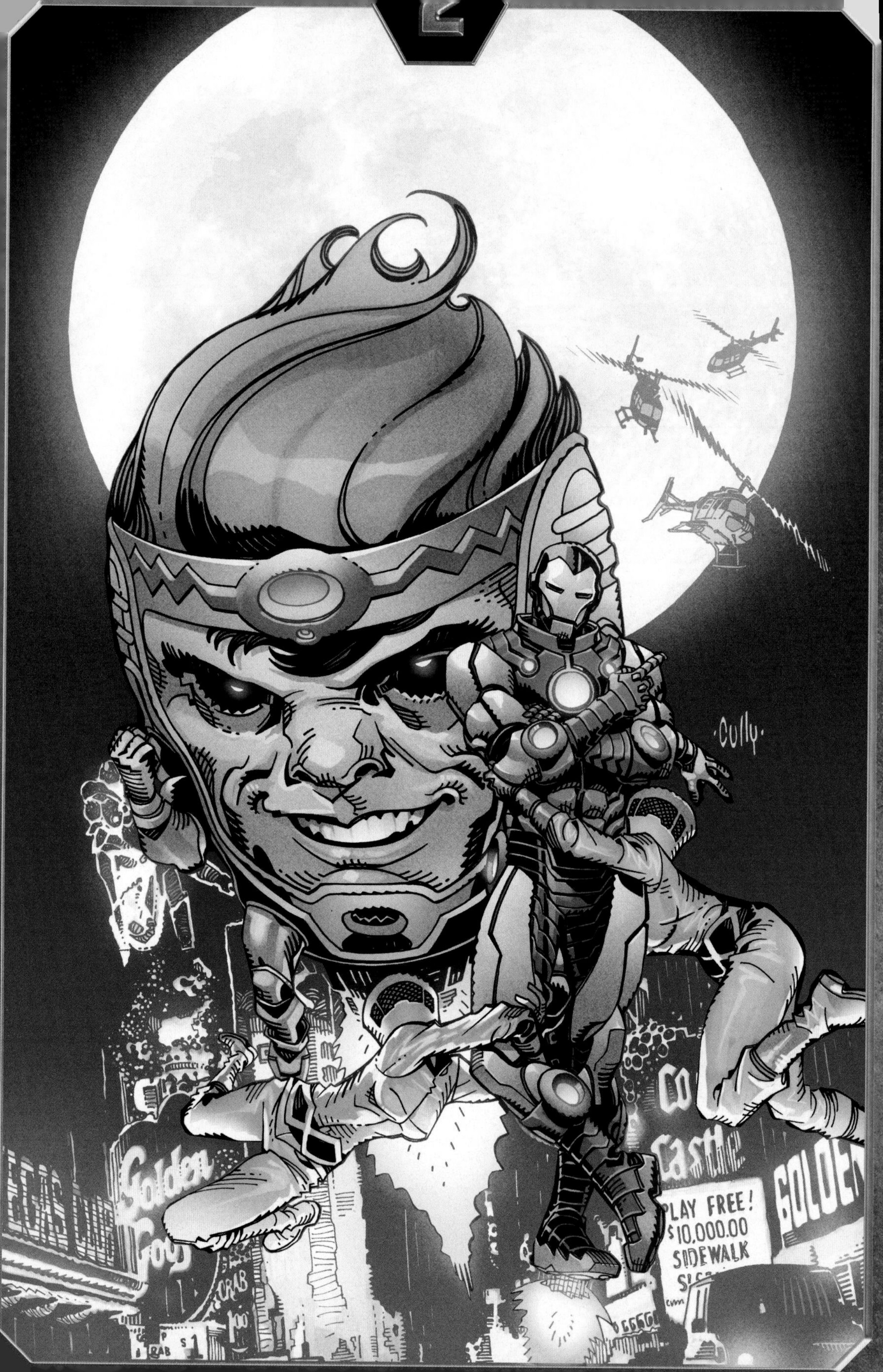

·Cully·
Golden
Castle
GOLDEN
PLAY FREE!
$10,000.00
SIDEWALK
CRAB

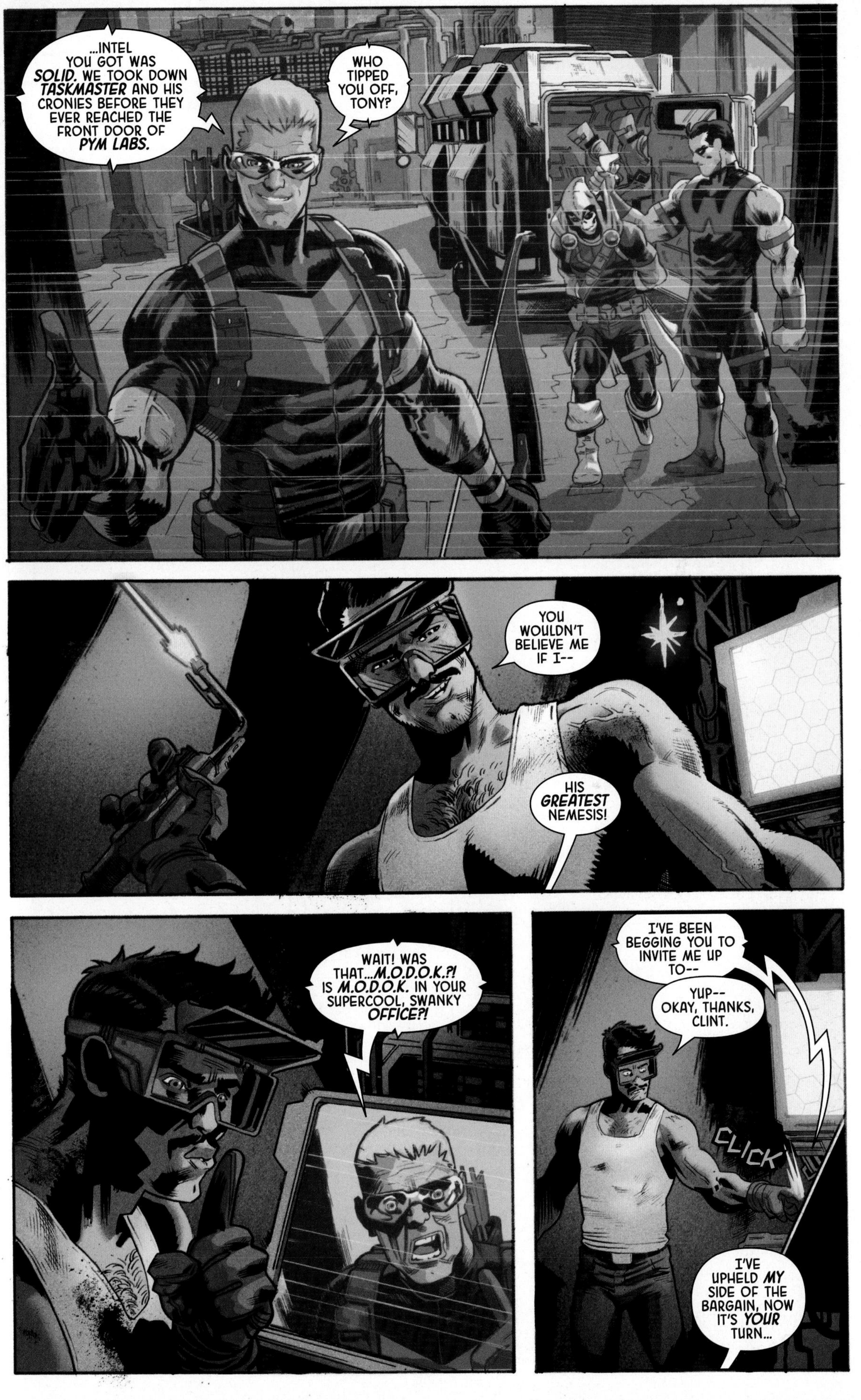
...INTEL YOU GOT WAS SOLID. WE TOOK DOWN TASKMASTER AND HIS CRONIES BEFORE THEY EVER REACHED THE FRONT DOOR OF PYM LABS.
WHO TIPPED YOU OFF, TONY?
YOU WOULDN'T BELIEVE ME IF I--
HIS GREATEST NEMESIS!
WAIT! WAS THAT...M.O.D.O.K.?! IS M.O.D.O.K. IN YOUR SUPERCOOL, SWANKY OFFICE?!
I'VE BEEN BEGGING YOU TO INVITE ME UP TO--
YUP-- OKAY, THANKS, CLINT.
CLICK
I'VE UPHELD MY SIDE OF THE BARGAIN, NOW IT'S YOUR TURN...

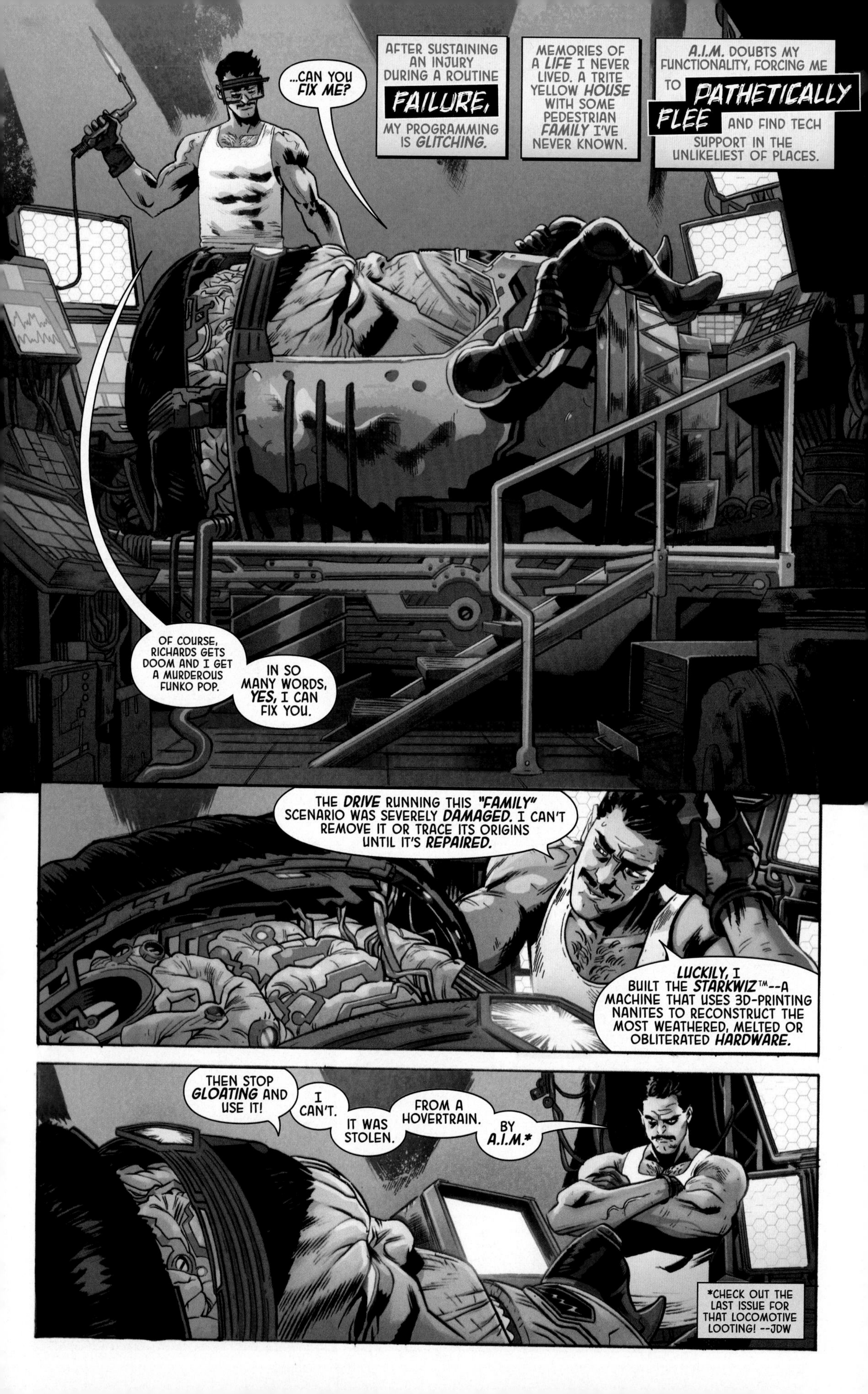
...CAN YOU FIX ME?
AFTER SUSTAINING AN INJURY DURING A ROUTINE FAILURE, MY PROGRAMMING IS GLITCHING.
MEMORIES OF A LIFE I NEVER LIVED. A TRITE YELLOW HOUSE WITH SOME PEDESTRIAN FAMILY I'VE NEVER KNOWN.
A.I.M. DOUBTS MY FUNCTIONALITY, FORCING ME TO PATHETICALLY FLEE AND FIND TECH SUPPORT IN THE UNLIKELIEST OF PLACES.
OF COURSE, RICHARDS GETS DOOM AND I GET A MURDEROUS FUNKO POP.
IN SO MANY WORDS, YES, I CAN FIX YOU.
THE DRIVE RUNNING THIS "FAMILY" SCENARIO WAS SEVERELY DAMAGED. I CAN'T REMOVE IT OR TRACE ITS ORIGINS UNTIL IT'S REPAIRED.
LUCKILY, I BUILT THE STARKWIZ™--A MACHINE THAT USES 3D-PRINTING NANITES TO RECONSTRUCT THE MOST WEATHERED, MELTED OR OBLITERATED HARDWARE.
THEN STOP GLOATING AND USE IT!
I CAN'T.
IT WAS STOLEN.
FROM A HOVERTRAIN.
BY A.I.M.*
*CHECK OUT THE LAST ISSUE FOR THAT LOCOMOTIVE LOOTING! --JDW

I KNOW WHERE YOUR STOLEN MACHINE IS.

OH GOOD.

LAS VEGAS.

MONICA WILL BE AUCTIONING IT OFF AT THE *CTS EXPO*.

THE WHAT-- WHAT NOW?

THE *CRIMINAL TECHNOLOGY SHOW*-- A TRADE SHOW WHERE ORGANIZATIONS LIKE A.I.M. AND HYDRA CAN SHOWCASE NEW WEAPONRY TO POTENTIAL BUYERS.

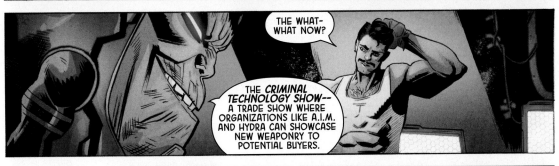

BUT THE STARKWIZ™ ISN'T A WEAPON.

AND A KITCHEN KNIFE IS JUST CUTLERY UNTIL YOU PLUNGE IT INTO SOMEONE'S CHEST.

YOUR DEVICE CAN REBUILD DESTROYED NUCLEAR LAUNCH CODES.

OH $&%@!

MONICA WILL MAKE SURE NEITHER OF US ARE WELCOME.

WE'LL HAVE TO RETRIEVE THE MACHINE...BY GOING *INCOGNITO*.

AND HOW EXACTLY DO *YOU* DO THAT?

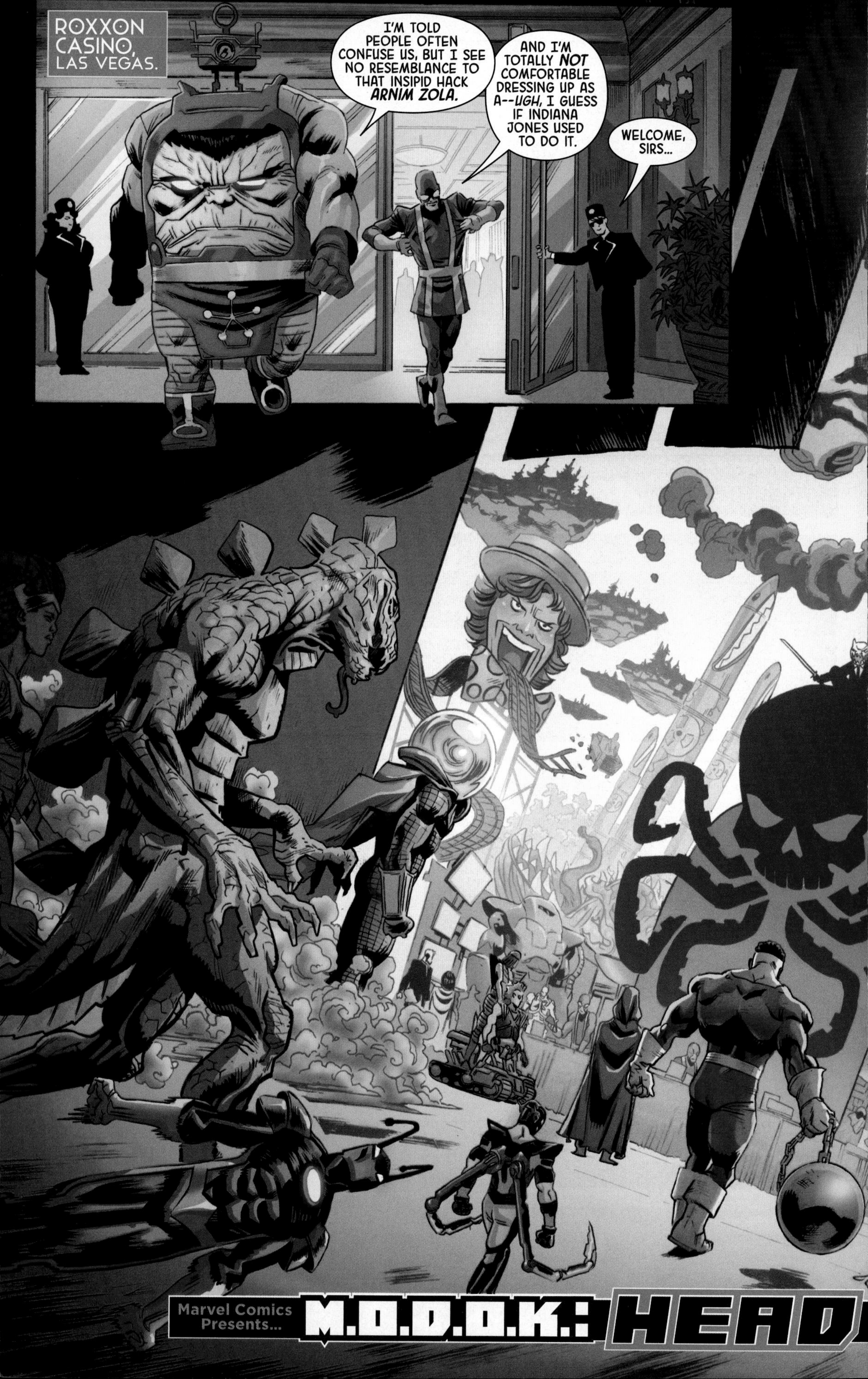
ROXXON CASINO, LAS VEGAS.
I'M TOLD PEOPLE OFTEN CONFUSE US, BUT I SEE NO RESEMBLANCE TO THAT INSIPID HACK ARNIM ZOLA.
AND I'M TOTALLY NOT COMFORTABLE DRESSING UP AS A--UGH, I GUESS IF INDIANA JONES USED TO DO IT.
WELCOME, SIRS...
Marvel Comics Presents...
M.O.D.O.K.: HEAD

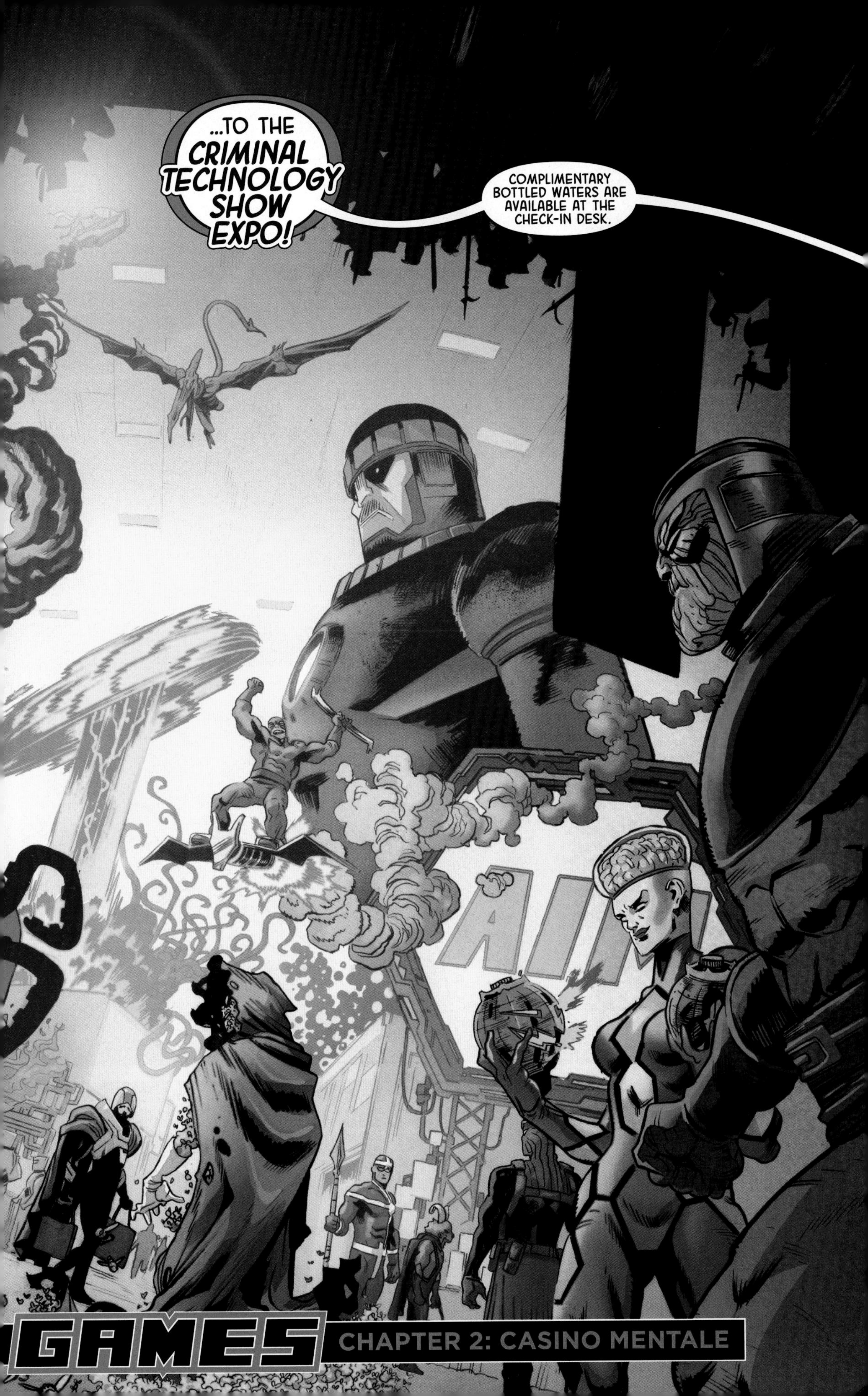
...TO THE CRIMINAL TECHNOLOGY SHOW EXPO!
COMPLIMENTARY BOTTLED WATERS ARE AVAILABLE AT THE CHECK-IN DESK.
GAMES
CHAPTER 2: CASINO MENTALE

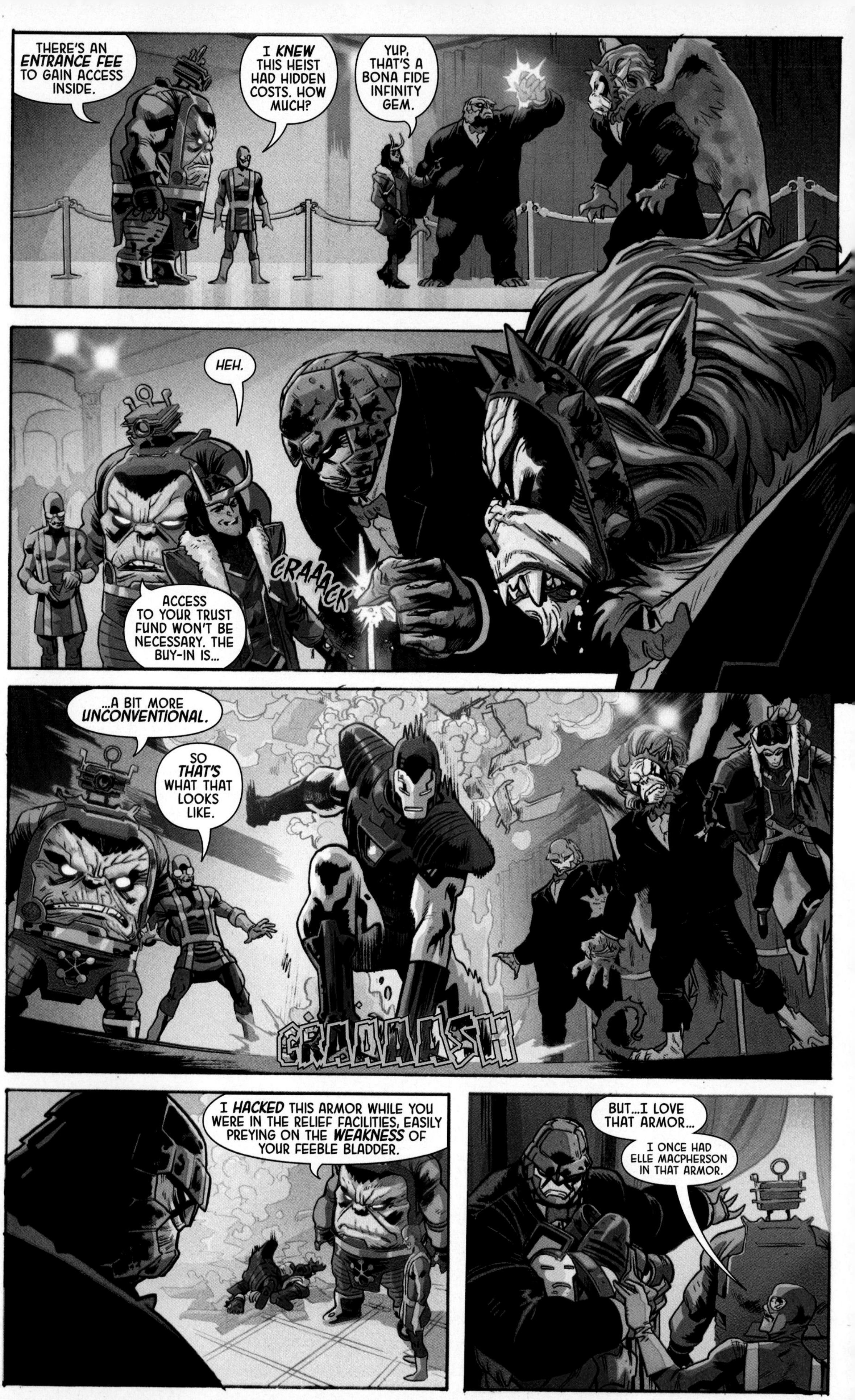
THERE'S AN ENTRANCE FEE TO GAIN ACCESS INSIDE.
I KNEW THIS HEIST HAD HIDDEN COSTS. HOW MUCH?
YUP, THAT'S A BONA FIDE INFINITY GEM.
HEH.
CRAAACK
ACCESS TO YOUR TRUST FUND WON'T BE NECESSARY. THE BUY-IN IS...
...A BIT MORE UNCONVENTIONAL.
SO THAT'S WHAT THAT LOOKS LIKE.
CRAAAASH
I HACKED THIS ARMOR WHILE YOU WERE IN THE RELIEF FACILITIES, EASILY PREYING ON THE WEAKNESS OF YOUR FEEBLE BLADDER.
BUT...I LOVE THAT ARMOR...
I ONCE HAD ELLE MACPHERSON IN THAT ARMOR.

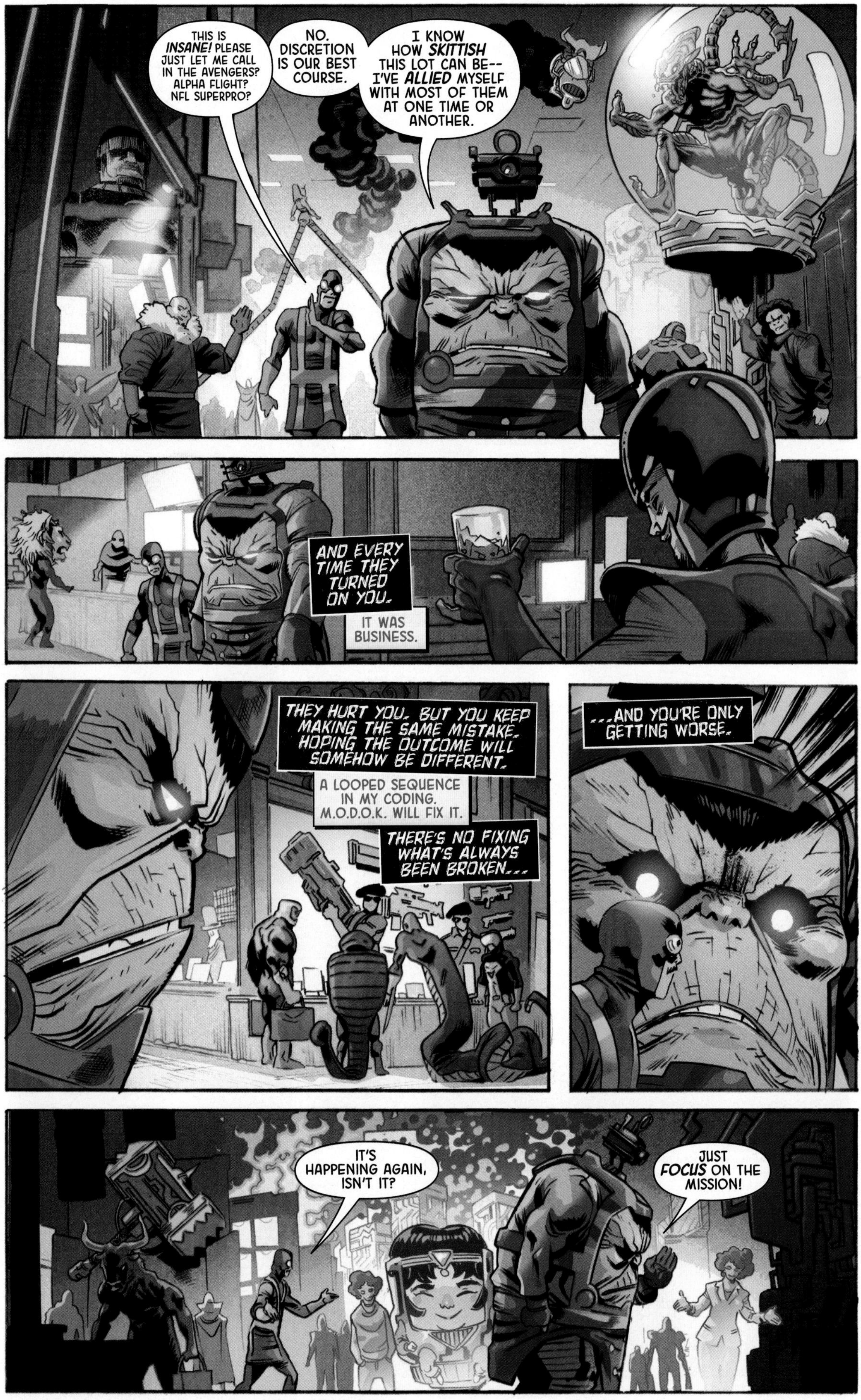
THIS IS INSANE! PLEASE JUST LET ME CALL IN THE AVENGERS? ALPHA FLIGHT? NFL SUPERPRO?
NO. DISCRETION IS OUR BEST COURSE.
I KNOW HOW SKITTISH THIS LOT CAN BE-- I'VE ALLIED MYSELF WITH MOST OF THEM AT ONE TIME OR ANOTHER.
AND EVERY TIME THEY TURNED ON YOU.
IT WAS BUSINESS.
THEY HURT YOU. BUT YOU KEEP MAKING THE SAME MISTAKE. HOPING THE OUTCOME WILL SOMEHOW BE DIFFERENT.
A LOOPED SEQUENCE IN MY CODING. M.O.D.O.K. WILL FIX IT.
THERE'S NO FIXING WHAT'S ALWAYS BEEN BROKEN...
...AND YOU'RE ONLY GETTING WORSE.
IT'S HAPPENING AGAIN, ISN'T IT?
JUST FOCUS ON THE MISSION!

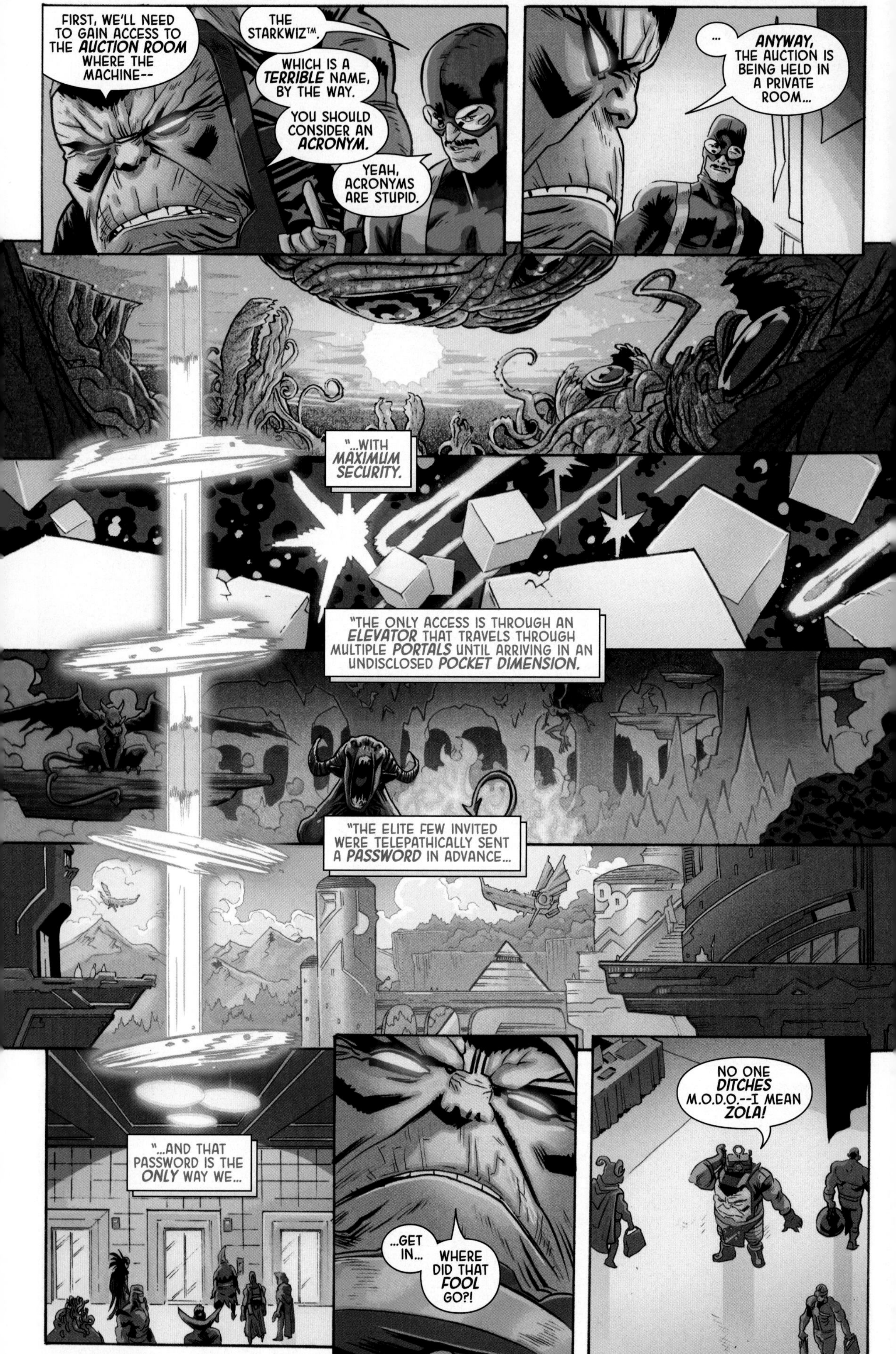
FIRST, WE'LL NEED TO GAIN ACCESS TO THE AUCTION ROOM WHERE THE MACHINE--
THE STARKWIZ™.
WHICH IS A TERRIBLE NAME, BY THE WAY.
YOU SHOULD CONSIDER AN ACRONYM.
YEAH, ACRONYMS ARE STUPID.
... ANYWAY, THE AUCTION IS BEING HELD IN A PRIVATE ROOM...
"...WITH MAXIMUM SECURITY.
"THE ONLY ACCESS IS THROUGH AN ELEVATOR THAT TRAVELS THROUGH MULTIPLE PORTALS UNTIL ARRIVING IN AN UNDISCLOSED POCKET DIMENSION.
"THE ELITE FEW INVITED WERE TELEPATHICALLY SENT A PASSWORD IN ADVANCE...
"...AND THAT PASSWORD IS THE ONLY WAY WE...
...GET IN...
WHERE DID THAT FOOL GO?!
NO ONE DITCHES M.O.D.O.--I MEAN ZOLA!

IMBECILE! I'VE BEEN LOOKING FOR YOU FOR AN HOUR! WHAT IS *THIS?!*

THAT IS 21-YEAR-OLD LATVERIAN PORTWOOD, DR. ZOLA.

COURTESY OF OUR NEW DRINKING COMPANION...

...THE *MASTER.*

...OF THE WORLD! YOU HAVE TO SAY THE WHOLE NAME!

I WOULD RATHER DRINK DITCH LIQUOR WITH A PIG FARMER.

YOU'RE THE PIG F--

NICE! BANTER BETWEEN *EQUALS!*

THIS IS HOW EDISON AND TESLA MUST'VE BUSTED EACH OTHER'S BEANS.

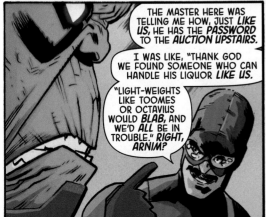

THE MASTER HERE WAS TELLING ME HOW, JUST *LIKE US,* HE HAS THE *PASSWORD* TO THE *AUCTION UPSTAIRS.*

I WAS LIKE, "THANK GOD WE FOUND SOMEONE WHO CAN HANDLE HIS LIQUOR *LIKE US.*

"LIGHT-WEIGHTS LIKE TOOMES OR OCTAVIUS WOULD *BLAB,* AND WE'D *ALL* BE IN TROUBLE." *RIGHT,* ARNIM?

Y-YES. I SEE WHERE YOU ARE GOING WITH THIS.

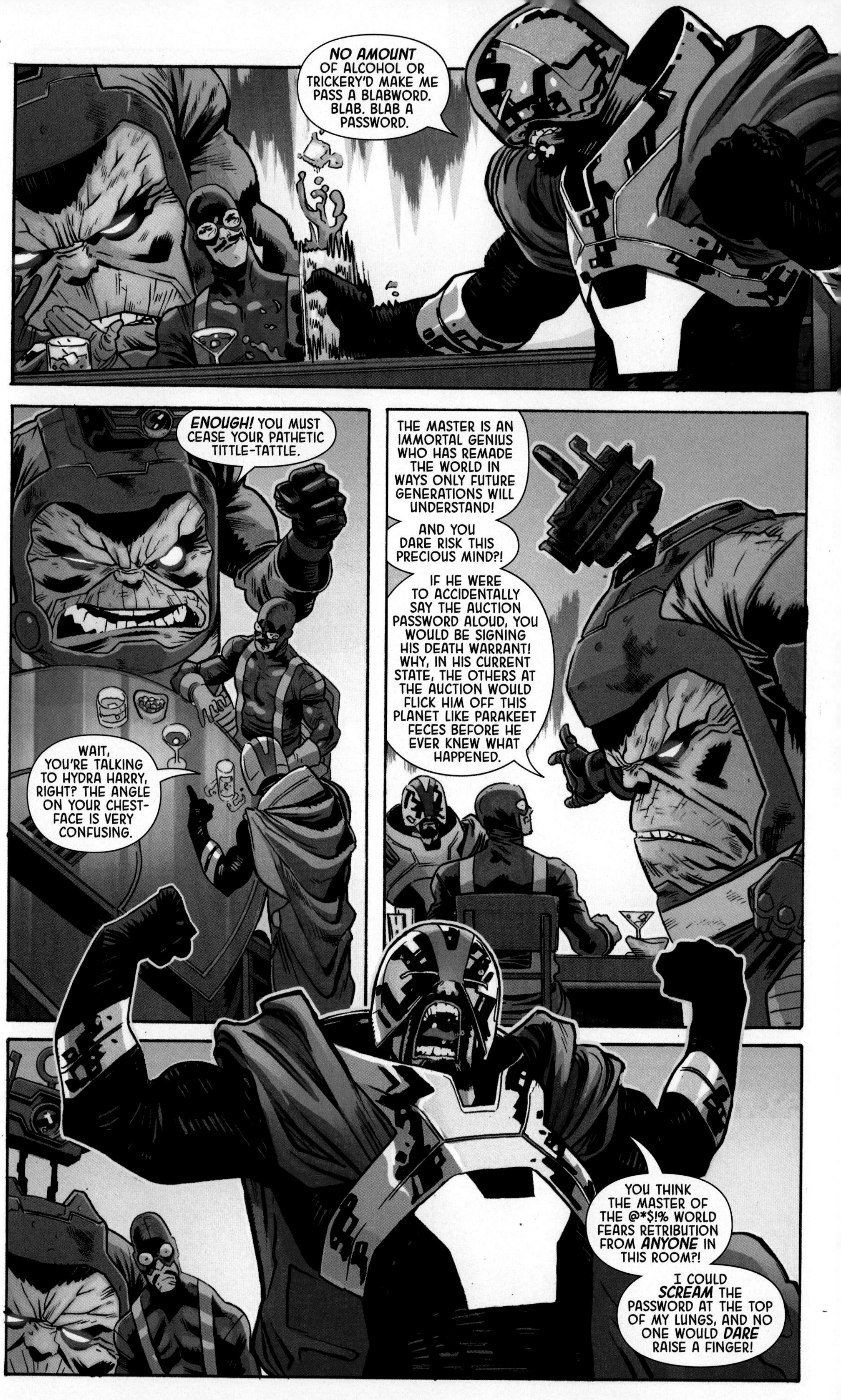
NO AMOUNT OF ALCOHOL OR TRICKERY'D MAKE ME PASS A BLABWORD. BLAB. BLAB A PASSWORD.
ENOUGH! YOU MUST CEASE YOUR PATHETIC TITTLE-TATTLE.
WAIT, YOU'RE TALKING TO HYDRA HARRY, RIGHT? THE ANGLE ON YOUR CHEST-FACE IS VERY CONFUSING.
THE MASTER IS AN IMMORTAL GENIUS WHO HAS REMADE THE WORLD IN WAYS ONLY FUTURE GENERATIONS WILL UNDERSTAND!
AND YOU DARE RISK THIS PRECIOUS MIND?!
IF HE WERE TO ACCIDENTALLY SAY THE AUCTION PASSWORD ALOUD, YOU WOULD BE SIGNING HIS DEATH WARRANT! WHY, IN HIS CURRENT STATE, THE OTHERS AT THE AUCTION WOULD FLICK HIM OFF THIS PLANET LIKE PARAKEET FECES BEFORE HE EVER KNEW WHAT HAPPENED.
YOU THINK THE MASTER OF THE @*$!% WORLD FEARS RETRIBUTION FROM ANYONE IN THIS ROOM?!
I COULD SCREAM THE PASSWORD AT THE TOP OF MY LUNGS, AND NO ONE WOULD DARE RAISE A FINGER!

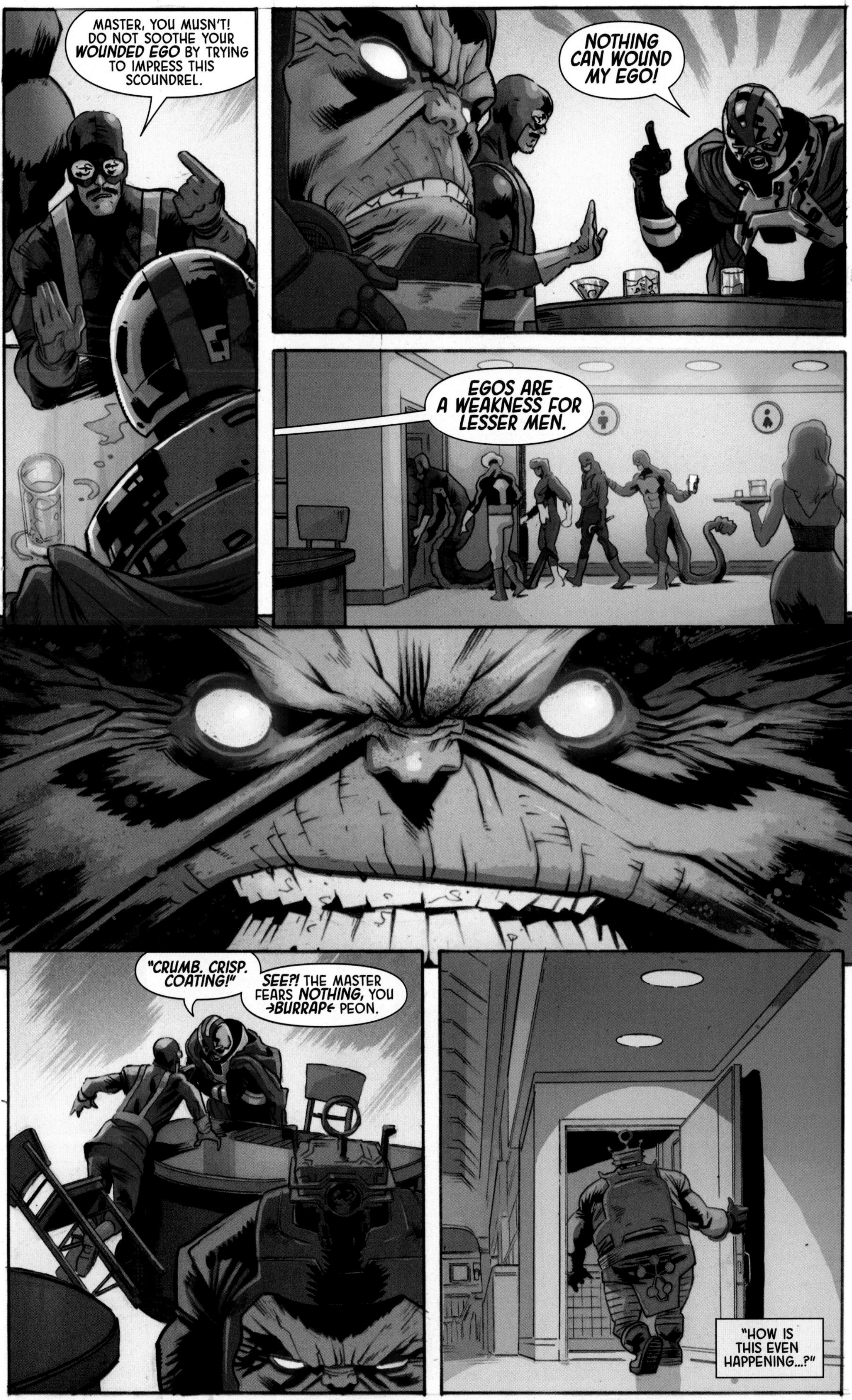
MASTER, YOU MUSN'T! DO NOT SOOTHE YOUR WOUNDED EGO BY TRYING TO IMPRESS THIS SCOUNDREL.
NOTHING CAN WOUND MY EGO!
EGOS ARE A WEAKNESS FOR LESSER MEN.
"CRUMB. CRISP. COATING!"
SEE?! THE MASTER FEARS NOTHING, YOU →BURRAP← PEON.
"HOW IS THIS EVEN HAPPENING...?"

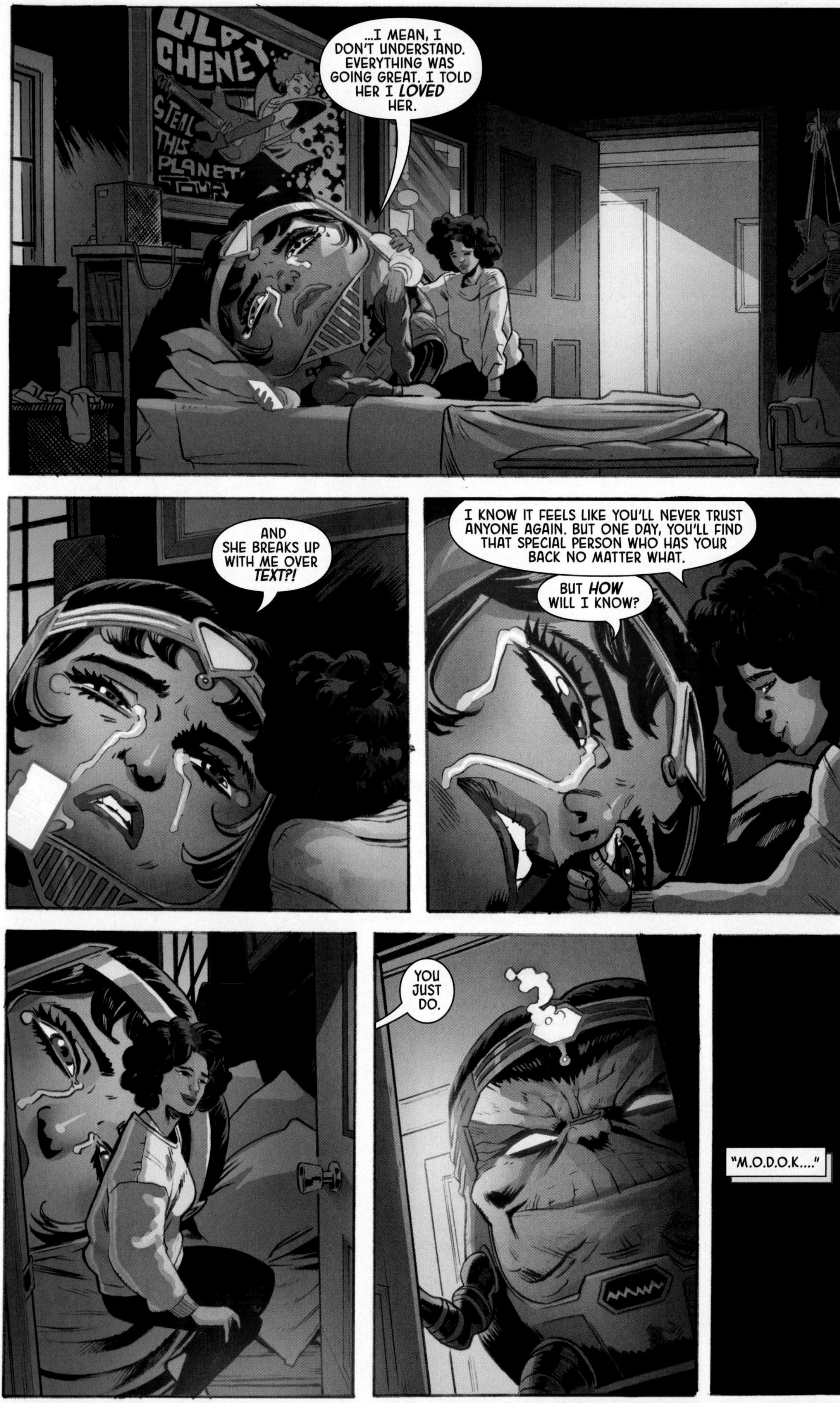
...I MEAN, I DON'T UNDERSTAND. EVERYTHING WAS GOING GREAT. I TOLD HER I *LOVED* HER.
STEAL THIS PLANET TOUR
AND SHE BREAKS UP WITH ME OVER ***TEXT?!***
I KNOW IT FEELS LIKE YOU'LL NEVER TRUST ANYONE AGAIN. BUT ONE DAY, YOU'LL FIND THAT SPECIAL PERSON WHO HAS YOUR BACK NO MATTER WHAT.
BUT *HOW* WILL I KNOW?
YOU JUST DO.
"M.O.D.O.K...."

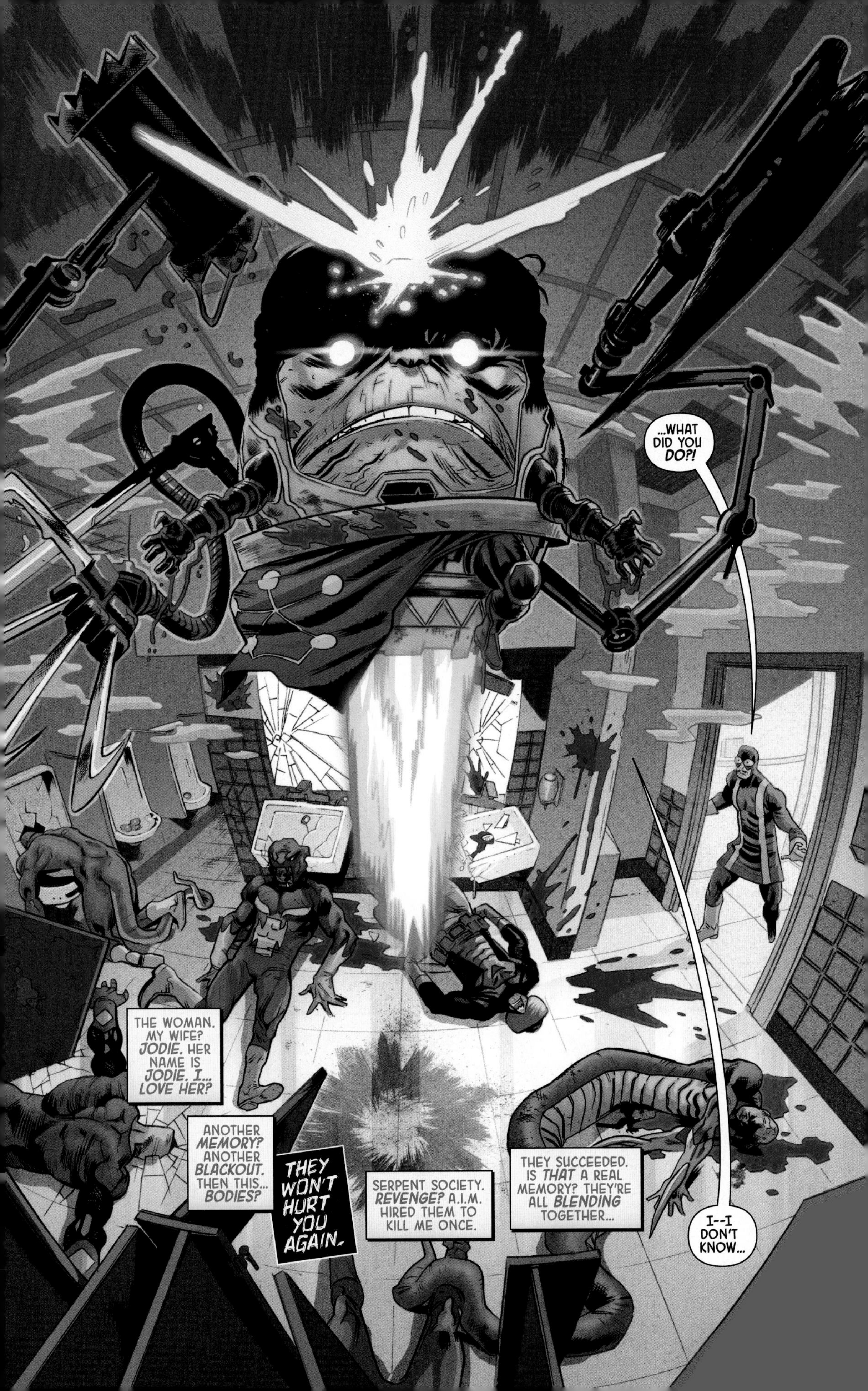

...WHAT DID YOU *DO?!*
THE WOMAN. MY WIFE? *JODIE.* HER NAME IS *JODIE. I... LOVE HER?*
ANOTHER *MEMORY?* ANOTHER *BLACKOUT.* THEN THIS... *BODIES?*
THEY WON'T HURT YOU AGAIN.
SERPENT SOCIETY. *REVENGE?* A.I.M. HIRED THEM TO KILL ME ONCE.
THEY SUCCEEDED. IS *THAT* A REAL MEMORY? THEY'RE ALL *BLENDING* TOGETHER...
I--I DON'T KNOW...

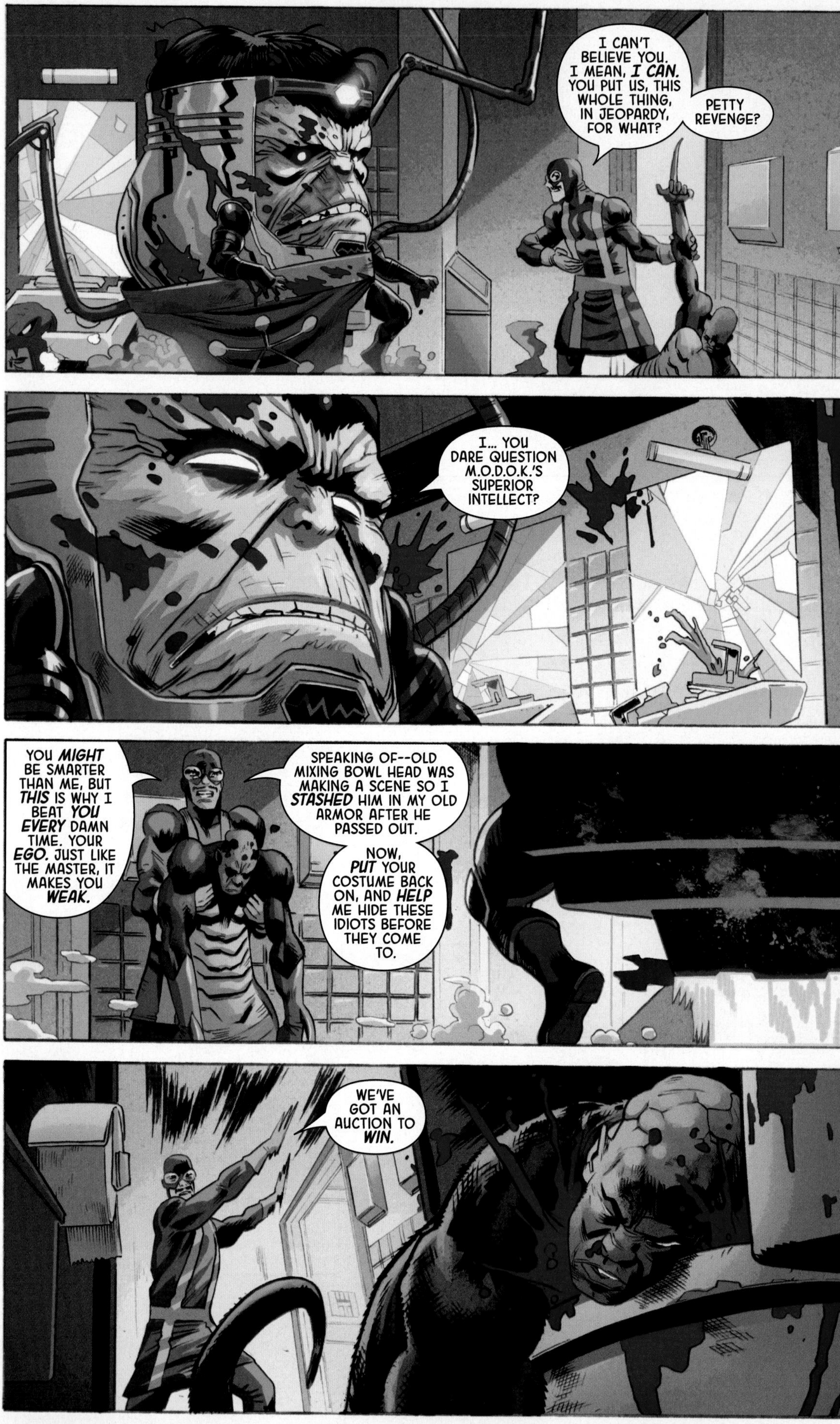
I CAN'T BELIEVE YOU. I MEAN, I CAN. YOU PUT US, THIS WHOLE THING, IN JEOPARDY, FOR WHAT?
PETTY REVENGE?
I... YOU DARE QUESTION M.O.D.O.K.'S SUPERIOR INTELLECT?
YOU MIGHT BE SMARTER THAN ME, BUT THIS IS WHY I BEAT YOU EVERY DAMN TIME. YOUR EGO. JUST LIKE THE MASTER, IT MAKES YOU WEAK.
SPEAKING OF--OLD MIXING BOWL HEAD WAS MAKING A SCENE SO I STASHED HIM IN MY OLD ARMOR AFTER HE PASSED OUT.
NOW, PUT YOUR COSTUME BACK ON, AND HELP ME HIDE THESE IDIOTS BEFORE THEY COME TO.
WE'VE GOT AN AUCTION TO WIN.

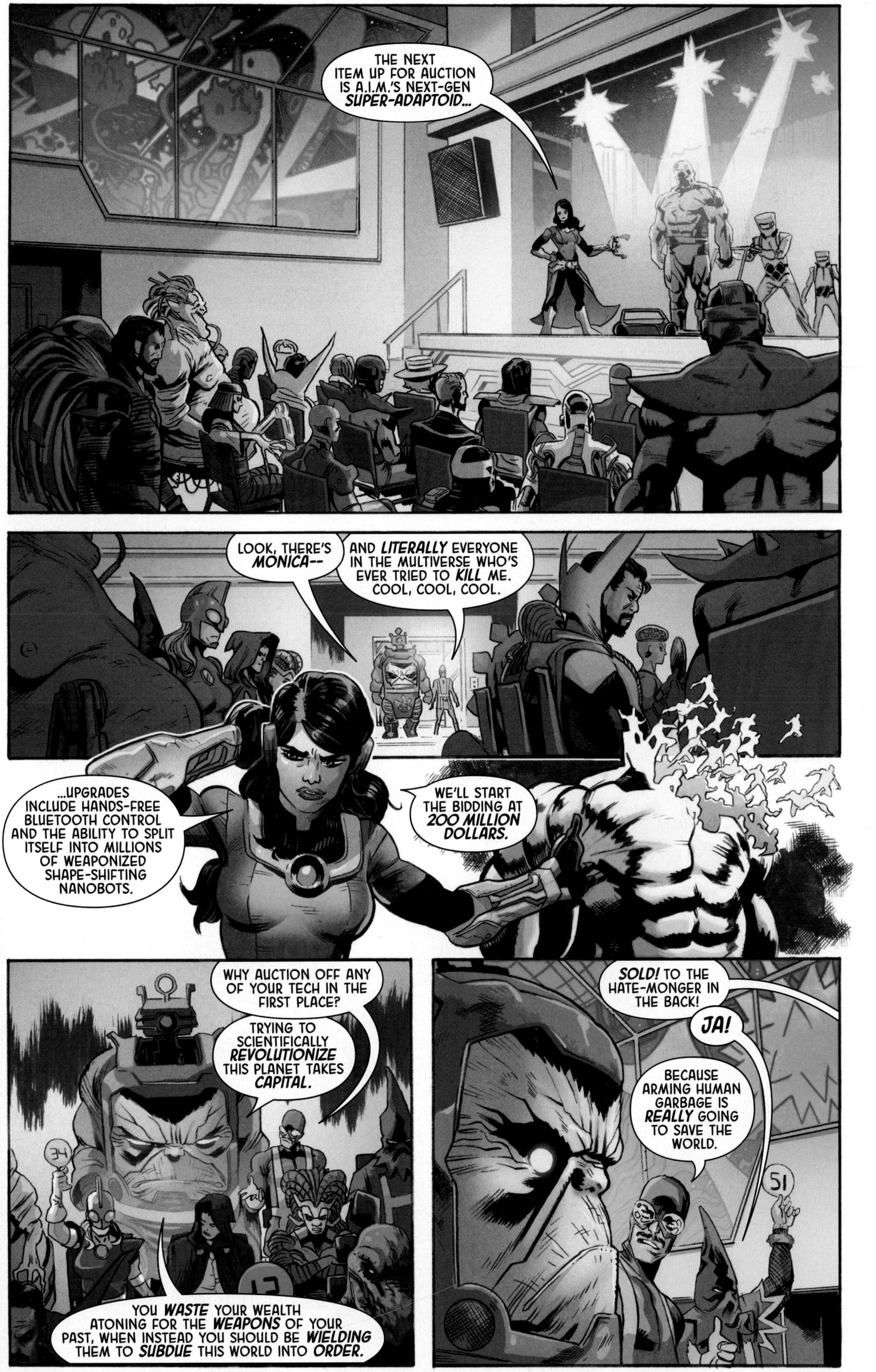
THE NEXT ITEM UP FOR AUCTION IS A.I.M.'S NEXT-GEN SUPER-ADAPTOID...
LOOK, THERE'S MONICA--
AND LITERALLY EVERYONE IN THE MULTIVERSE WHO'S EVER TRIED TO KILL ME. COOL, COOL, COOL.
...UPGRADES INCLUDE HANDS-FREE BLUETOOTH CONTROL AND THE ABILITY TO SPLIT ITSELF INTO MILLIONS OF WEAPONIZED SHAPE-SHIFTING NANOBOTS.
WE'LL START THE BIDDING AT 200 MILLION DOLLARS.
WHY AUCTION OFF ANY OF YOUR TECH IN THE FIRST PLACE?
TRYING TO SCIENTIFICALLY REVOLUTIONIZE THIS PLANET TAKES CAPITAL.
34
13
YOU WASTE YOUR WEALTH ATONING FOR THE WEAPONS OF YOUR PAST, WHEN INSTEAD YOU SHOULD BE WIELDING THEM TO SUBDUE THIS WORLD INTO ORDER.
SOLD! TO THE HATE-MONGER IN THE BACK!
JA!
BECAUSE ARMING HUMAN GARBAGE IS REALLY GOING TO SAVE THE WORLD.
51

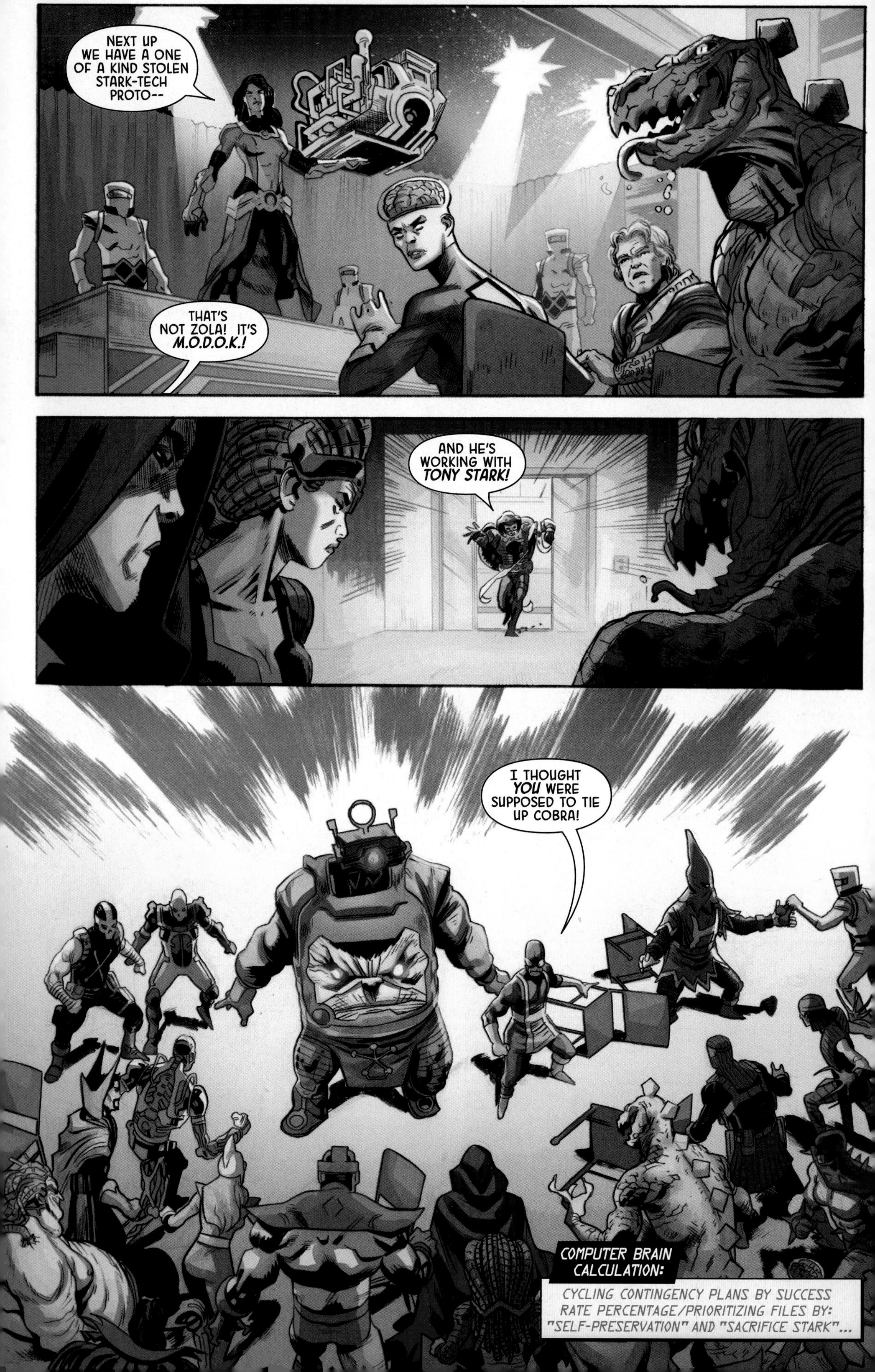
NEXT UP WE HAVE A ONE OF A KIND STOLEN STARK-TECH PROTO--
THAT'S NOT ZOLA! IT'S M.O.D.O.K.!
AND HE'S WORKING WITH TONY STARK!
I THOUGHT YOU WERE SUPPOSED TO TIE UP COBRA!
COMPUTER BRAIN CALCULATION:
CYCLING CONTINGENCY PLANS BY SUCCESS RATE PERCENTAGE/PRIORITIZING FILES BY: "SELF-PRESERVATION" AND "SACRIFICE STARK"...

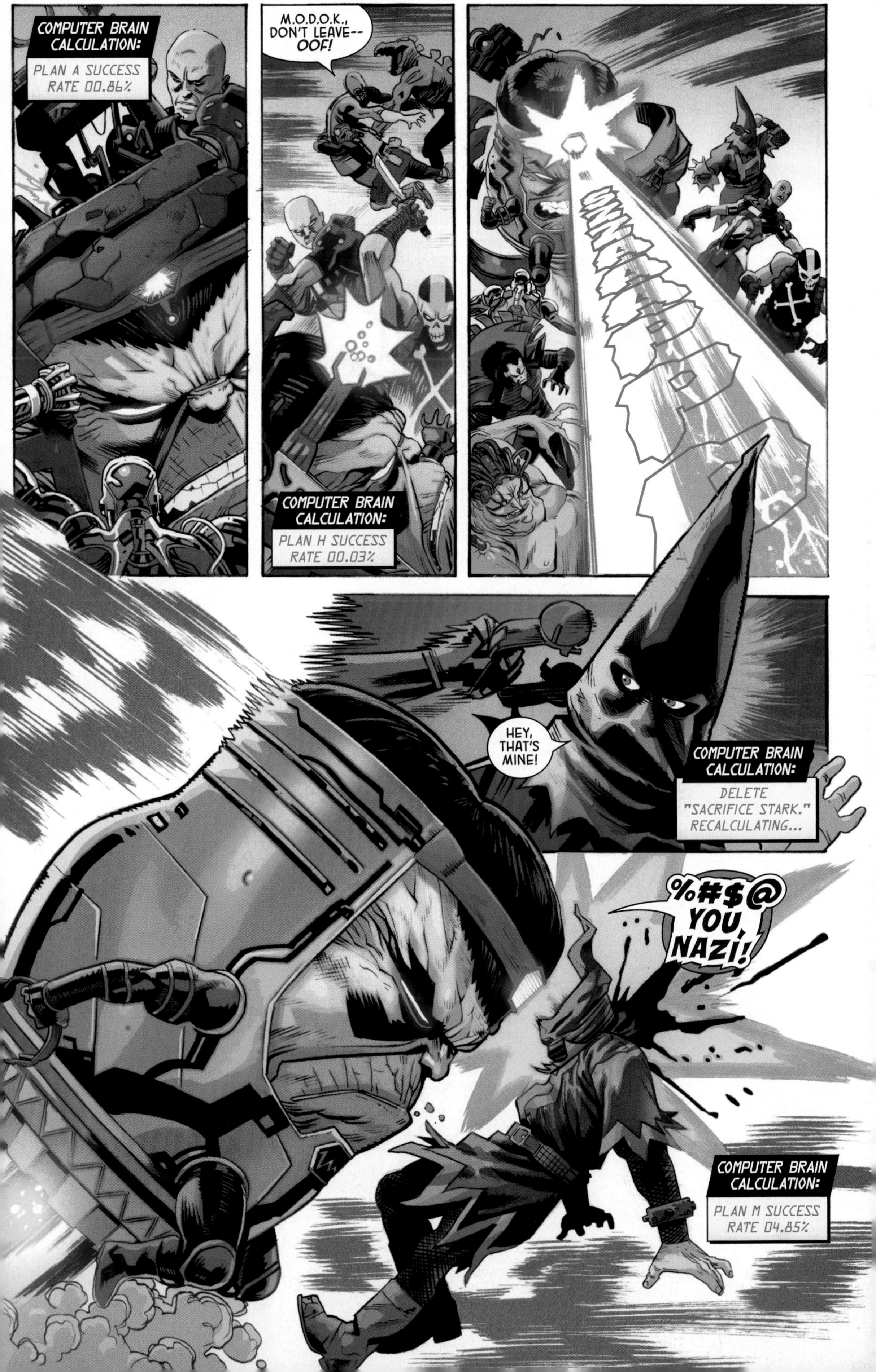
COMPUTER BRAIN CALCULATION:
PLAN A SUCCESS RATE 00.86%
M.O.D.O.K., DON'T LEAVE-- OOF!
COMPUTER BRAIN CALCULATION:
PLAN H SUCCESS RATE 00.03%
HEY, THAT'S MINE!
COMPUTER BRAIN CALCULATION:
DELETE "SACRIFICE STARK." RECALCULATING...
%#$@ YOU, NAZI!
COMPUTER BRAIN CALCULATION:
PLAN M SUCCESS RATE 04.85%

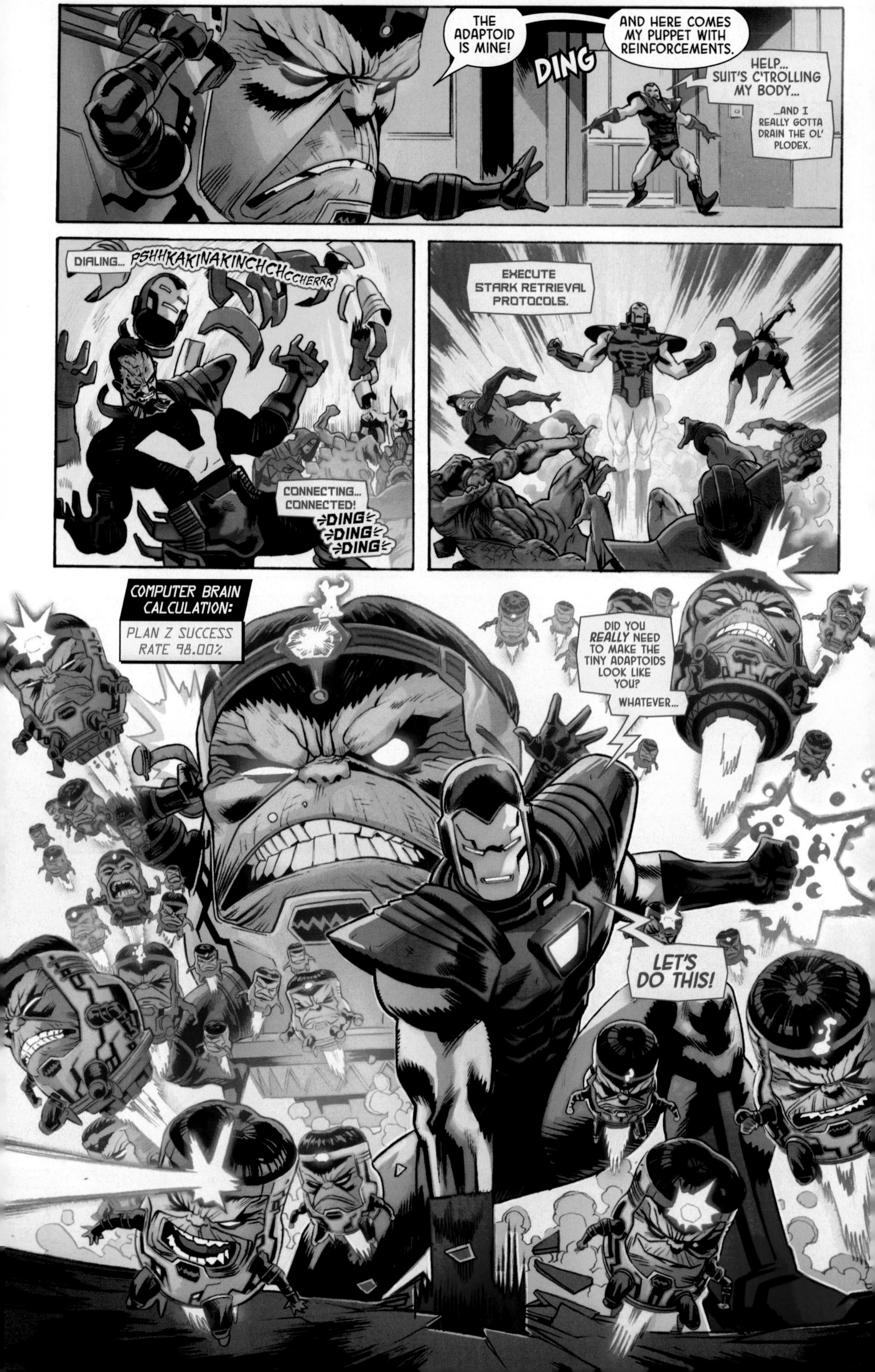
THE ADAPTOID IS MINE!
AND HERE COMES MY PUPPET WITH REINFORCEMENTS.
DING
HELP... SUIT'S C'TROLLING MY BODY...
...AND I REALLY GOTTA DRAIN THE OL' PLODEX.
DIALING...
PSHHKAKINAKINCHCHCCHERRR
CONNECTING... CONNECTED!
DING DING DING
EXECUTE STARK RETRIEVAL PROTOCOLS.
COMPUTER BRAIN CALCULATION:
PLAN Z SUCCESS RATE 98.00%
DID YOU REALLY NEED TO MAKE THE TINY ADAPTOIDS LOOK LIKE YOU?
WHATEVER...
LET'S DO THIS!

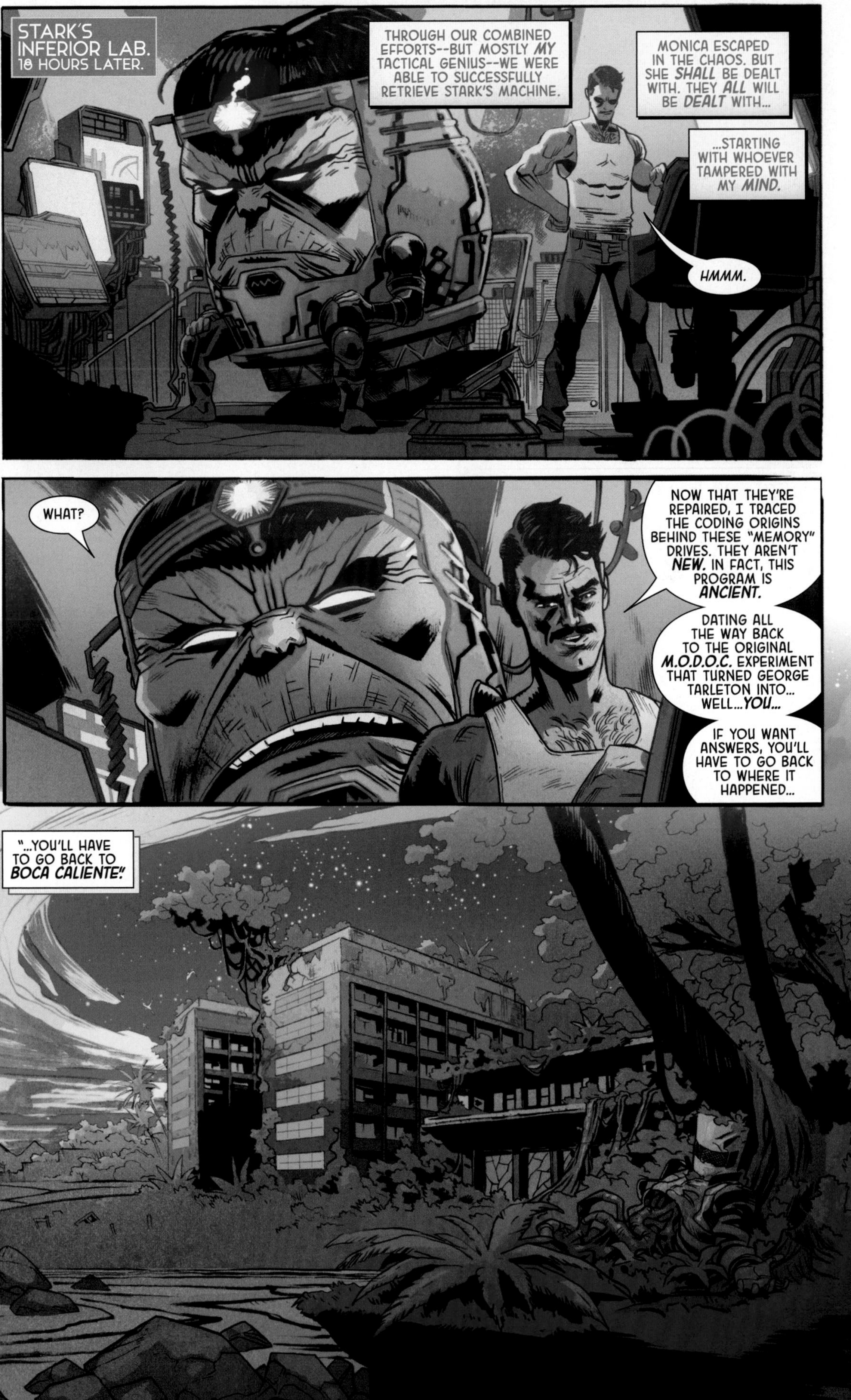
STARK'S INFERIOR LAB. 18 HOURS LATER.
THROUGH OUR COMBINED EFFORTS--BUT MOSTLY MY TACTICAL GENIUS--WE WERE ABLE TO SUCCESSFULLY RETRIEVE STARK'S MACHINE.
MONICA ESCAPED IN THE CHAOS. BUT SHE SHALL BE DEALT WITH. THEY ALL WILL BE DEALT WITH...
...STARTING WITH WHOEVER TAMPERED WITH MY MIND.
HMMM.
WHAT?
NOW THAT THEY'RE REPAIRED, I TRACED THE CODING ORIGINS BEHIND THESE "MEMORY" DRIVES. THEY AREN'T NEW. IN FACT, THIS PROGRAM IS ANCIENT.
DATING ALL THE WAY BACK TO THE ORIGINAL M.O.D.O.C. EXPERIMENT THAT TURNED GEORGE TARLETON INTO... WELL...YOU...
IF YOU WANT ANSWERS, YOU'LL HAVE TO GO BACK TO WHERE IT HAPPENED...
"...YOU'LL HAVE TO GO BACK TO BOCA CALIENTE!"

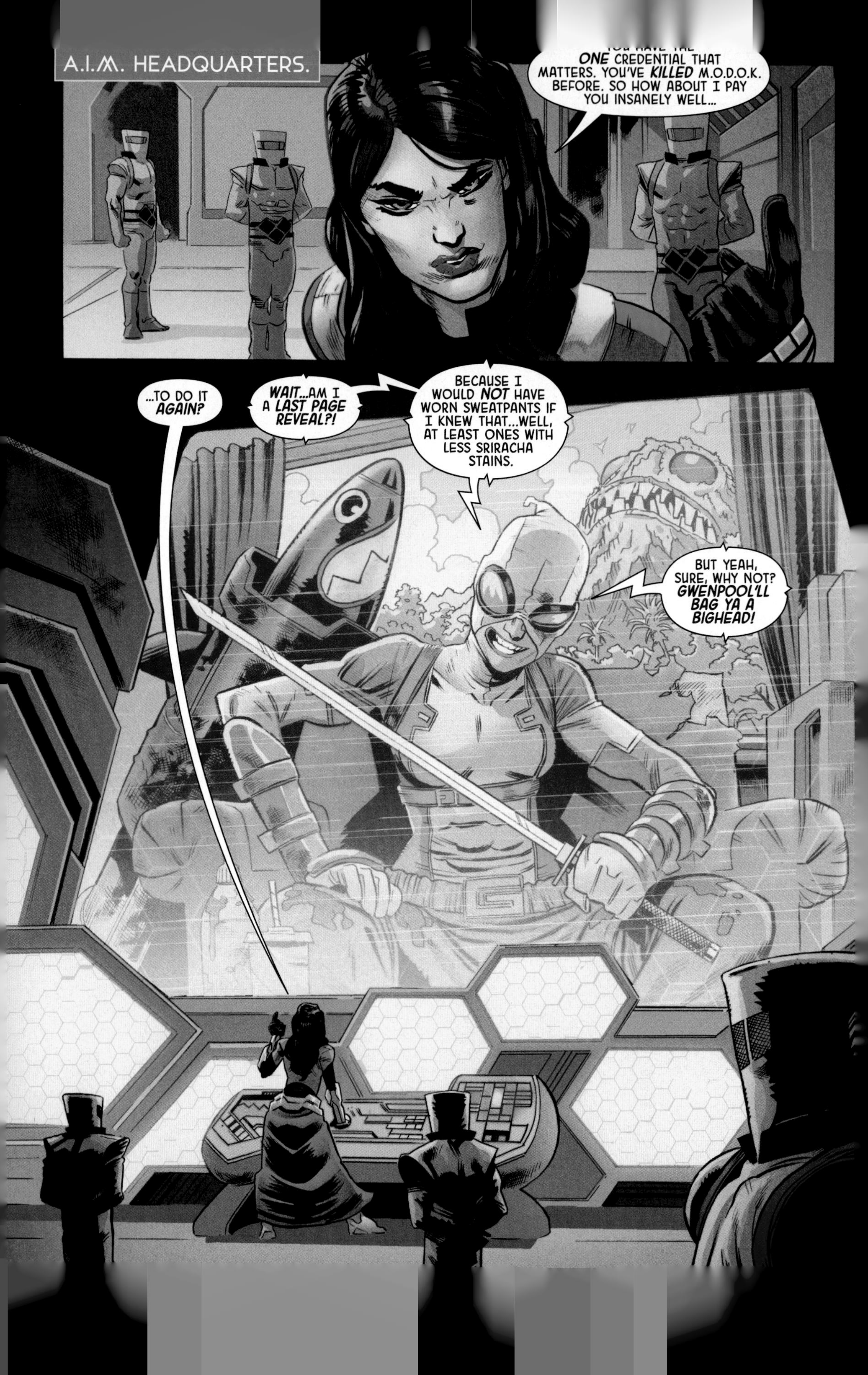
A.I.M. HEADQUARTERS.
ONE CREDENTIAL THAT MATTERS. YOU'VE KILLED M.O.D.O.K. BEFORE. SO HOW ABOUT I PAY YOU INSANELY WELL...
...TO DO IT AGAIN?
WAIT...AM I A LAST PAGE REVEAL?!
BECAUSE I WOULD NOT HAVE WORN SWEATPANTS IF I KNEW THAT...WELL, AT LEAST ONES WITH LESS SRIRACHA STAINS.
BUT YEAH, SURE, WHY NOT? GWENPOOL'LL BAG YA A BIGHEAD!

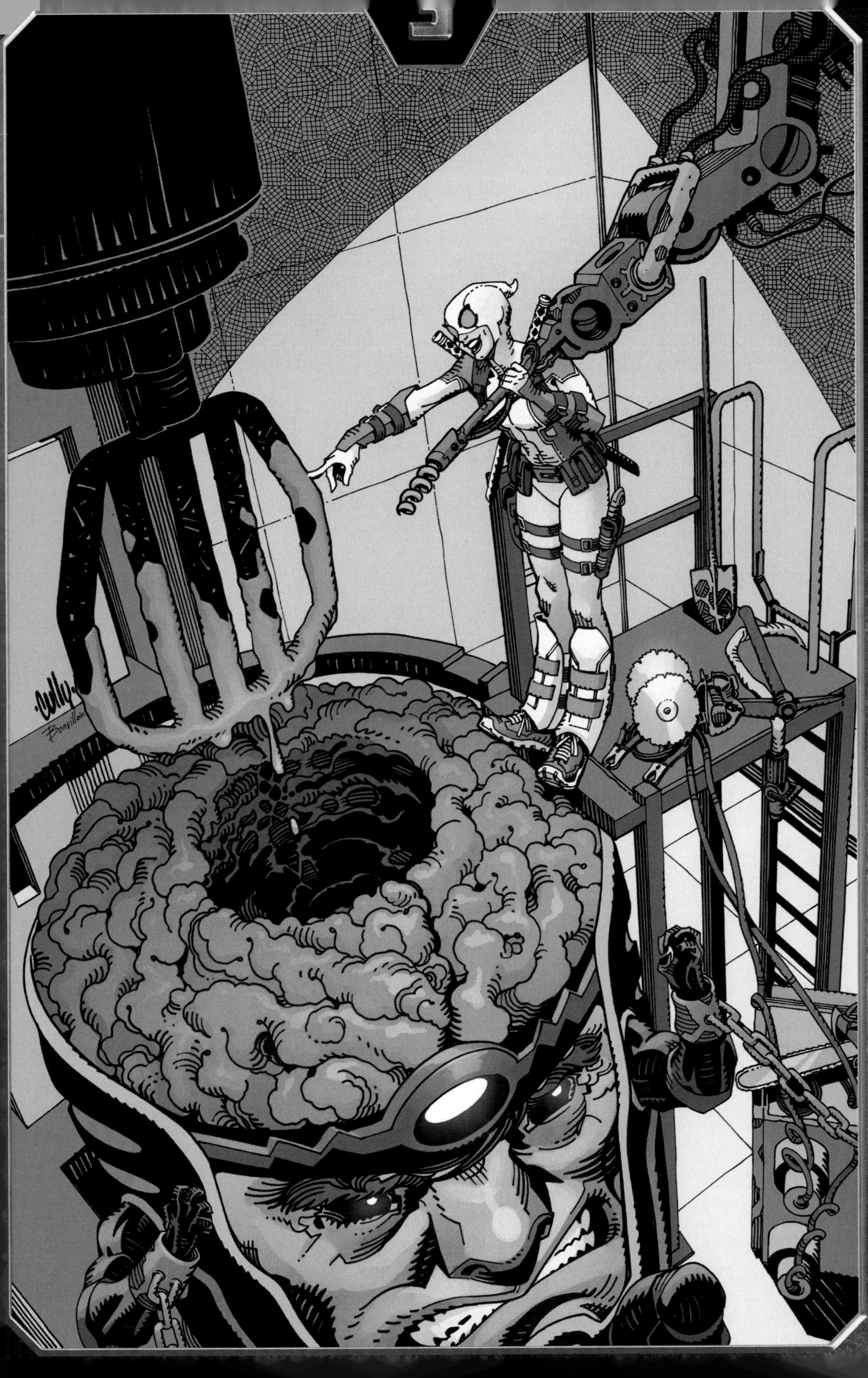
Bonvillain

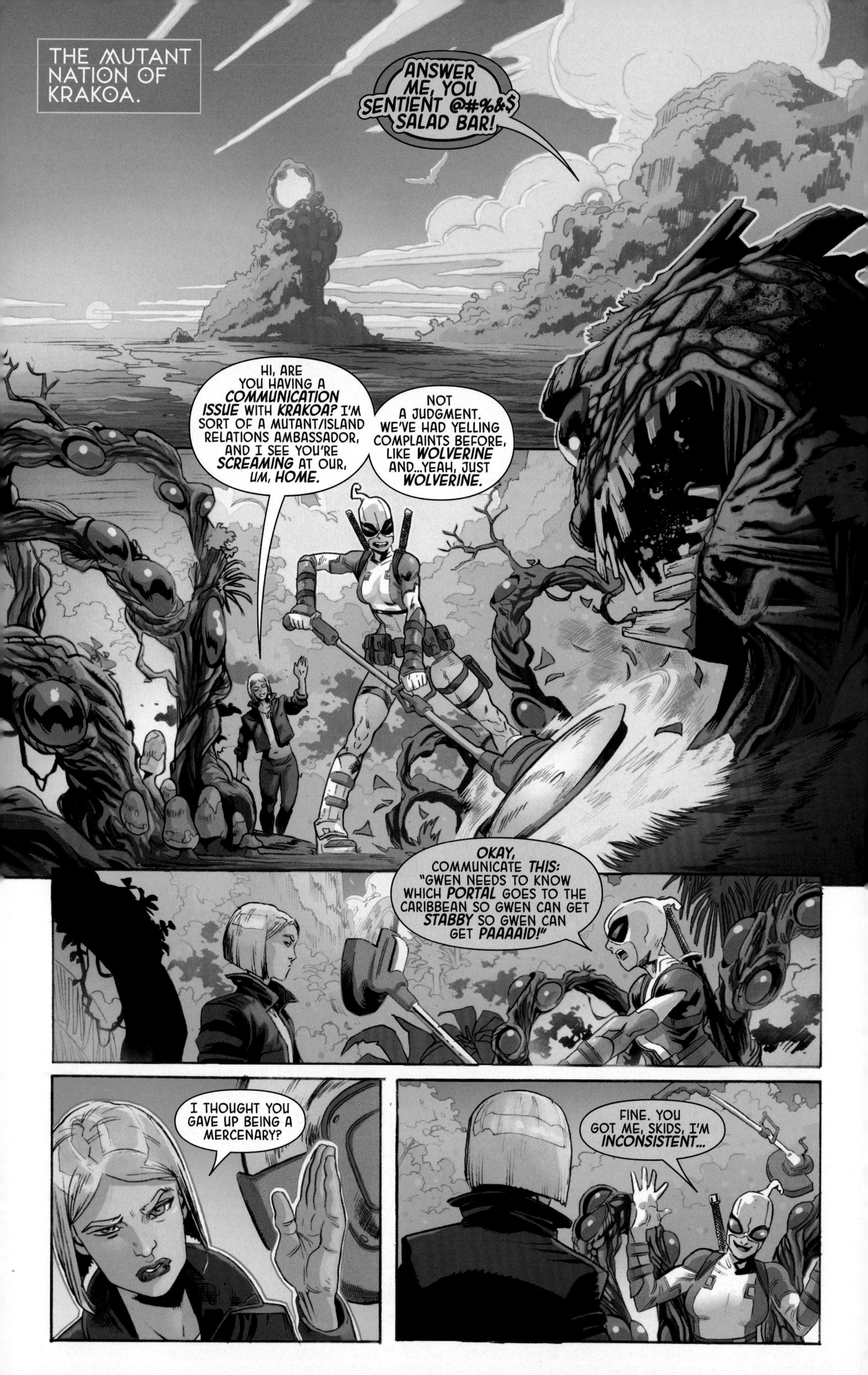
THE MUTANT NATION OF KRAKOA.
ANSWER ME, YOU SENTIENT @#%&$ SALAD BAR!
HI, ARE YOU HAVING A COMMUNICATION ISSUE WITH KRAKOA? I'M SORT OF A MUTANT/ISLAND RELATIONS AMBASSADOR, AND I SEE YOU'RE SCREAMING AT OUR, UM, HOME.
NOT A JUDGMENT. WE'VE HAD YELLING COMPLAINTS BEFORE, LIKE WOLVERINE AND...YEAH, JUST WOLVERINE.
OKAY, COMMUNICATE THIS: "GWEN NEEDS TO KNOW WHICH PORTAL GOES TO THE CARIBBEAN SO GWEN CAN GET STABBY SO GWEN CAN GET PAAAAID!"
I THOUGHT YOU GAVE UP BEING A MERCENARY?
FINE. YOU GOT ME, SKIDS, I'M INCONSISTENT...

...BUT WEREN'T YOU ONCE, LIKE, A MADONNA PASTICHE?*

*X-FACTOR #7 VOL. 1 --JORDAN "DON'T DO THIS BIT" WHITE

THEN AN M.L.F. TERRORIST?**

*X-FACTOR #7 VOL. 1 --JORDAN "DON'T DO THIS BIT" WHITE

**NEW MUTANTS #77 VOL. 1 -- JORDAN "DAMMIT, MORE?!" WHITE

*X-FA-- --JORDAN "DON'T DO THIS BIT" WHITE

AND THEN AN UNDERCOVER S.H.I.E.L.D. AGENT?***

**NEW MUTANTS #77 VOL. 1 -- JORDAN "DAMMIT, MORE?!" WHITE

***UNCANNY X-MEN #487 VOL. 1 -- JORDAN "DELETING WRITERS' CONTACTS FROM PHONE" WHITE

BUT, HEY, CONGRATS ON BEING DUSTED OFF AND TAKEN OUT OF MUTANT LOWERCASE-L LIMBO. OOH, MAYBE HICKMAN'LL PUT YOU IN A CHART!

DAMMIT," WHITE

X-MEN .1 -- ETING TACTS WHITE

... UM... HAVE YOU TRIED ASKING KRAKOA IN KRAKOAN?

-FACTOR #7 VOL-- --JORDAN "DON'T DO THIS BIT" WHITE

**NEW MUTANTS #77 VOL. 1 -- JORDAN "DAMMIT, MORE?!" WHITE

***UNCANNY X-MEN #487 VOL. 1 -- JORDAN "DELETING WRITERS' CONTACTS FROM PHONE WHITE

OH YEAH--FONT CHANGE!

OKAY, GOTTA GO MURDER A BABY-MAN-CHAIR-THING!

WHAT WAS THAT ABOUT?

I WANT A NEW @#%&$ JOB.

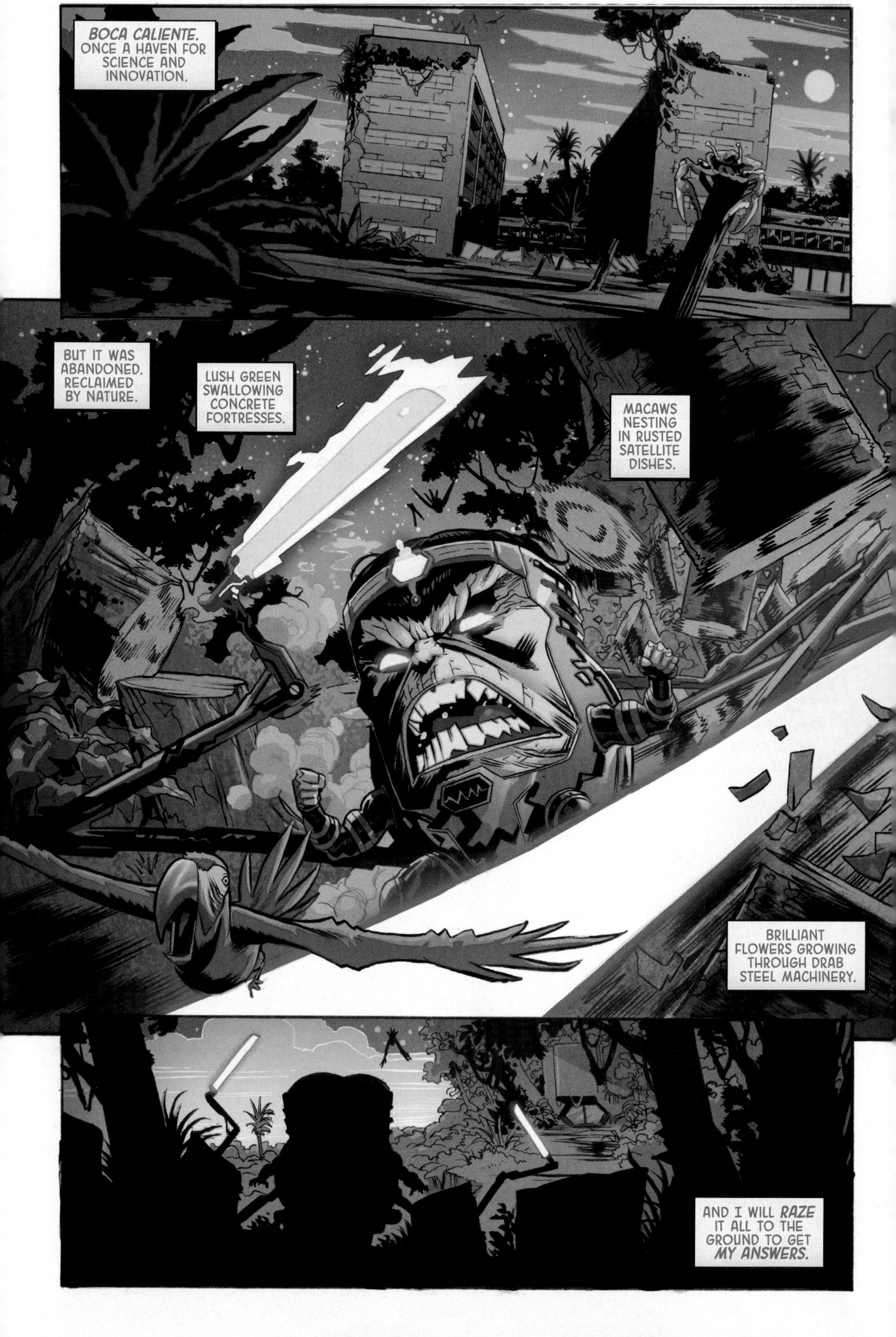
BOCA CALIENTE. ONCE A HAVEN FOR SCIENCE AND INNOVATION.
BUT IT WAS ABANDONED. RECLAIMED BY NATURE.
LUSH GREEN SWALLOWING CONCRETE FORTRESSES.
MACAWS NESTING IN RUSTED SATELLITE DISHES.
BRILLIANT FLOWERS GROWING THROUGH DRAB STEEL MACHINERY.
AND I WILL RAZE IT ALL TO THE GROUND TO GET MY ANSWERS.

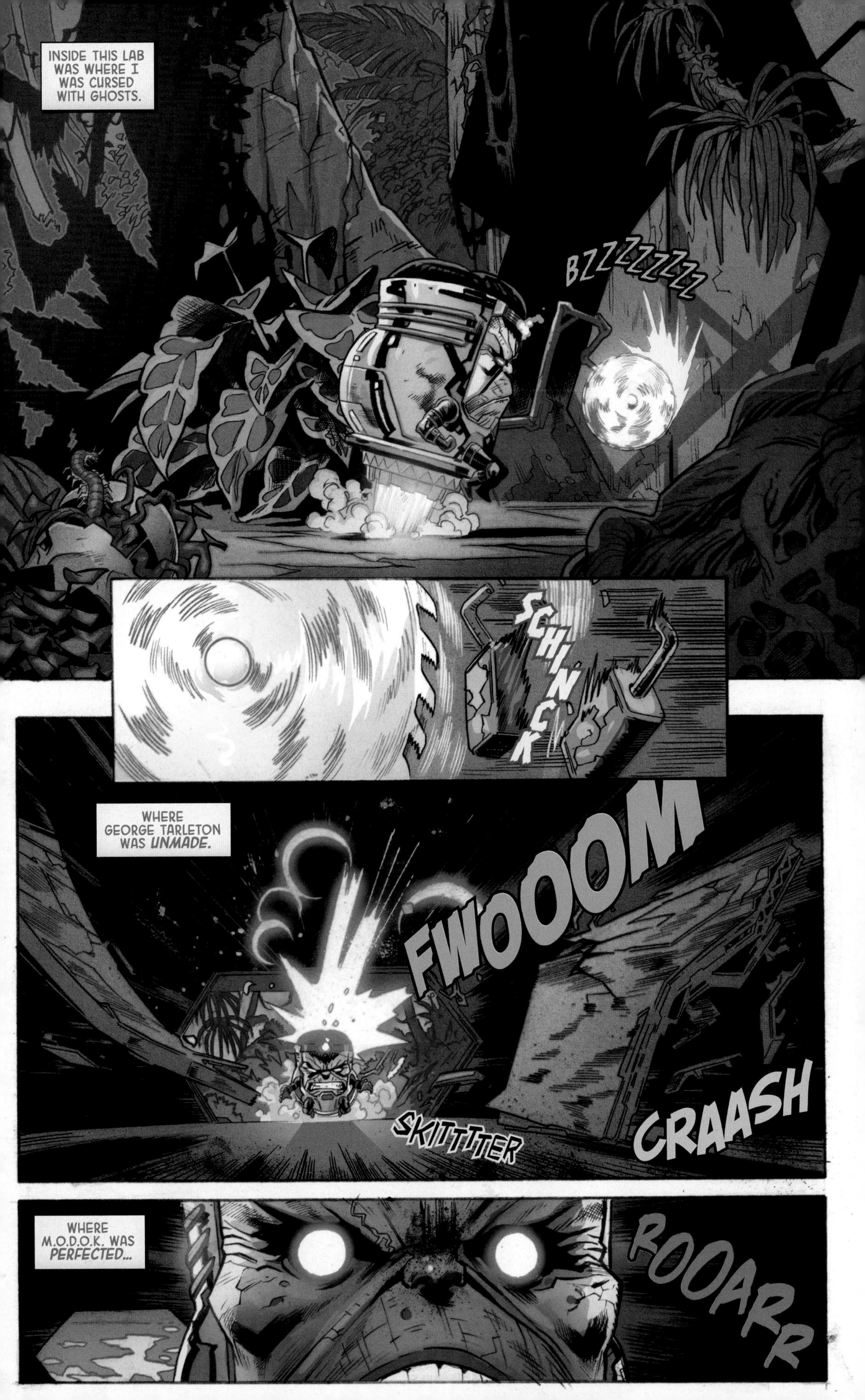
INSIDE THIS LAB WAS WHERE I WAS CURSED WITH GHOSTS.
BZZZZZZZZ
SCHINCK
WHERE GEORGE TARLETON WAS *UNMADE.*
FWOOOM
SKITTTTER
CRAASH
WHERE M.O.D.O.K. WAS *PERFECTED...*
ROOARR

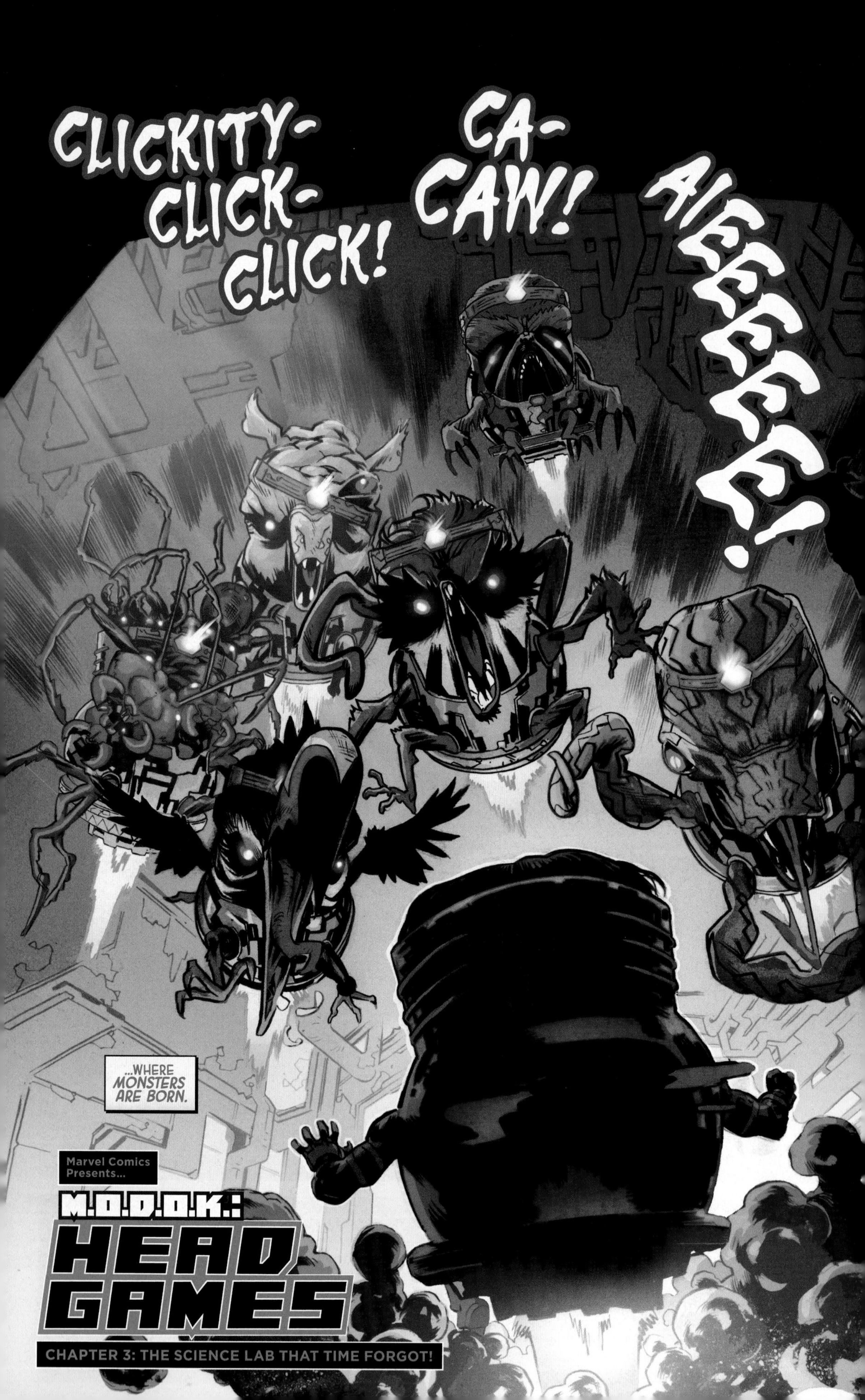
CLICKITY-CLICK-CLICK!
CA-CAW!
AIEEEEE!
...WHERE MONSTERS ARE BORN.
Marvel Comics Presents...
M.O.D.O.K.: HEAD GAMES
CHAPTER 3: THE SCIENCE LAB THAT TIME FORGOT!

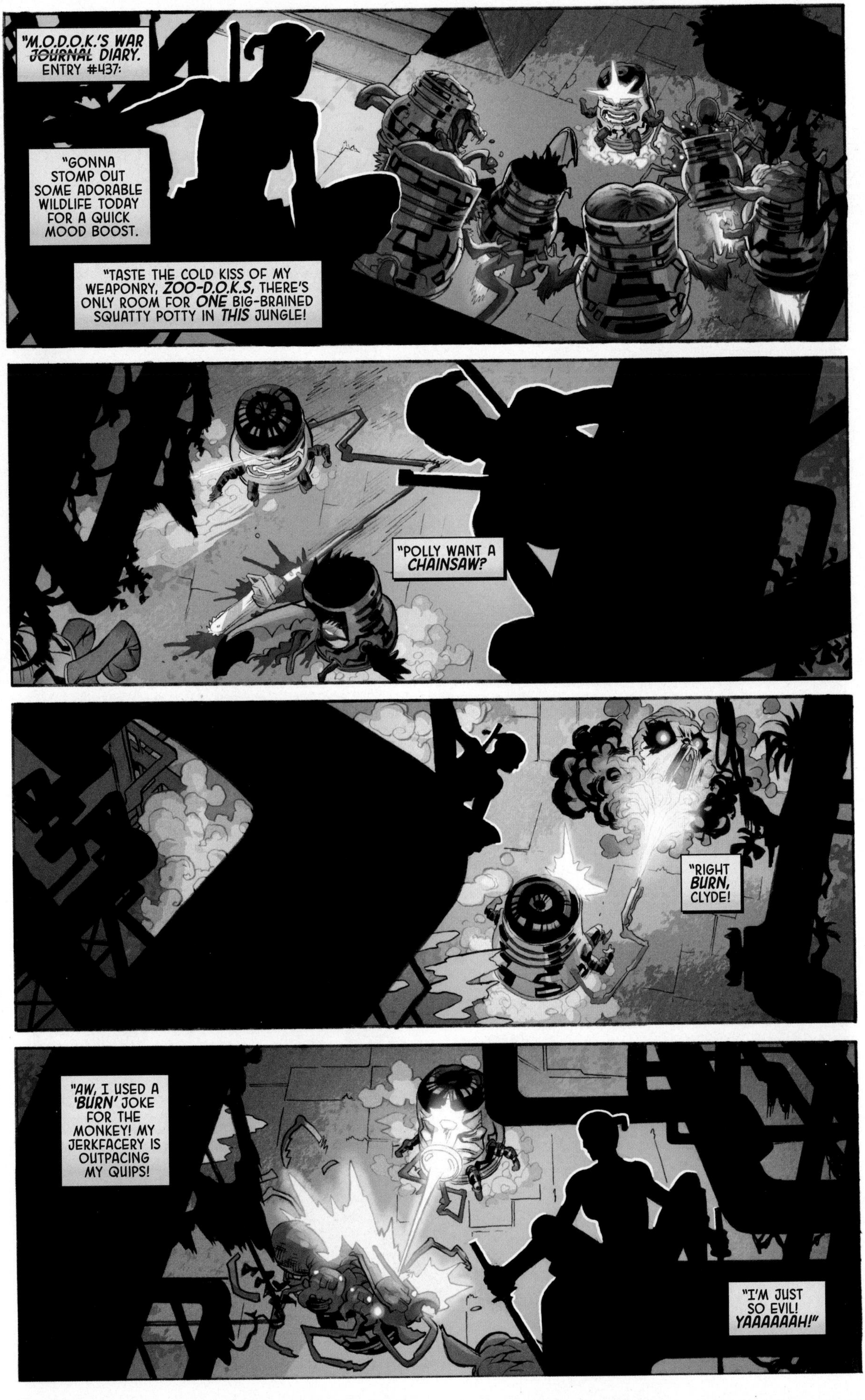
"M.O.D.O.K.'S WAR JOURNAL DIARY. ENTRY #437:
"GONNA STOMP OUT SOME ADORABLE WILDLIFE TODAY FOR A QUICK MOOD BOOST.
"TASTE THE COLD KISS OF MY WEAPONRY, ZOO-D.O.K.S, THERE'S ONLY ROOM FOR ONE BIG-BRAINED SQUATTY POTTY IN THIS JUNGLE!
"POLLY WANT A CHAINSAW?
"RIGHT BURN, CLYDE!
"AW, I USED A 'BURN' JOKE FOR THE MONKEY! MY JERKFACERY IS OUTPACING MY QUIPS!
"I'M JUST SO EVIL! YAAAAAAH!"

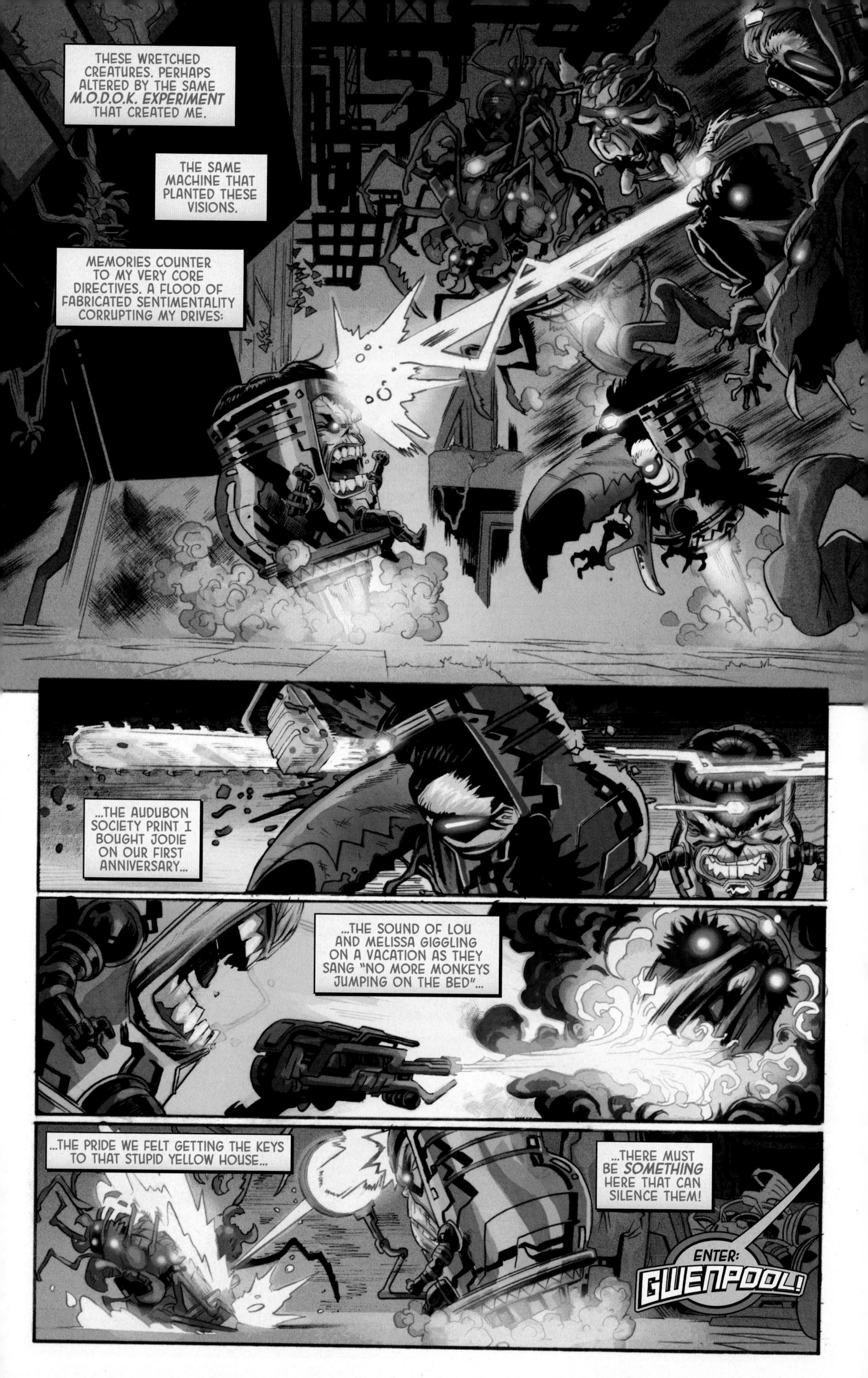
THESE WRETCHED CREATURES. PERHAPS ALTERED BY THE SAME *M.O.D.O.K. EXPERIMENT* THAT CREATED ME.
THE SAME MACHINE THAT PLANTED THESE VISIONS.
MEMORIES COUNTER TO MY VERY CORE DIRECTIVES. A FLOOD OF FABRICATED SENTIMENTALITY CORRUPTING MY DRIVES:
...THE AUDUBON SOCIETY PRINT I BOUGHT JODIE ON OUR FIRST ANNIVERSARY...
...THE SOUND OF LOU AND MELISSA GIGGLING ON A VACATION AS THEY SANG "NO MORE MONKEYS JUMPING ON THE BED"...
...THE PRIDE WE FELT GETTING THE KEYS TO THAT STUPID YELLOW HOUSE...
...THERE MUST BE *SOMETHING* HERE THAT CAN SILENCE THEM!
ENTER:
GWENPOOL!

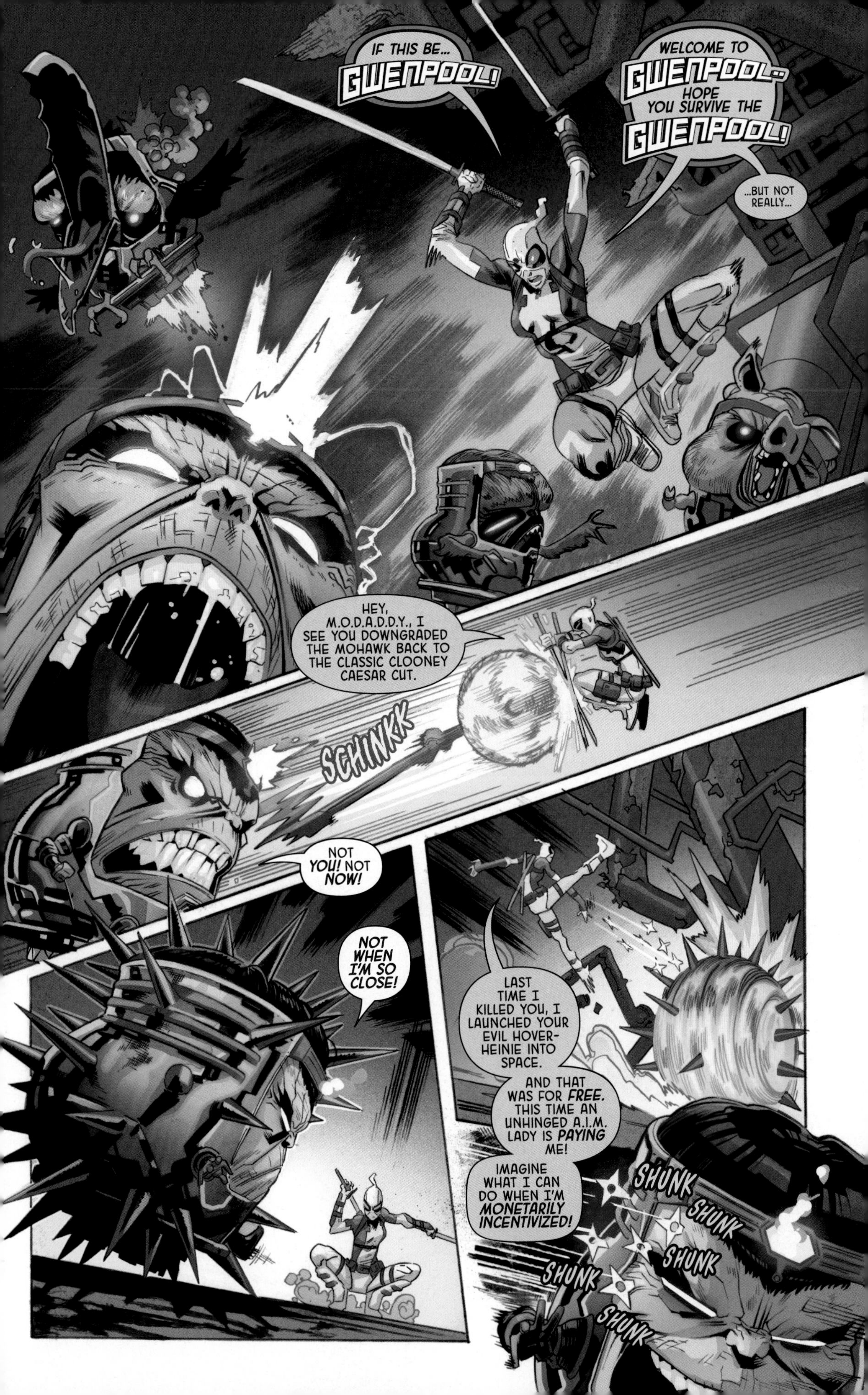
IF THIS BE... GWENPOOL!
WELCOME TO GWENPOOL... HOPE YOU SURVIVE THE GWENPOOL!
...BUT NOT REALLY...
HEY, M.O.D.A.D.D.Y., I SEE YOU DOWNGRADED THE MOHAWK BACK TO THE CLASSIC CLOONEY CAESAR CUT.
SCHINKK
NOT YOU! NOT NOW!
NOT WHEN I'M SO CLOSE!
LAST TIME I KILLED YOU, I LAUNCHED YOUR EVIL HOVER-HEINIE INTO SPACE.
AND THAT WAS FOR FREE. THIS TIME AN UNHINGED A.I.M. LADY IS PAYING ME!
IMAGINE WHAT I CAN DO WHEN I'M MONETARILY INCENTIVIZED!
SHUNK
SHUNK
SHUNK
SHUNK
SHUNK

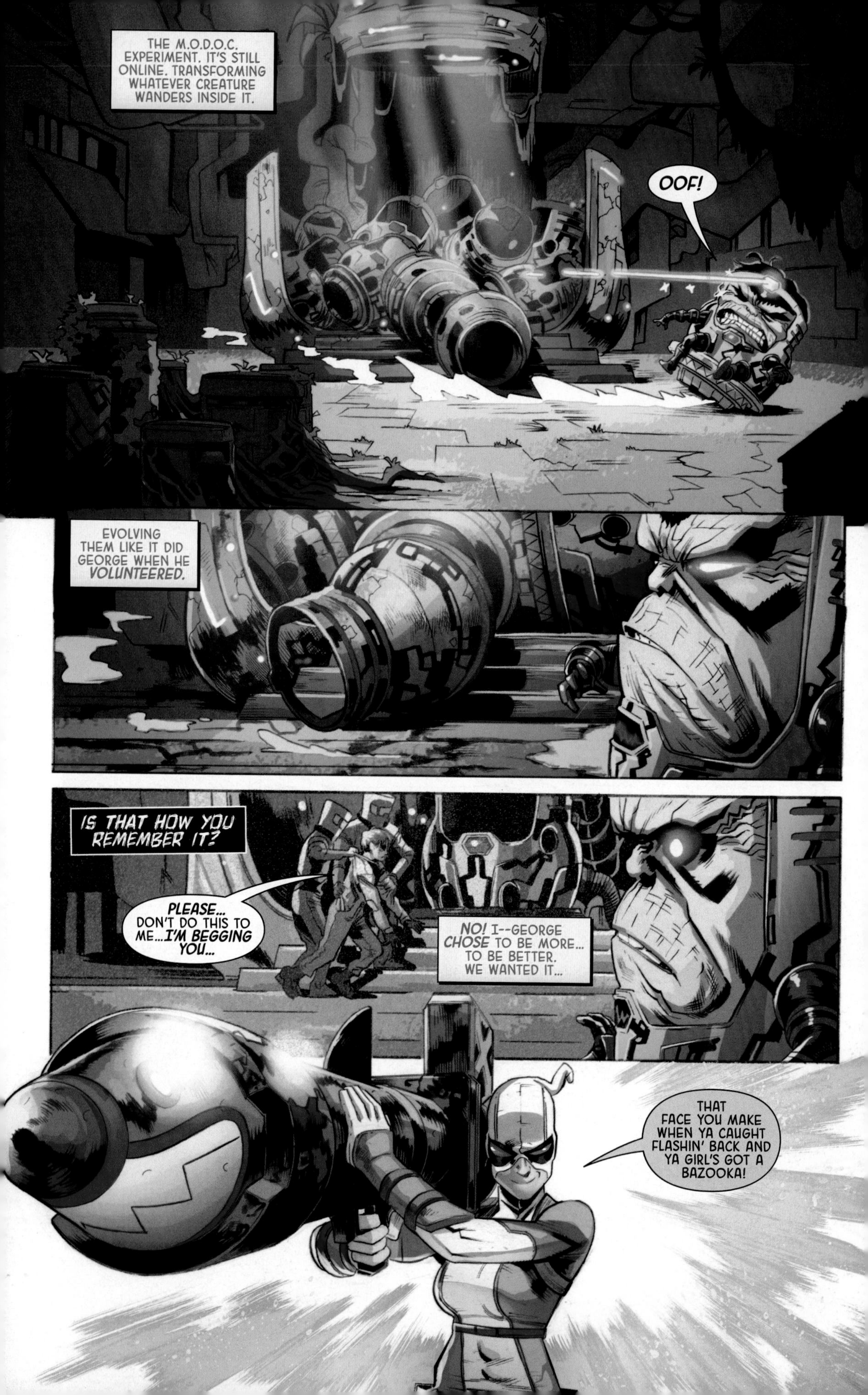
THE M.O.D.O.C. EXPERIMENT. IT'S STILL ONLINE. TRANSFORMING WHATEVER CREATURE WANDERS INSIDE IT.
OOF!
EVOLVING THEM LIKE IT DID GEORGE WHEN HE VOLUNTEERED.
IS THAT HOW YOU REMEMBER IT?
PLEASE... DON'T DO THIS TO ME...I'M BEGGING YOU...
NO! I--GEORGE CHOSE TO BE MORE... TO BE BETTER. WE WANTED IT...
THAT FACE YOU MAKE WHEN YA CAUGHT FLASHIN' BACK AND YA GIRL'S GOT A BAZOOKA!

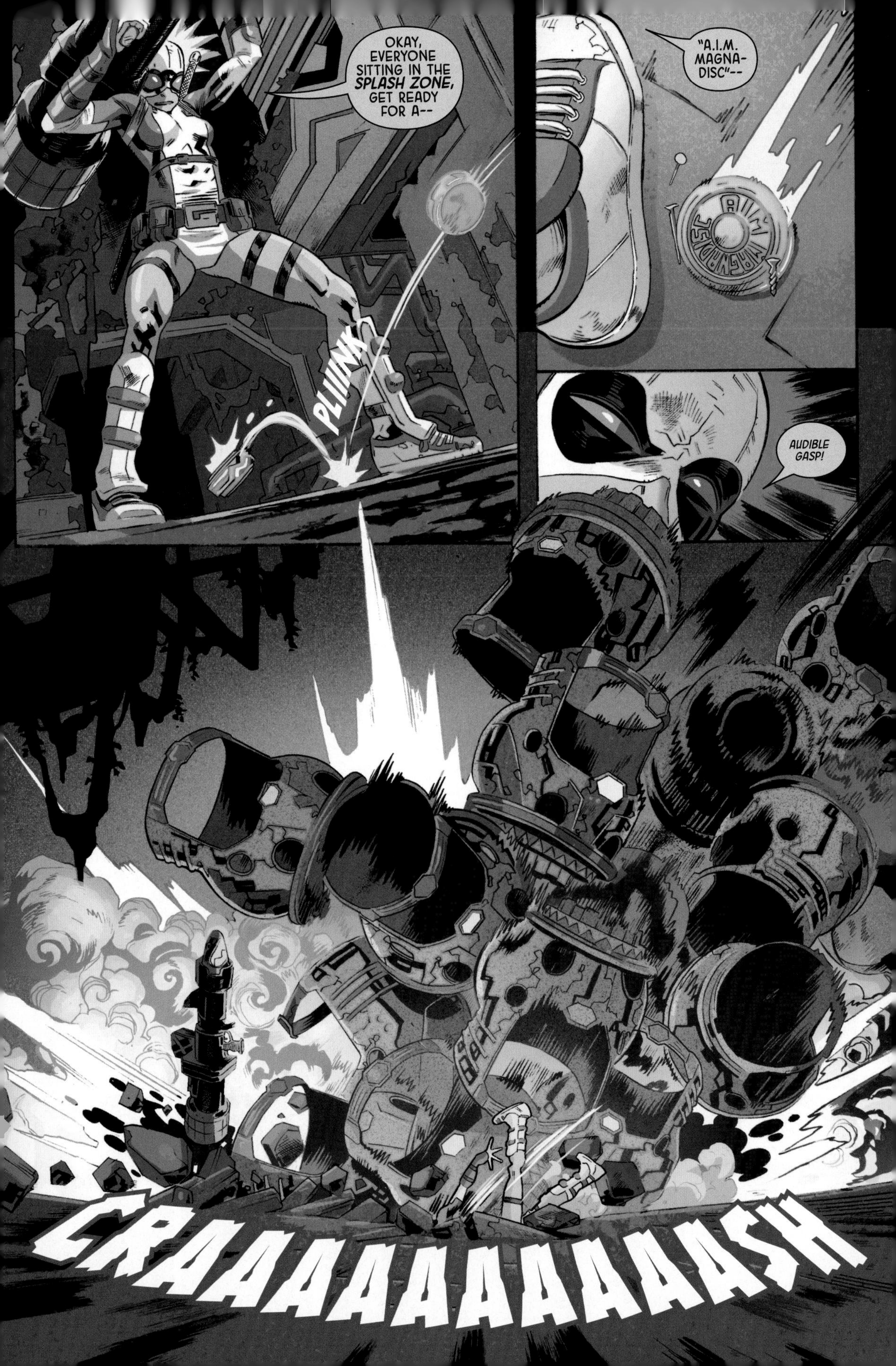
OKAY, EVERYONE SITTING IN THE SPLASH ZONE, GET READY FOR A--
PLIINK
"A.I.M. MAGNA-DISC"--
AIM MAGNADISC
AUDIBLE GASP!
CRAAAAAAAAAAASH

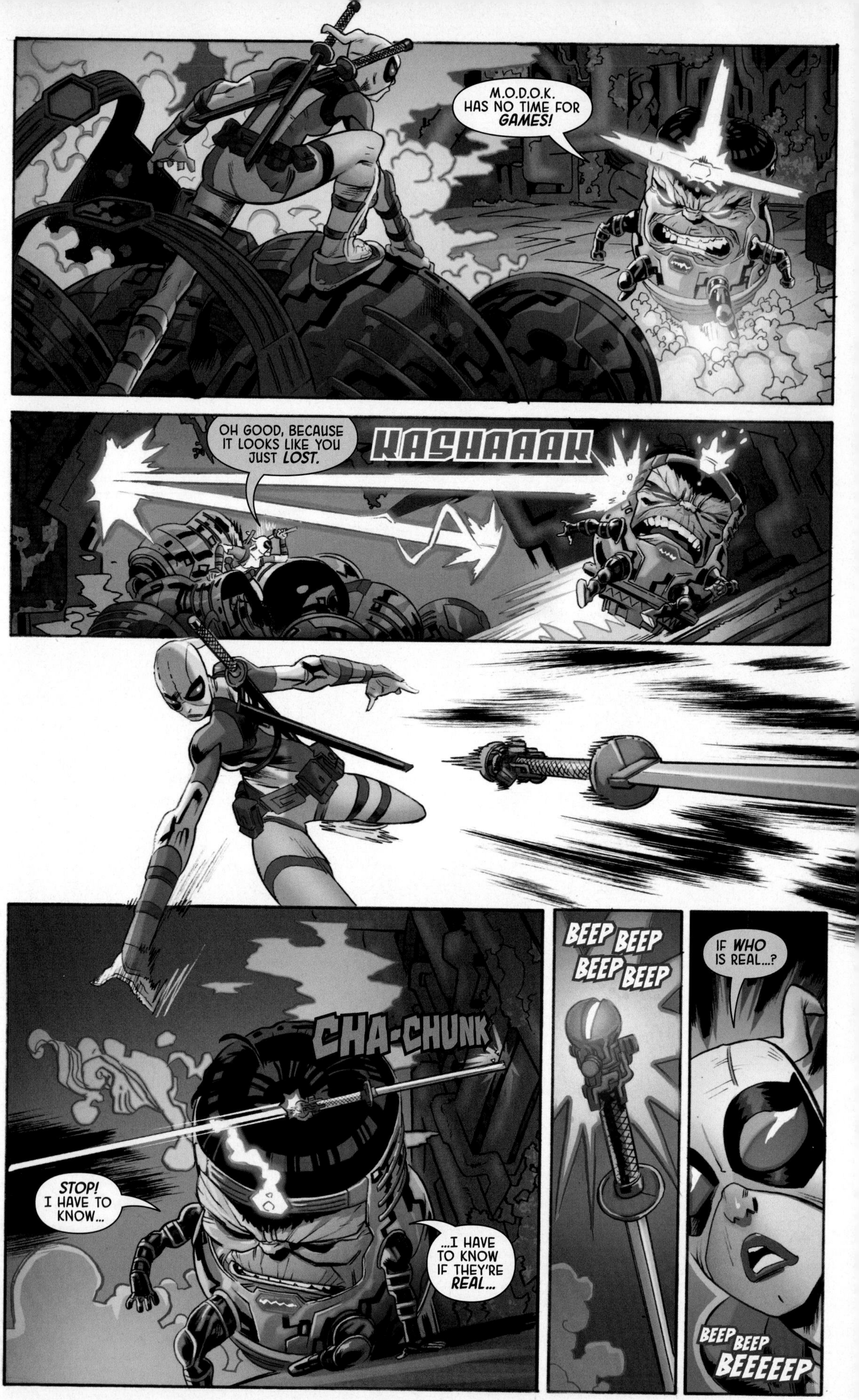
M.O.D.O.K. HAS NO TIME FOR GAMES!
OH GOOD, BECAUSE IT LOOKS LIKE YOU JUST LOST.
KASHAAAK
CHA-CHUNK
STOP! I HAVE TO KNOW...
...I HAVE TO KNOW IF THEY'RE REAL...
BEEP BEEP BEEP BEEP
IF WHO IS REAL...?
BEEP BEEP BEEEEEP

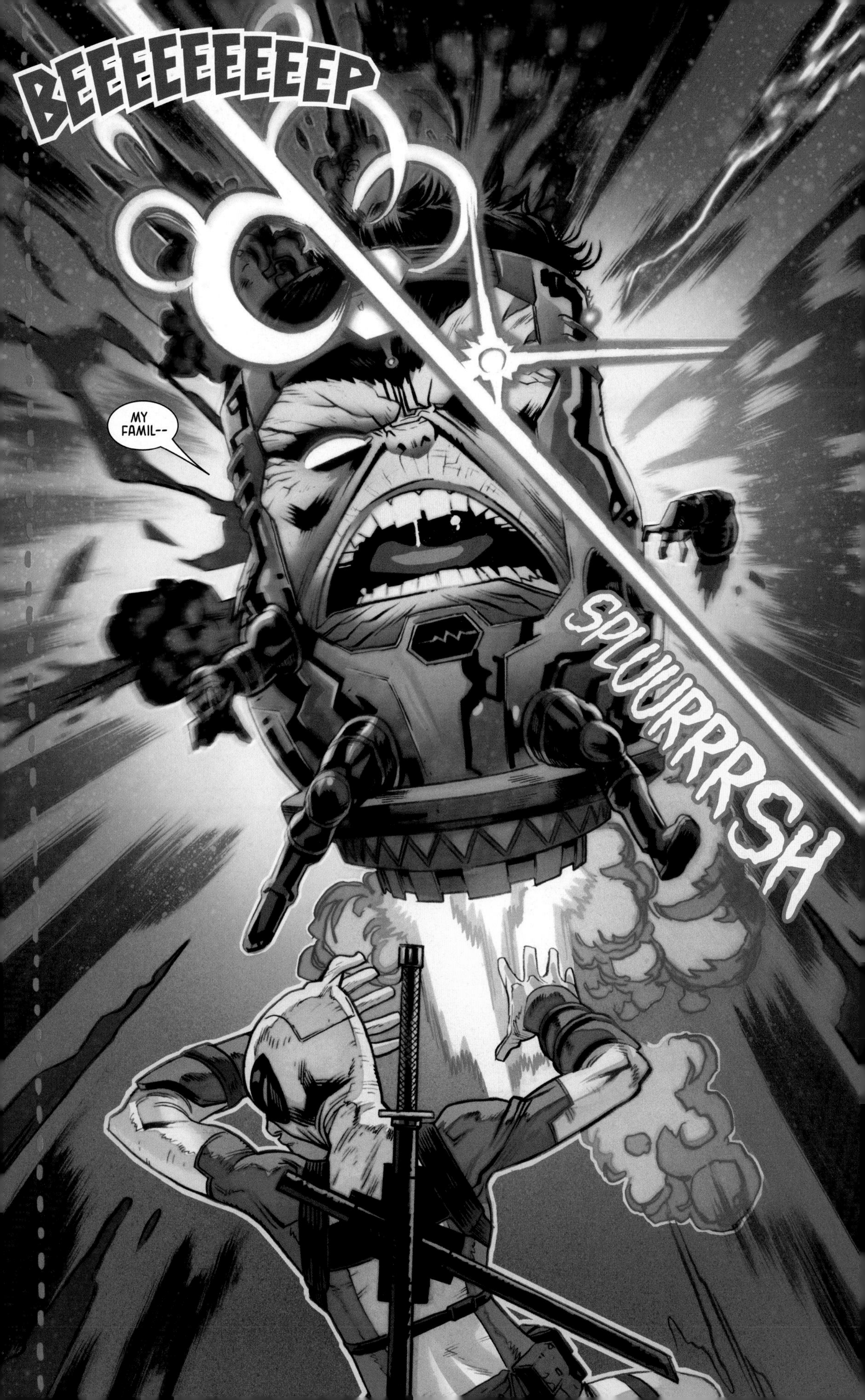
BEEEEEEEEEP
MY FAMIL--
SPLUURRRSH

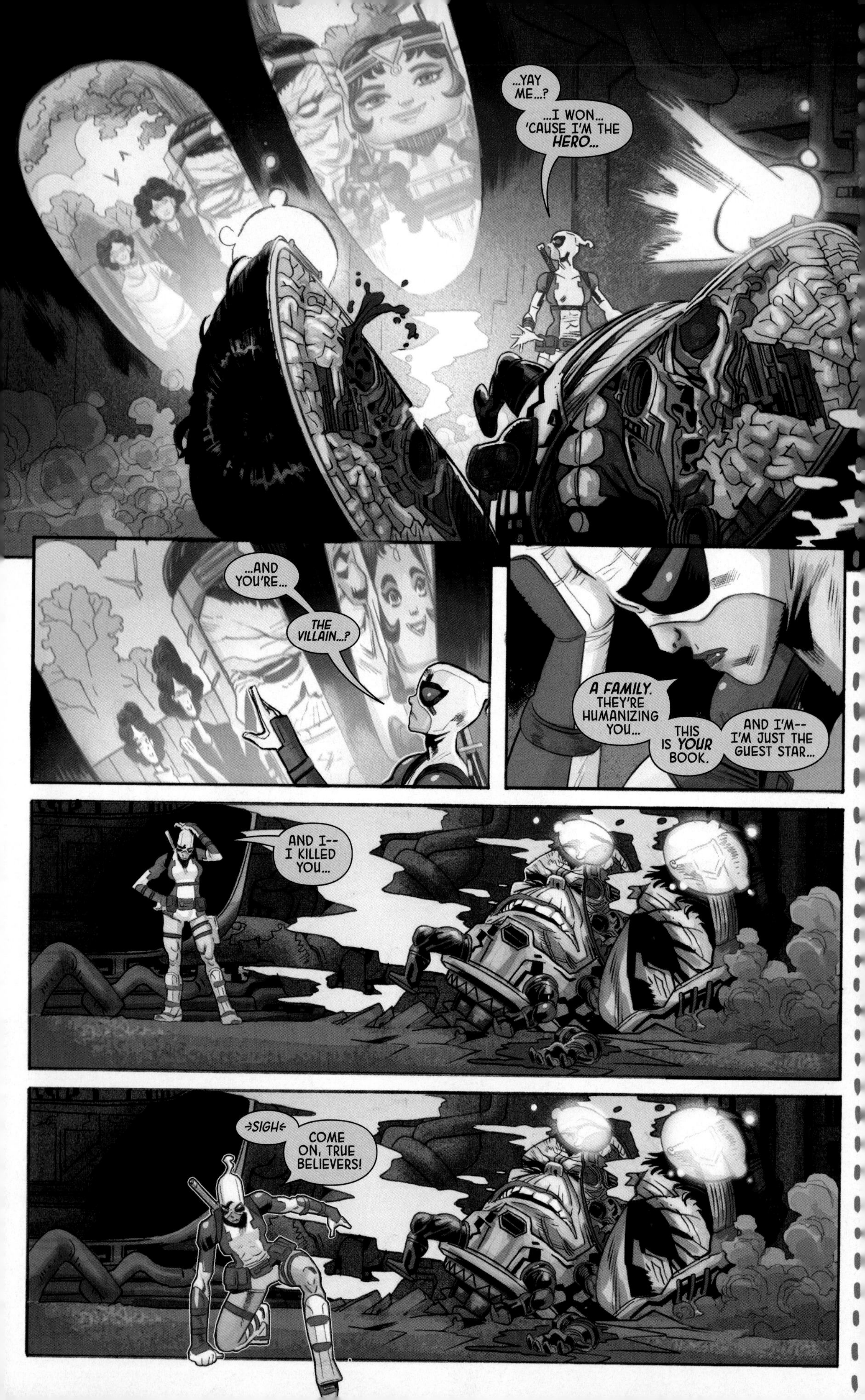
...YAY ME...?
...I WON... 'CAUSE I'M THE HERO...
...AND YOU'RE...
THE VILLAIN...?
A FAMILY. THEY'RE HUMANIZING YOU...
THIS IS YOUR BOOK.
AND I'M-- I'M JUST THE GUEST STAR...
AND I-- I KILLED YOU...
SIGH
COME ON, TRUE BELIEVERS!

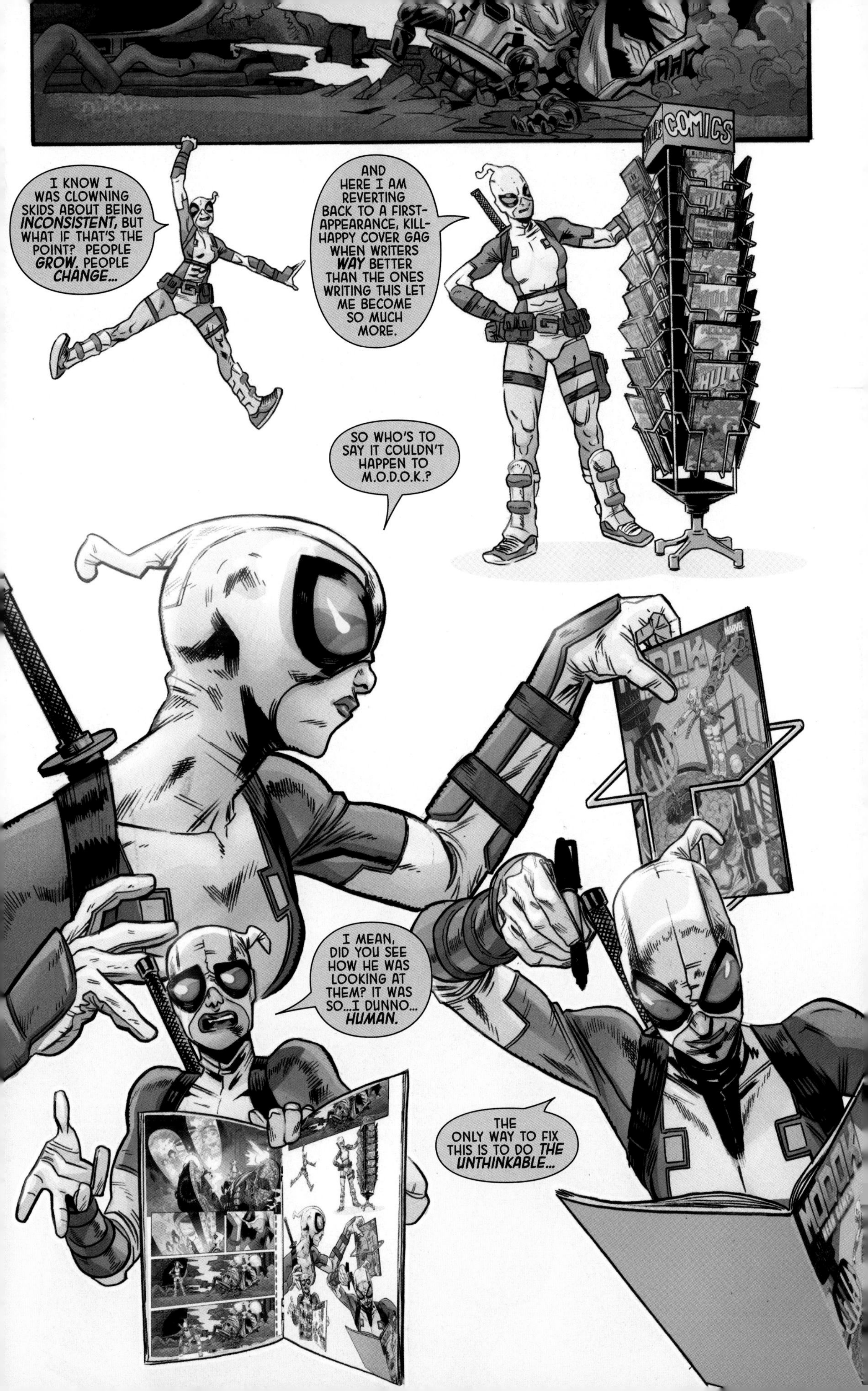

COMICS
I KNOW I WAS CLOWNING SKIDS ABOUT BEING INCONSISTENT, BUT WHAT IF THAT'S THE POINT? PEOPLE GROW. PEOPLE CHANGE...
AND HERE I AM REVERTING BACK TO A FIRST-APPEARANCE, KILL-HAPPY COVER GAG WHEN WRITERS WAY BETTER THAN THE ONES WRITING THIS LET ME BECOME SO MUCH MORE.
SO WHO'S TO SAY IT COULDN'T HAPPEN TO M.O.D.O.K.?
I MEAN, DID YOU SEE HOW HE WAS LOOKING AT THEM? IT WAS SO...I DUNNO... HUMAN.
THE ONLY WAY TO FIX THIS IS TO DO THE UNTHINKABLE...

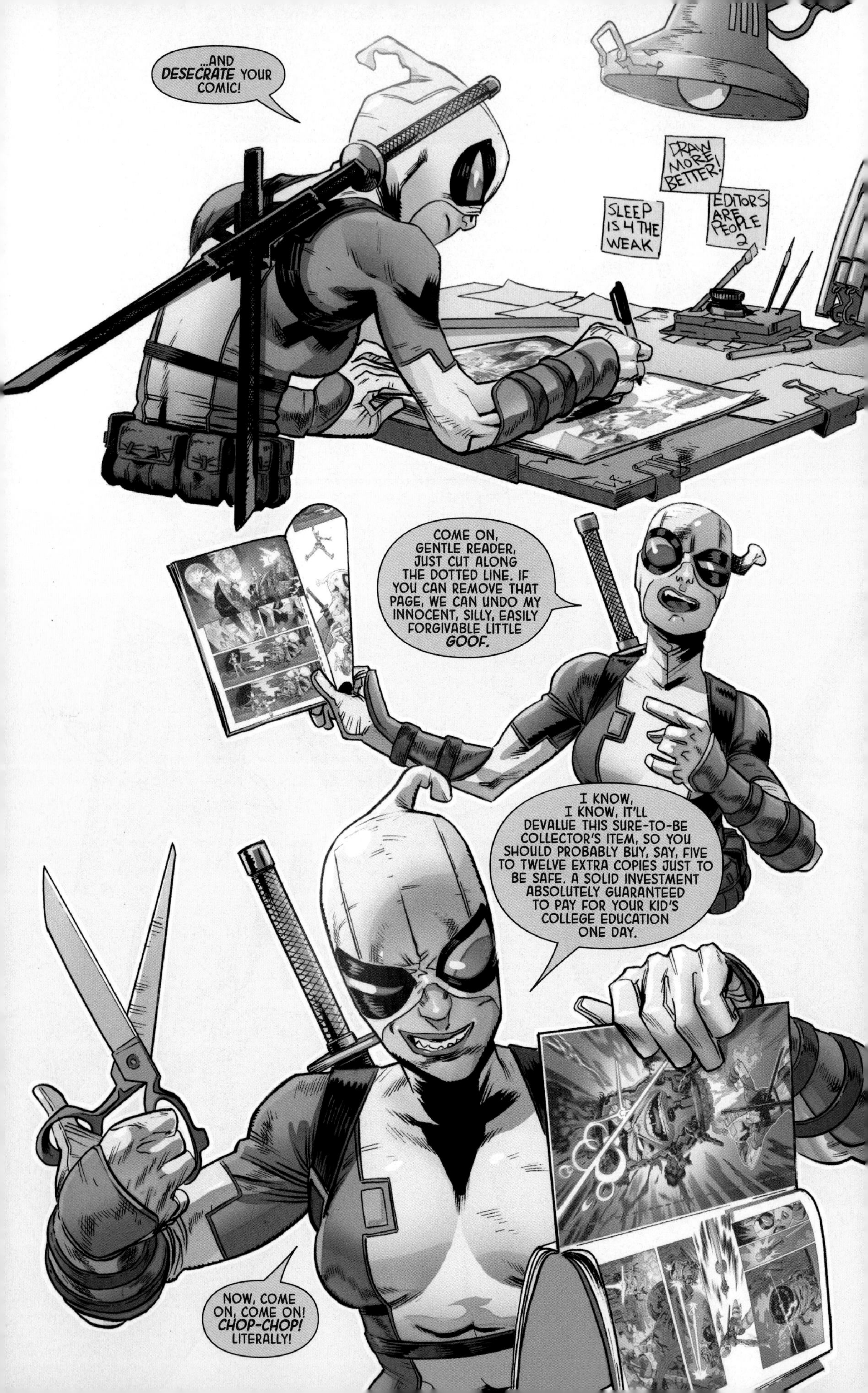

...AND DESECRATE YOUR COMIC!
DRAW MORE BETTER!
SLEEP IS 4 THE WEAK
EDITORS ARE PEOPLE 2
COME ON, GENTLE READER, JUST CUT ALONG THE DOTTED LINE. IF YOU CAN REMOVE THAT PAGE, WE CAN UNDO MY INNOCENT, SILLY, EASILY FORGIVABLE LITTLE GOOF.
I KNOW, I KNOW, IT'LL DEVALUE THIS SURE-TO-BE COLLECTOR'S ITEM, SO YOU SHOULD PROBABLY BUY, SAY, FIVE TO TWELVE EXTRA COPIES JUST TO BE SAFE. A SOLID INVESTMENT ABSOLUTELY GUARANTEED TO PAY FOR YOUR KID'S COLLEGE EDUCATION ONE DAY.
NOW, COME ON, COME ON! CHOP-CHOP! LITERALLY!

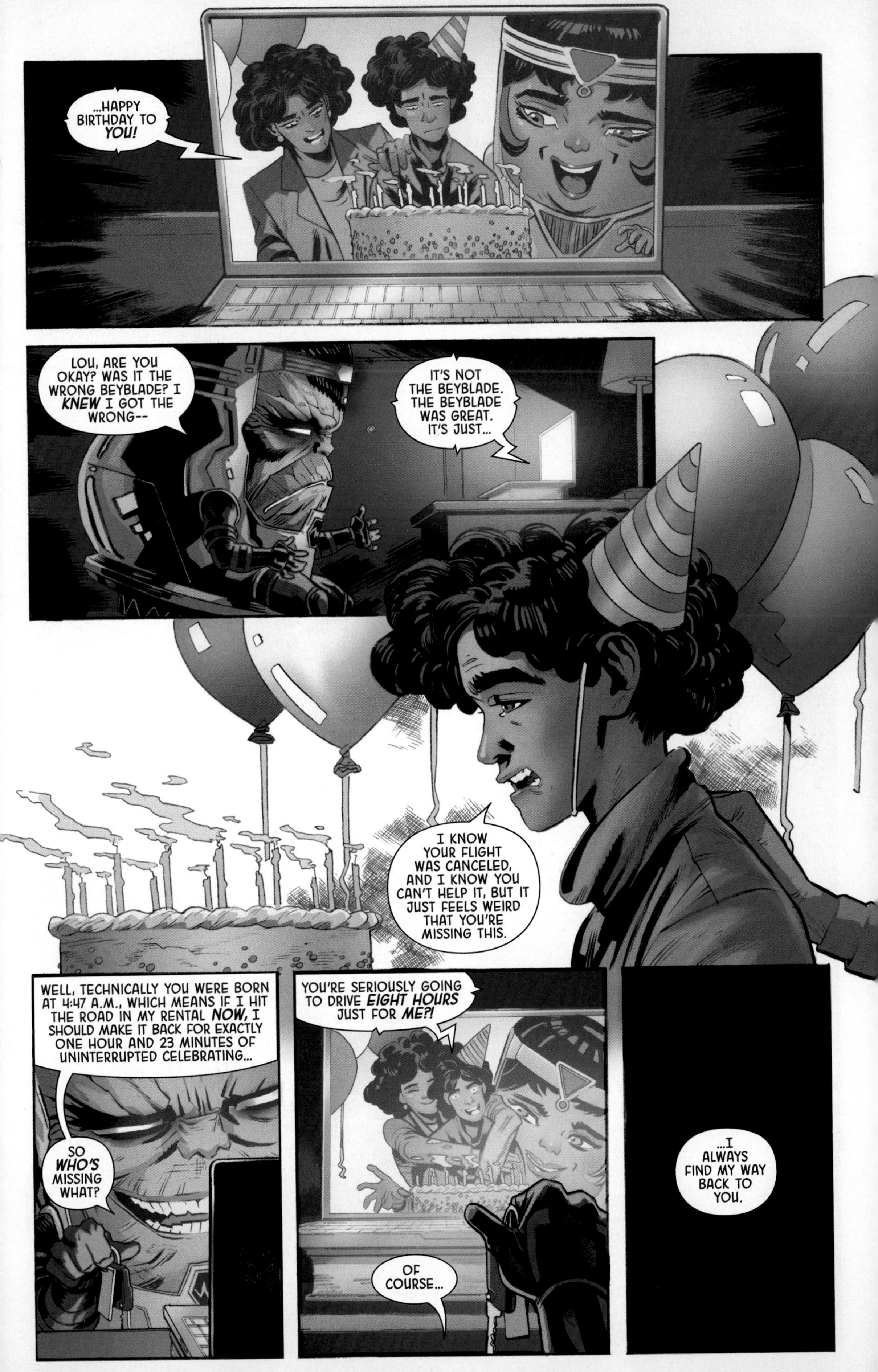
...HAPPY BIRTHDAY TO YOU!
LOU, ARE YOU OKAY? WAS IT THE WRONG BEYBLADE? I KNEW I GOT THE WRONG--
IT'S NOT THE BEYBLADE. THE BEYBLADE WAS GREAT. IT'S JUST...
I KNOW YOUR FLIGHT WAS CANCELED, AND I KNOW YOU CAN'T HELP IT, BUT IT JUST FEELS WEIRD THAT YOU'RE MISSING THIS.
WELL, TECHNICALLY YOU WERE BORN AT 4:47 A.M., WHICH MEANS IF I HIT THE ROAD IN MY RENTAL NOW, I SHOULD MAKE IT BACK FOR EXACTLY ONE HOUR AND 23 MINUTES OF UNINTERRUPTED CELEBRATING...
SO WHO'S MISSING WHAT?
YOU'RE SERIOUSLY GOING TO DRIVE EIGHT HOURS JUST FOR ME?!
OF COURSE...
...I ALWAYS FIND MY WAY BACK TO YOU.

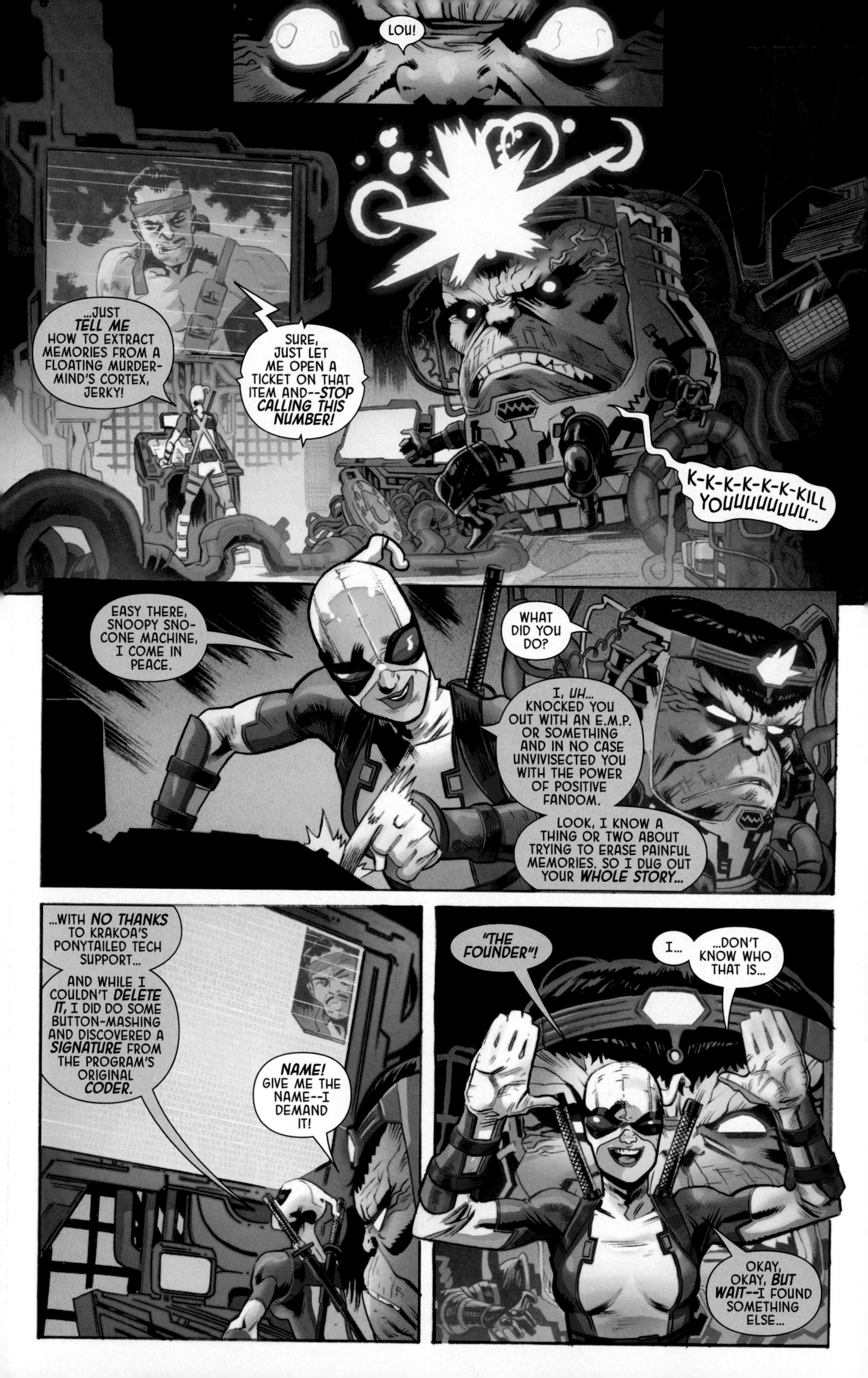
LOU!
...JUST TELL ME HOW TO EXTRACT MEMORIES FROM A FLOATING MURDER-MIND'S CORTEX, JERKY!
SURE, JUST LET ME OPEN A TICKET ON THAT ITEM AND--STOP CALLING THIS NUMBER!
K-K-K-K-K-K-KILL YOUUUUUUUU...
EASY THERE, SNOOPY SNO-CONE MACHINE, I COME IN PEACE.
WHAT DID YOU DO?
I, UH... KNOCKED YOU OUT WITH AN E.M.P. OR SOMETHING AND IN NO CASE UNVIVISECTED YOU WITH THE POWER OF POSITIVE FANDOM.
LOOK, I KNOW A THING OR TWO ABOUT TRYING TO ERASE PAINFUL MEMORIES. SO I DUG OUT YOUR WHOLE STORY...
...WITH NO THANKS TO KRAKOA'S PONYTAILED TECH SUPPORT...
AND WHILE I COULDN'T DELETE IT, I DID DO SOME BUTTON-MASHING AND DISCOVERED A SIGNATURE FROM THE PROGRAM'S ORIGINAL CODER.
NAME! GIVE ME THE NAME--I DEMAND IT!
"THE FOUNDER"!
I...
...DON'T KNOW WHO THAT IS...
OKAY, OKAY, BUT WAIT--I FOUND SOMETHING ELSE...

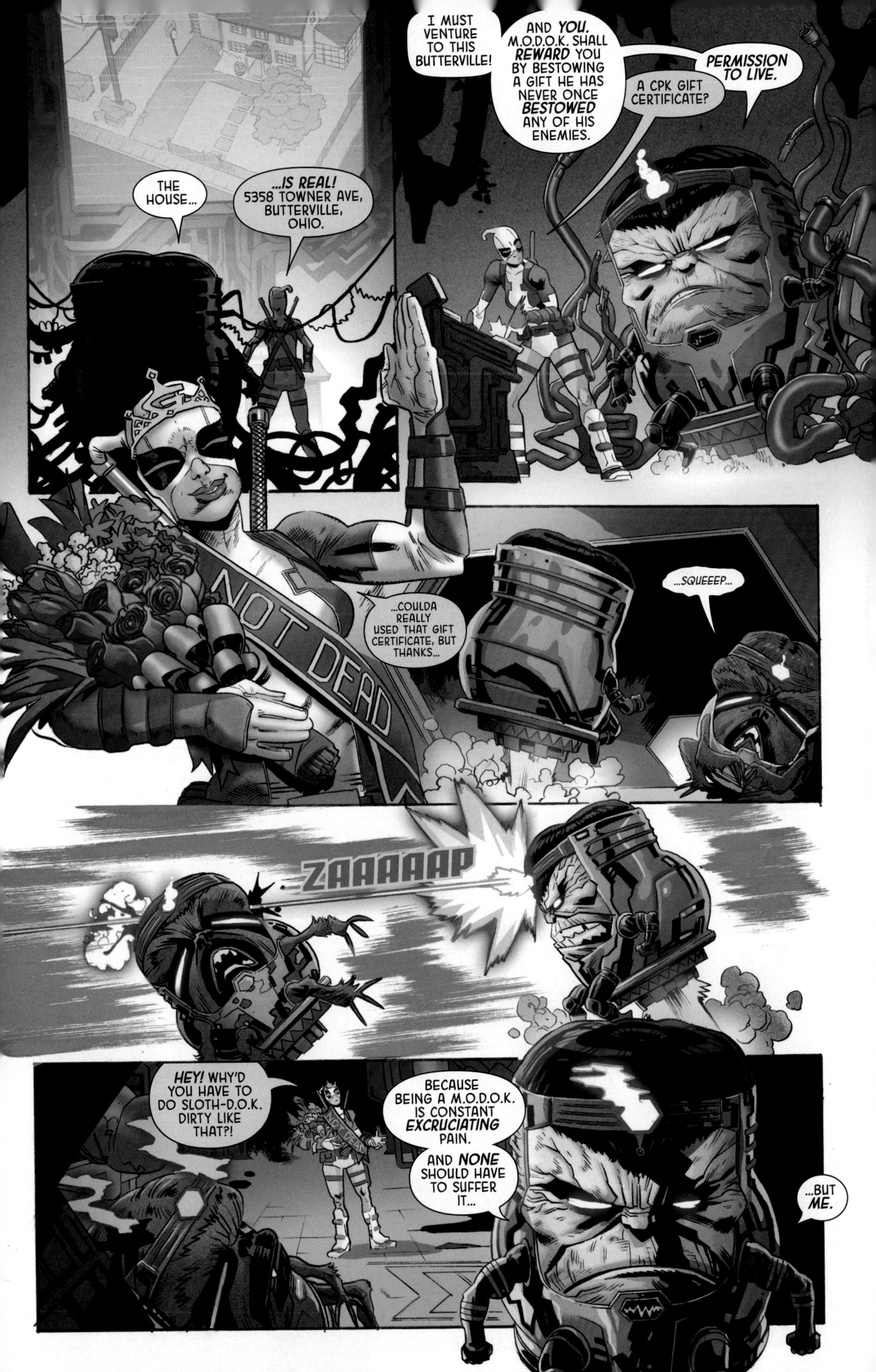
THE HOUSE...
...IS REAL! 5358 TOWNER AVE, BUTTERVILLE, OHIO.
I MUST VENTURE TO THIS BUTTERVILLE!
AND YOU. M.O.D.O.K. SHALL REWARD YOU BY BESTOWING A GIFT HE HAS NEVER ONCE BESTOWED ANY OF HIS ENEMIES.
A CPK GIFT CERTIFICATE?
PERMISSION TO LIVE.
NOT DEAD
...COULDA REALLY USED THAT GIFT CERTIFICATE, BUT THANKS...
...SQUEEEP...
ZAAAAAAP
HEY! WHY'D YOU HAVE TO DO SLOTH-D.O.K. DIRTY LIKE THAT?!
BECAUSE BEING A M.O.D.O.K. IS CONSTANT EXCRUCIATING PAIN.
AND NONE SHOULD HAVE TO SUFFER IT...
...BUT ME.

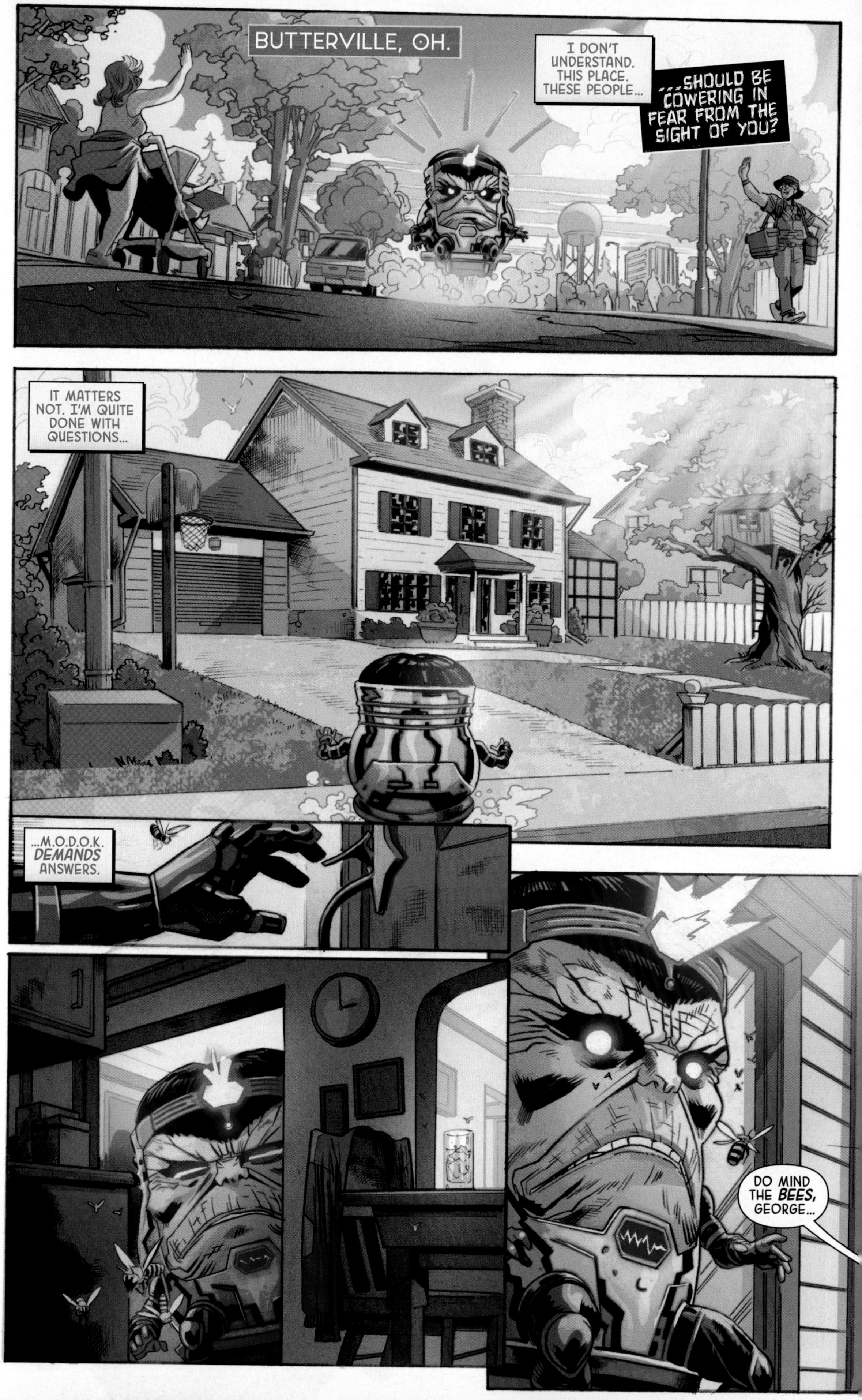
BUTTERVILLE, OH.
I DON'T UNDERSTAND. THIS PLACE. THESE PEOPLE...
...SHOULD BE COWERING IN FEAR FROM THE SIGHT OF YOU?
IT MATTERS NOT. I'M QUITE DONE WITH QUESTIONS...
...M.O.D.O.K. DEMANDS ANSWERS.
DO MIND THE BEES, GEORGE...

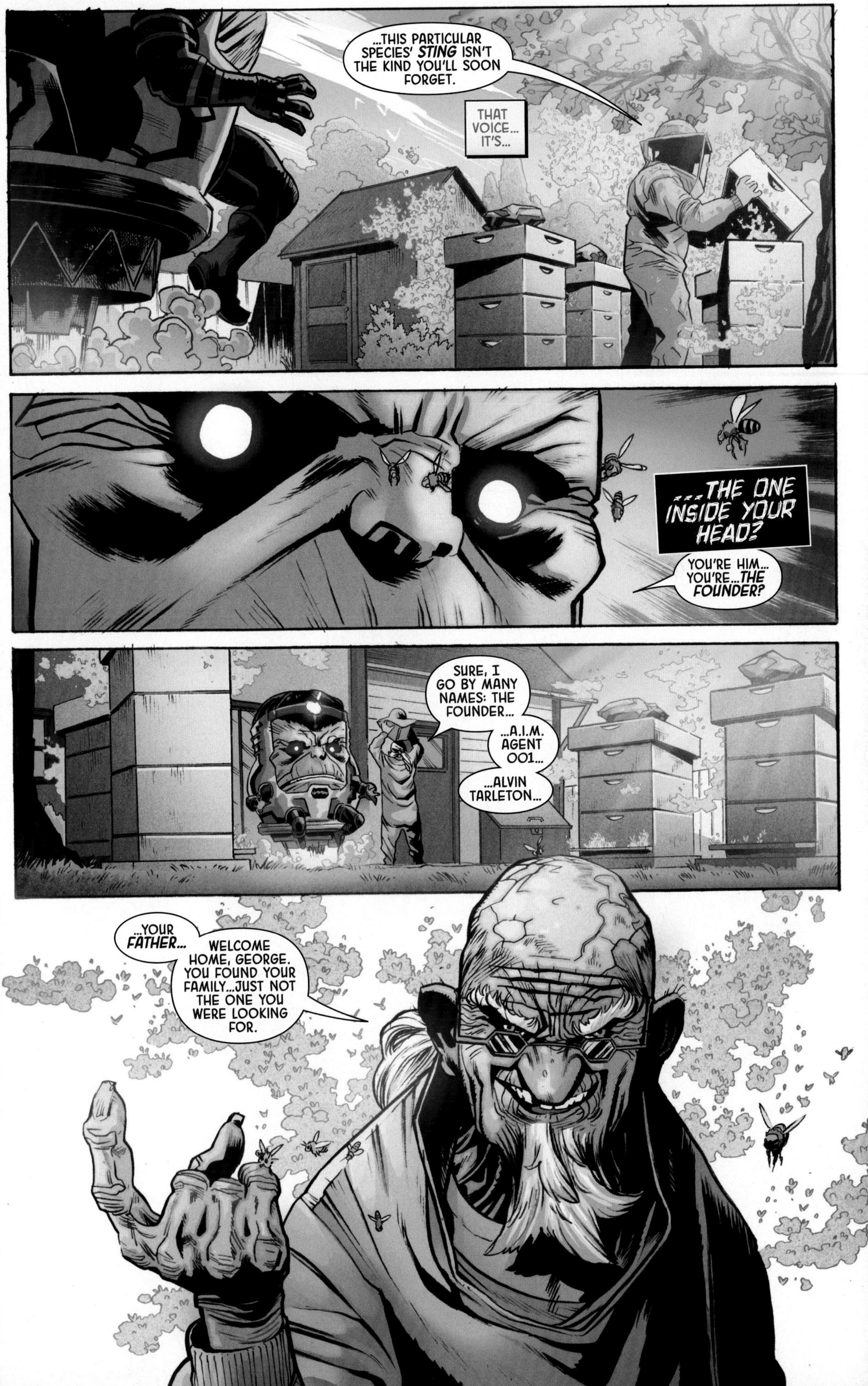
...THIS PARTICULAR SPECIES' STING ISN'T THE KIND YOU'LL SOON FORGET.
THAT VOICE... IT'S...
...THE ONE INSIDE YOUR HEAD?
YOU'RE HIM... YOU'RE...THE FOUNDER?
SURE, I GO BY MANY NAMES: THE FOUNDER...
...A.I.M. AGENT 001...
...ALVIN TARLETON...
...YOUR FATHER...
WELCOME HOME, GEORGE. YOU FOUND YOUR FAMILY...JUST NOT THE ONE YOU WERE LOOKING FOR.

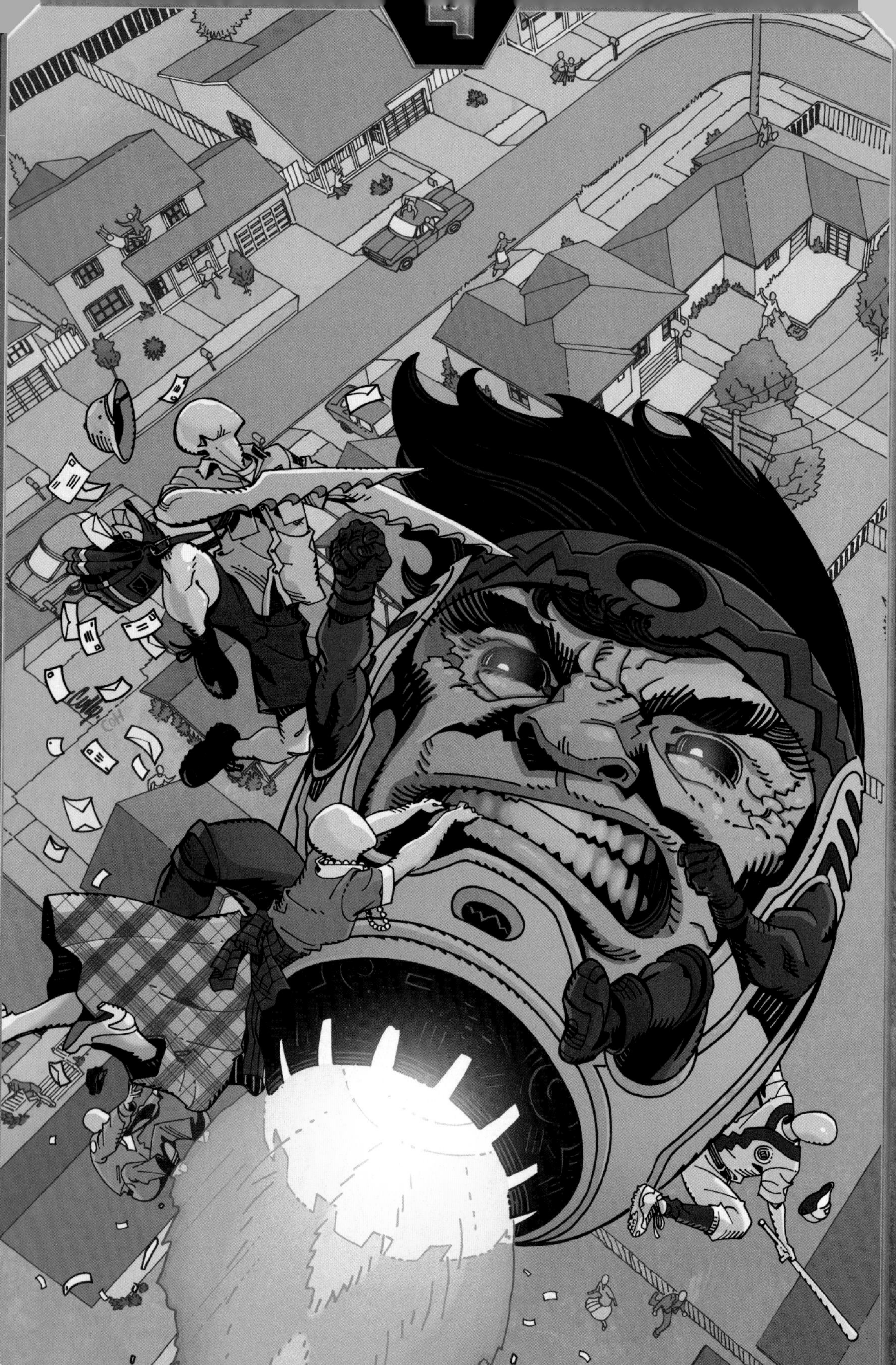

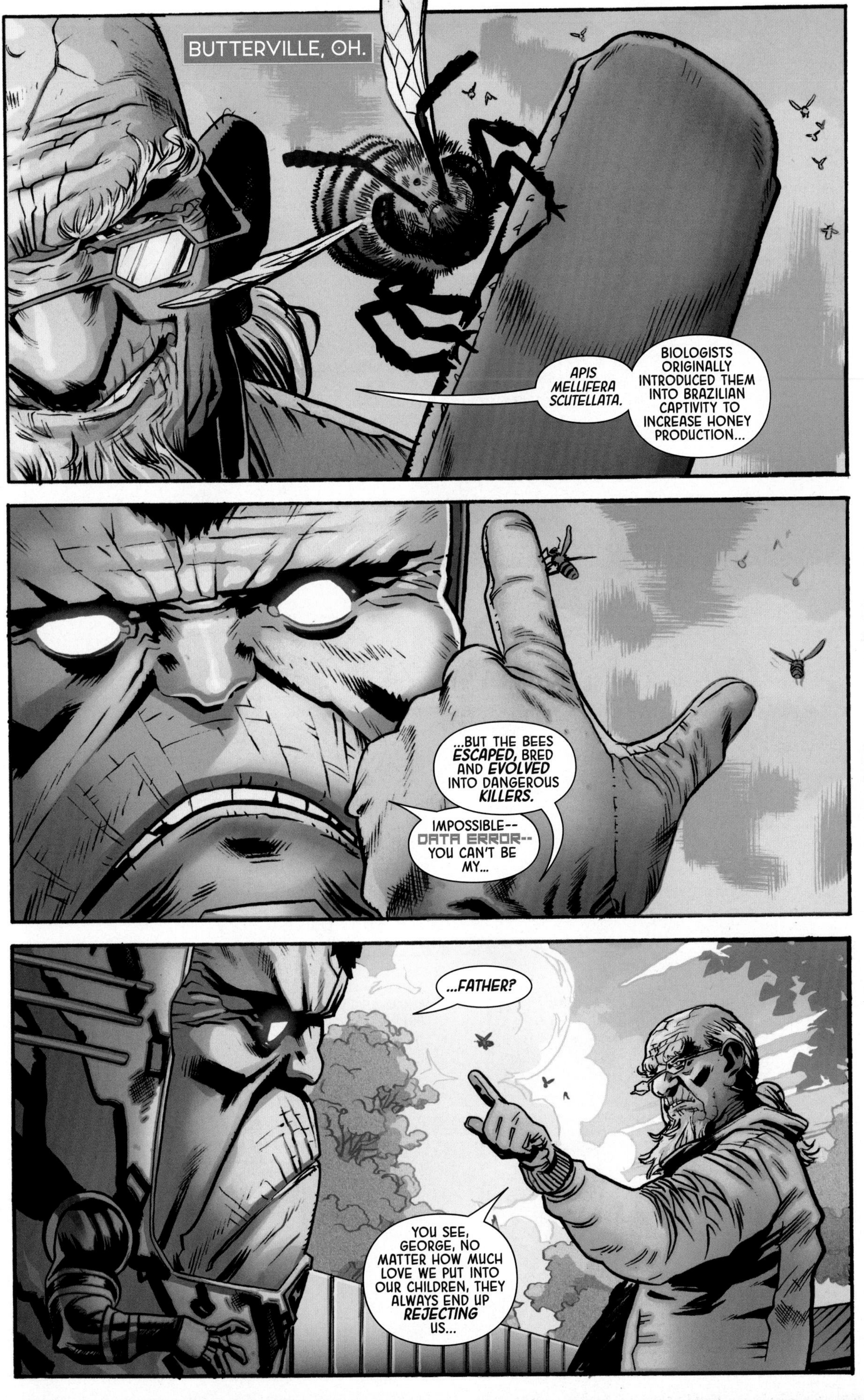
BUTTERVILLE, OH.
APIS MELLIFERA SCUTELLATA.
BIOLOGISTS ORIGINALLY INTRODUCED THEM INTO BRAZILIAN CAPTIVITY TO INCREASE HONEY PRODUCTION...
...BUT THE BEES ESCAPED, BRED AND EVOLVED INTO DANGEROUS KILLERS.
IMPOSSIBLE-- DATA ERROR-- YOU CAN'T BE MY...
...FATHER?
YOU SEE, GEORGE, NO MATTER HOW MUCH LOVE WE PUT INTO OUR CHILDREN, THEY ALWAYS END UP REJECTING US...

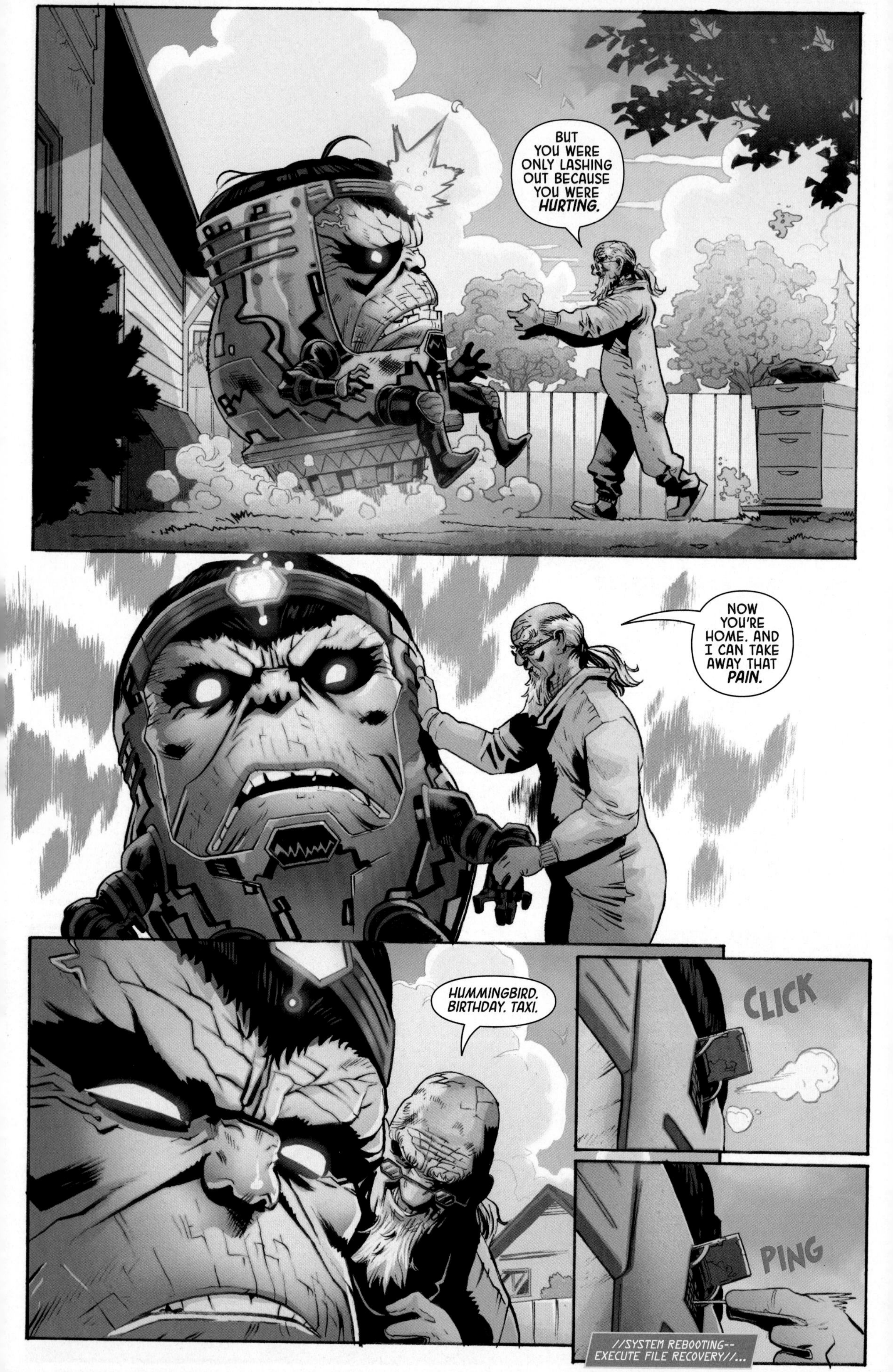
BUT YOU WERE ONLY LASHING OUT BECAUSE YOU WERE *HURTING.*
NOW YOU'RE HOME. AND I CAN TAKE AWAY THAT *PAIN.*
HUMMINGBIRD. BIRTHDAY. TAXI.
CLICK
PING
//SYSTEM REBOOTING--
EXECUTE FILE RECOVERY//...

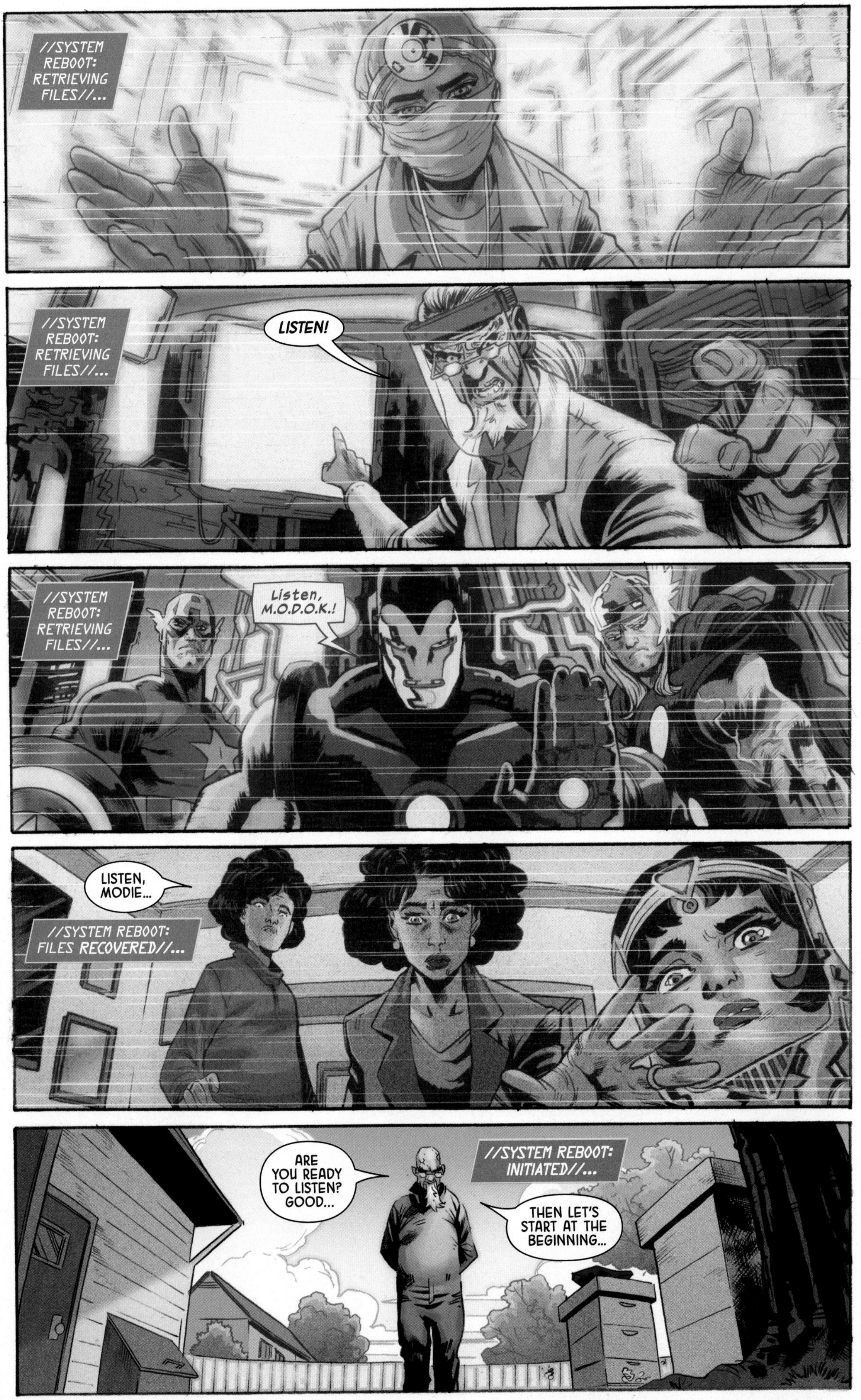
//SYSTEM REBOOT: RETRIEVING FILES//...
//SYSTEM REBOOT: RETRIEVING FILES//...
LISTEN!
//SYSTEM REBOOT: RETRIEVING FILES//...
Listen, M.O.D.O.K.!
LISTEN, MODIE...
//SYSTEM REBOOT: FILES RECOVERED//...
ARE YOU READY TO LISTEN? GOOD...
//SYSTEM REBOOT: INITIATED//...
THEN LET'S START AT THE BEGINNING...

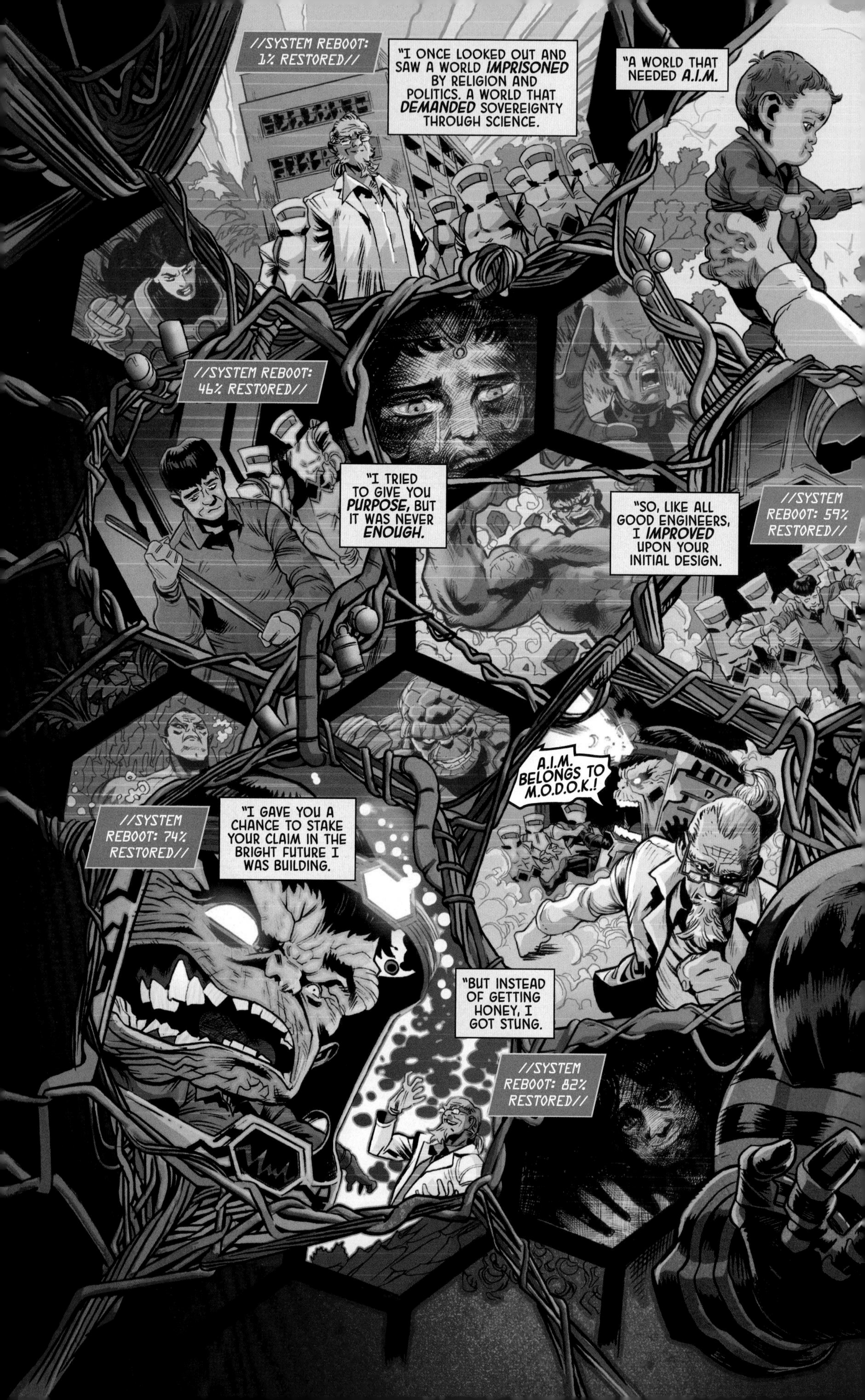

//SYSTEM REBOOT: 1% RESTORED//
"I ONCE LOOKED OUT AND SAW A WORLD IMPRISONED BY RELIGION AND POLITICS. A WORLD THAT DEMANDED SOVEREIGNTY THROUGH SCIENCE.
"A WORLD THAT NEEDED A.I.M.
//SYSTEM REBOOT: 46% RESTORED//
"I TRIED TO GIVE YOU PURPOSE, BUT IT WAS NEVER ENOUGH.
"SO, LIKE ALL GOOD ENGINEERS, I IMPROVED UPON YOUR INITIAL DESIGN.
//SYSTEM REBOOT: 59% RESTORED//
A.I.M. BELONGS TO M.O.D.O.K.!
//SYSTEM REBOOT: 74% RESTORED//
"I GAVE YOU A CHANCE TO STAKE YOUR CLAIM IN THE BRIGHT FUTURE I WAS BUILDING.
"BUT INSTEAD OF GETTING HONEY, I GOT STUNG.
//SYSTEM REBOOT: 82% RESTORED//

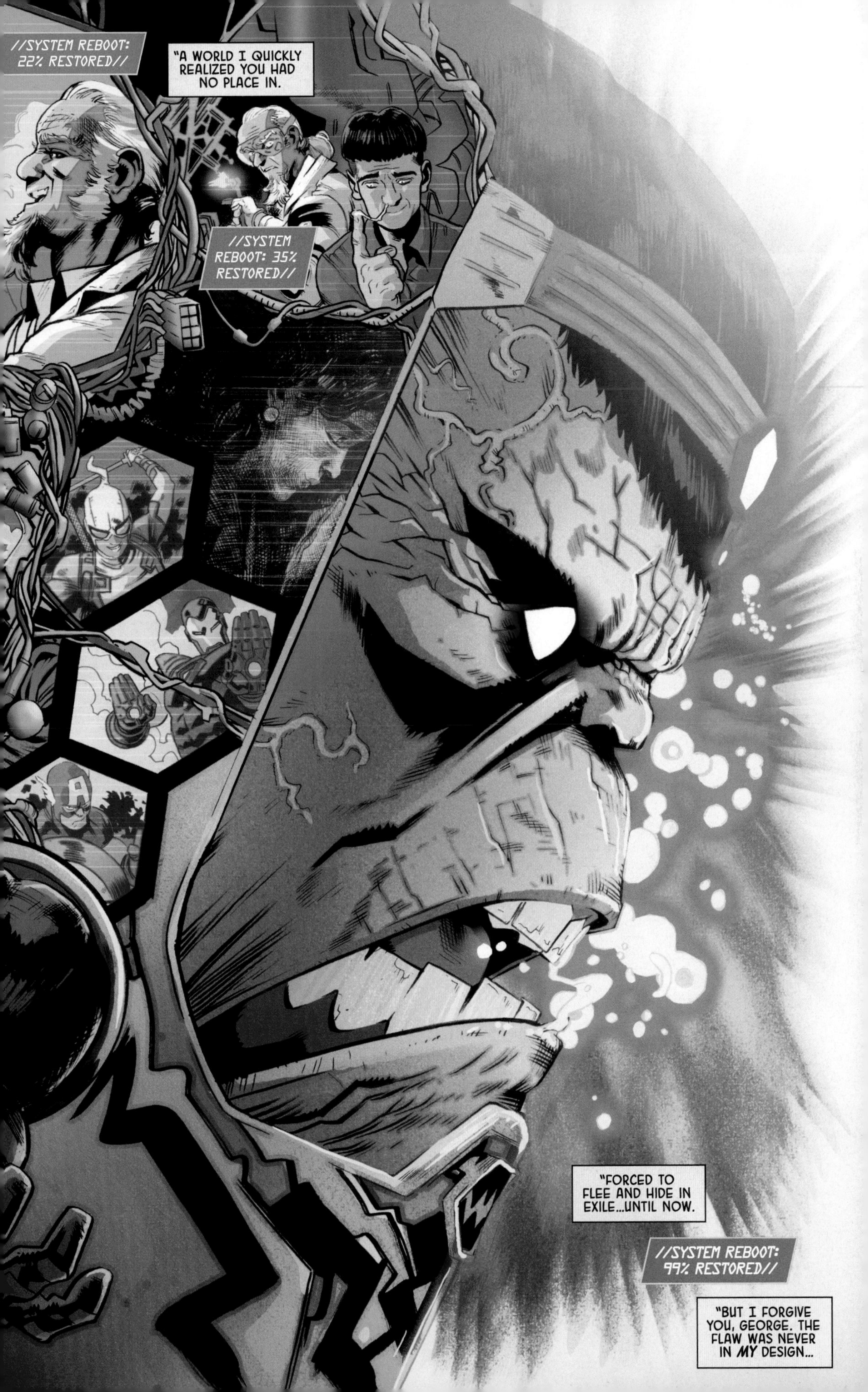
//SYSTEM REBOOT: 22% RESTORED//
"A WORLD I QUICKLY REALIZED YOU HAD NO PLACE IN.
//SYSTEM REBOOT: 35% RESTORED//
"FORCED TO FLEE AND HIDE IN EXILE...UNTIL NOW.
//SYSTEM REBOOT: 99% RESTORED//
"BUT I FORGIVE YOU, GEORGE. THE FLAW WAS NEVER IN *MY* DESIGN...

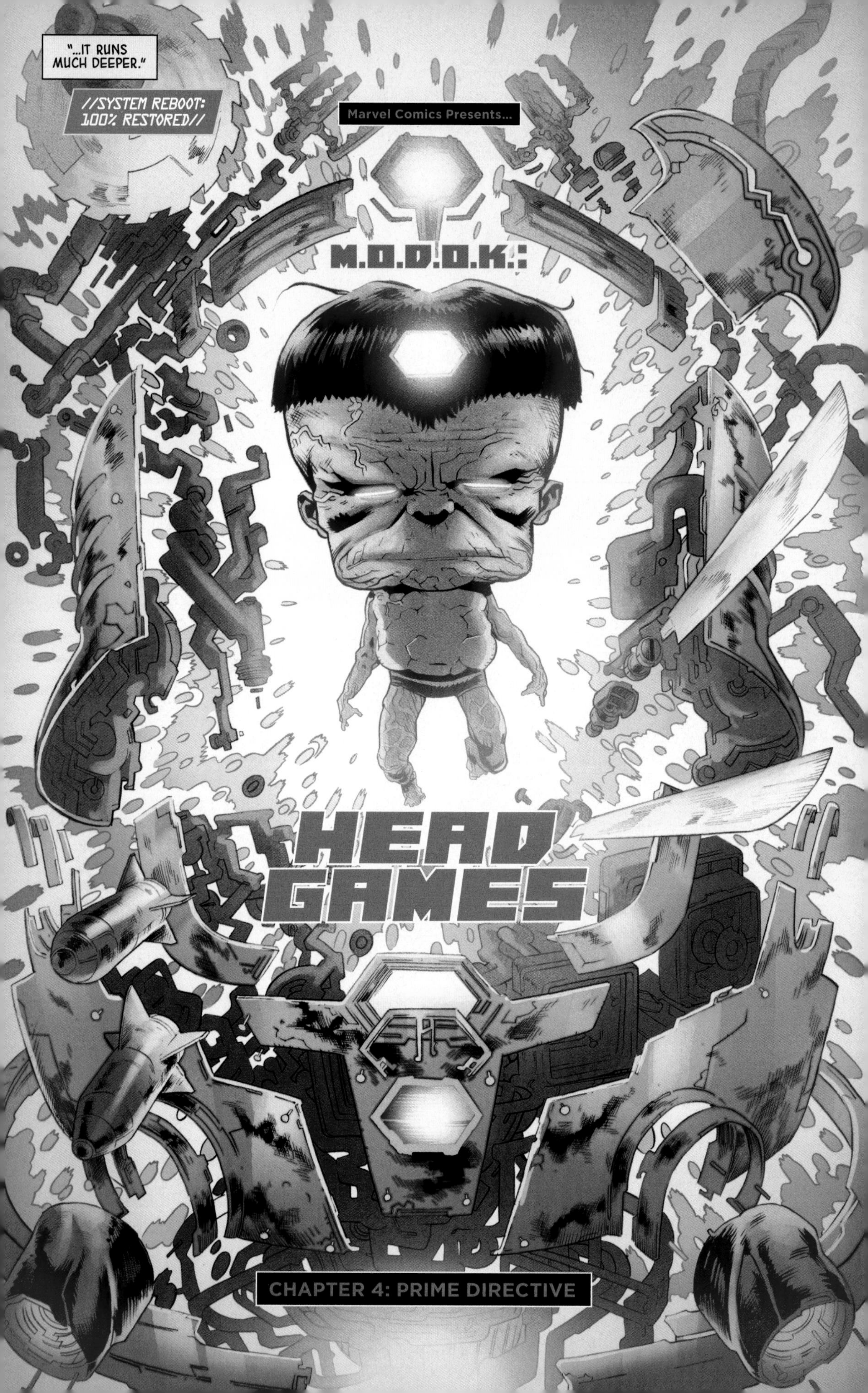
"...IT RUNS MUCH DEEPER."
//SYSTEM REBOOT: 100% RESTORED//
Marvel Comics Presents...
M.O.D.O.K.:
HEAD GAMES
CHAPTER 4: PRIME DIRECTIVE

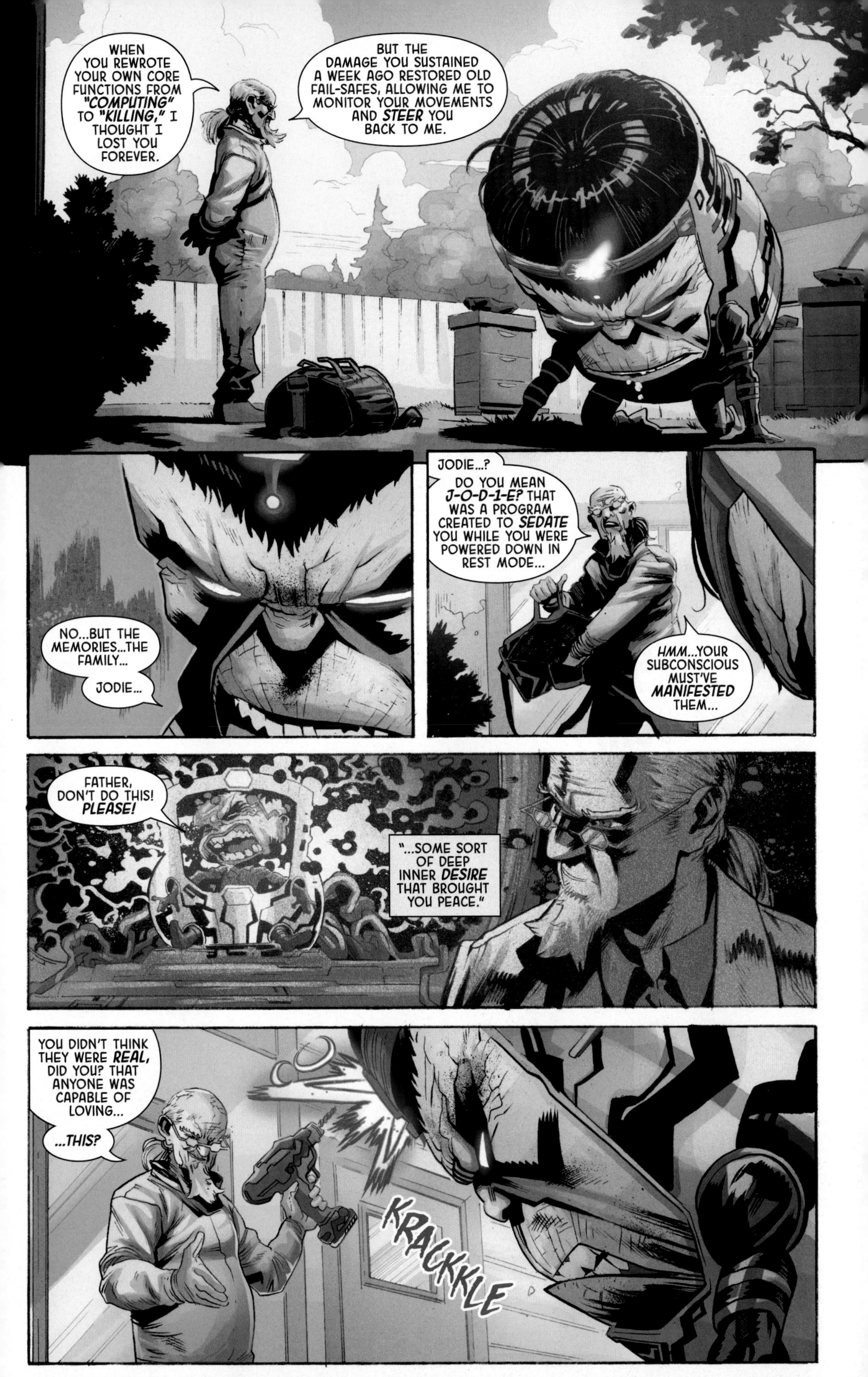
WHEN YOU REWROTE YOUR OWN CORE FUNCTIONS FROM "COMPUTING" TO "KILLING," I THOUGHT I LOST YOU FOREVER.
BUT THE DAMAGE YOU SUSTAINED A WEEK AGO RESTORED OLD FAIL-SAFES, ALLOWING ME TO MONITOR YOUR MOVEMENTS AND STEER YOU BACK TO ME.
NO...BUT THE MEMORIES...THE FAMILY...
JODIE...
JODIE...?
DO YOU MEAN J-O-D-1-E? THAT WAS A PROGRAM CREATED TO SEDATE YOU WHILE YOU WERE POWERED DOWN IN REST MODE...
HMM...YOUR SUBCONSCIOUS MUST'VE MANIFESTED THEM...
FATHER, DON'T DO THIS! PLEASE!
"...SOME SORT OF DEEP INNER DESIRE THAT BROUGHT YOU PEACE."
YOU DIDN'T THINK THEY WERE REAL, DID YOU? THAT ANYONE WAS CAPABLE OF LOVING...
...THIS?
KRACKKLE

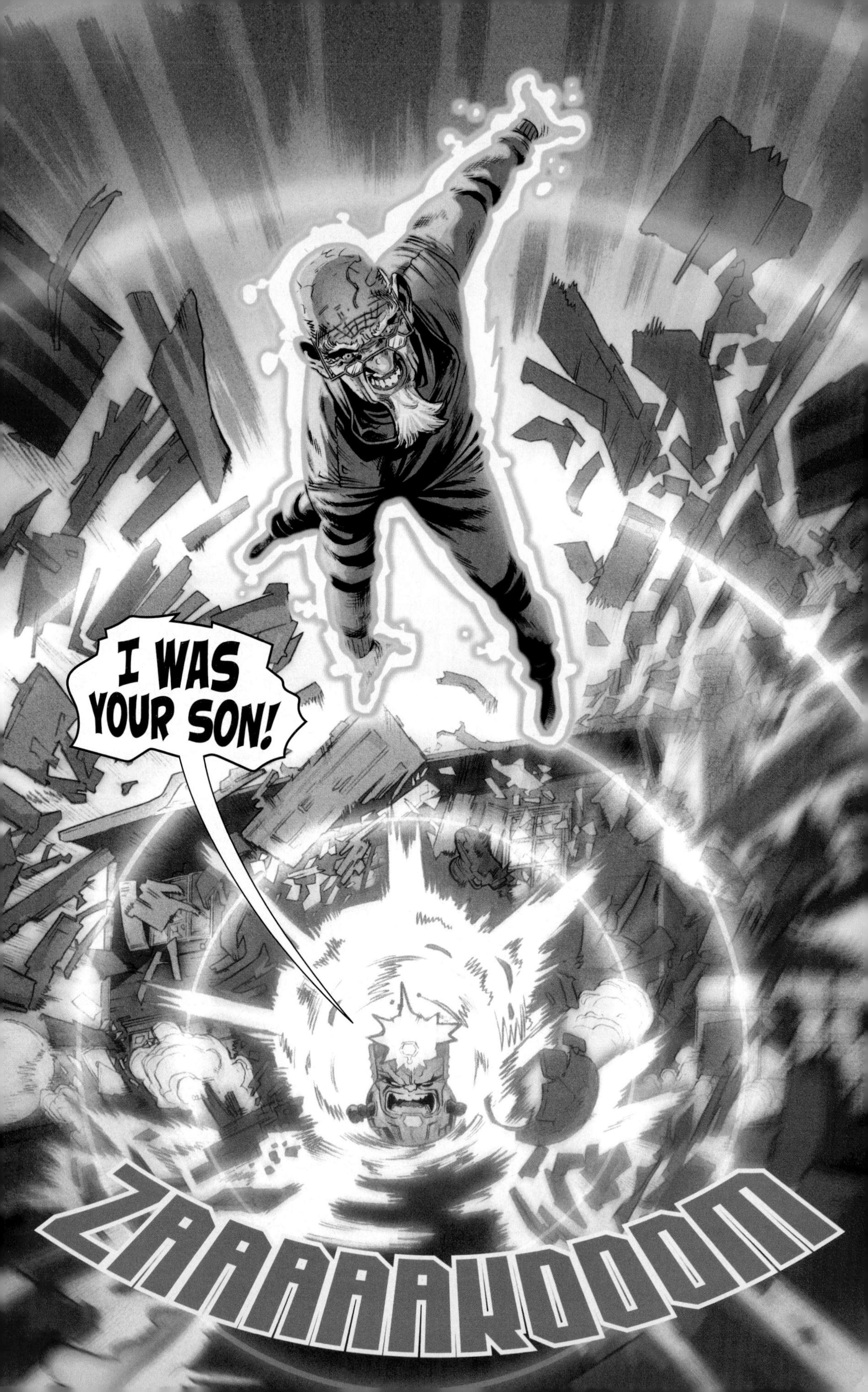
I WAS YOUR SON!
ZAAAAAKOOOOM

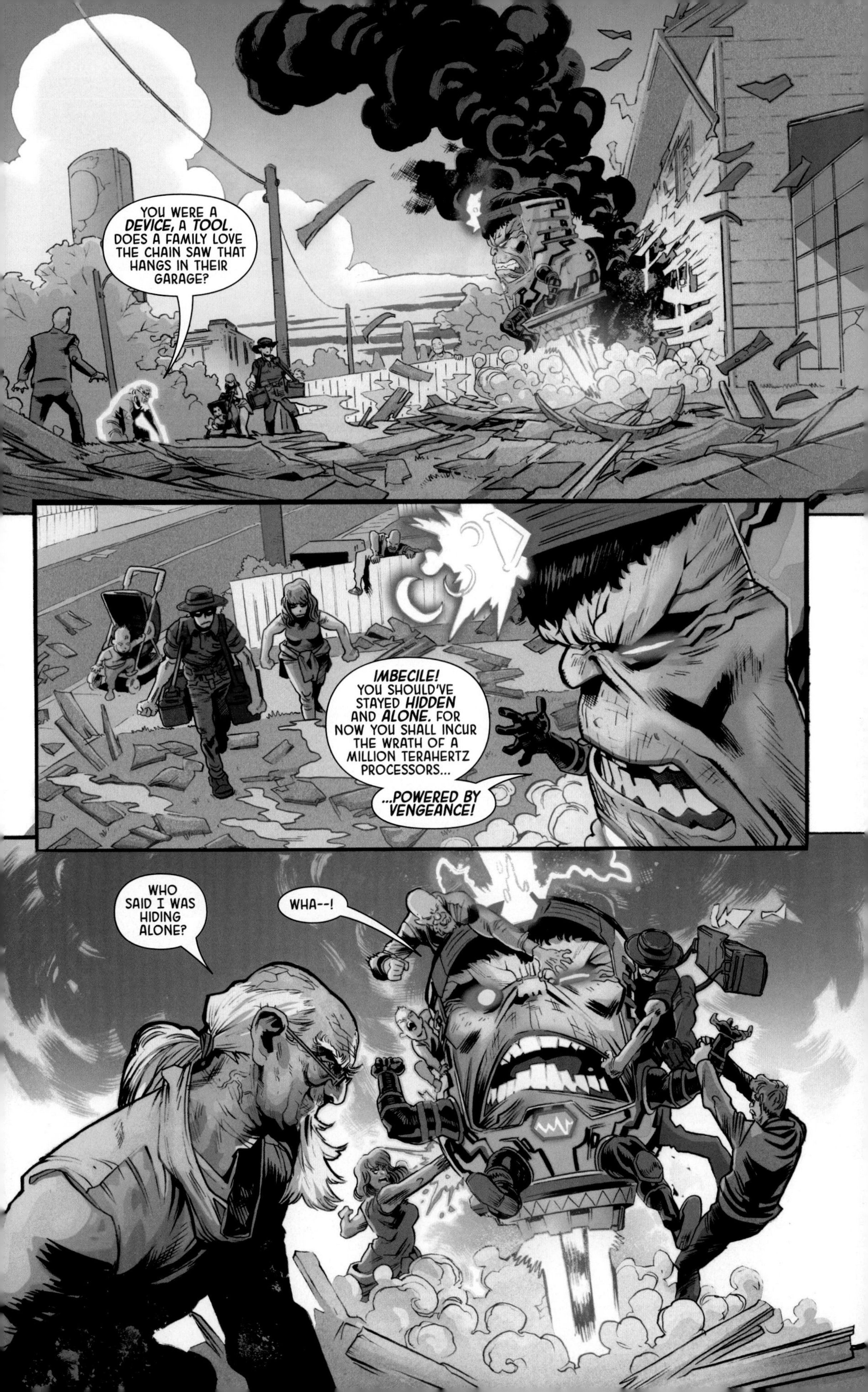
YOU WERE A DEVICE, A TOOL. DOES A FAMILY LOVE THE CHAIN SAW THAT HANGS IN THEIR GARAGE?
IMBECILE! YOU SHOULD'VE STAYED HIDDEN AND ALONE. FOR NOW YOU SHALL INCUR THE WRATH OF A MILLION TERAHERTZ PROCESSORS...
...POWERED BY VENGEANCE!
WHO SAID I WAS HIDING ALONE?
WHA--!

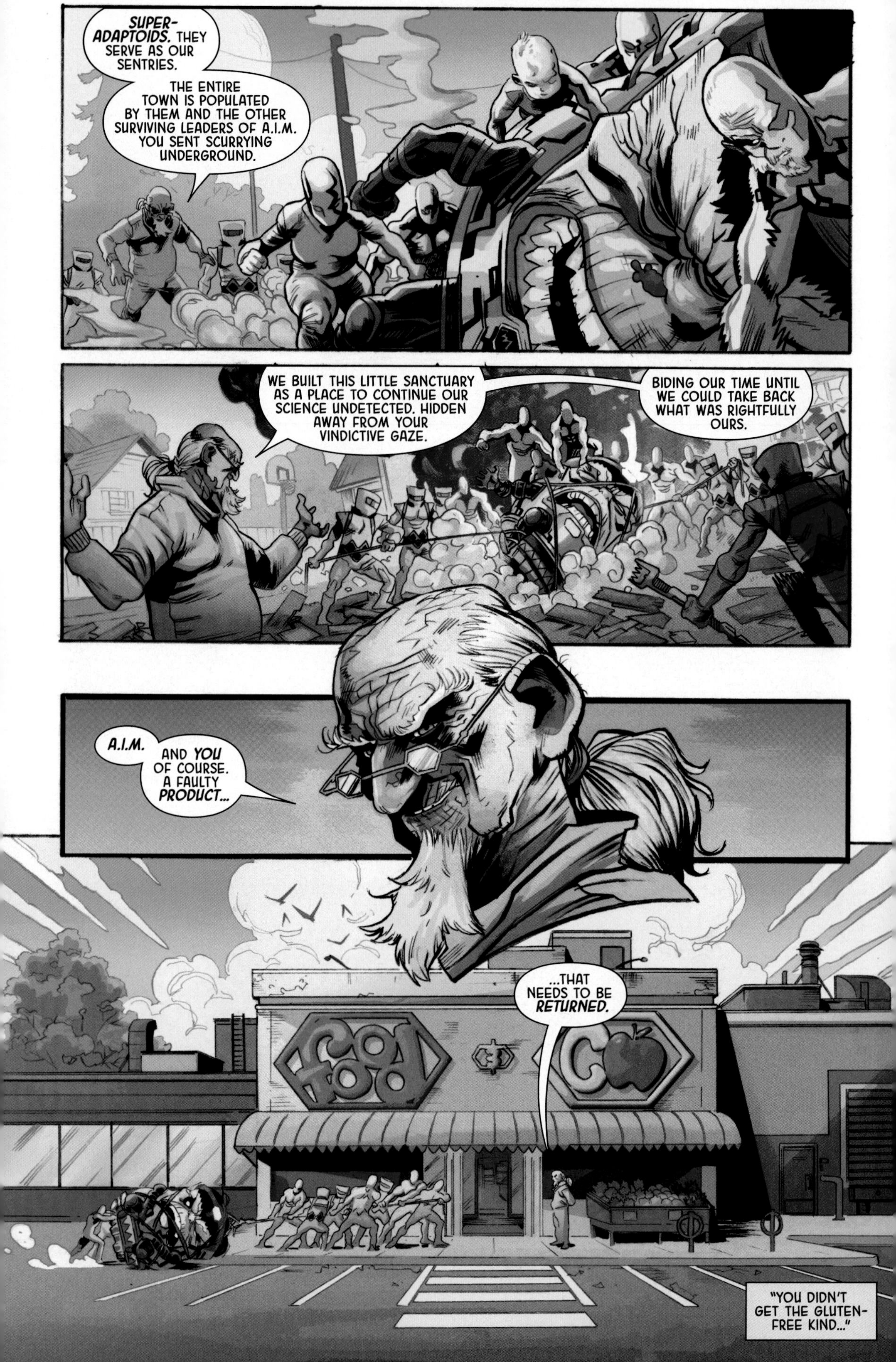
SUPER-ADAPTOIDS. THEY SERVE AS OUR SENTRIES.
THE ENTIRE TOWN IS POPULATED BY THEM AND THE OTHER SURVIVING LEADERS OF A.I.M. YOU SENT SCURRYING UNDERGROUND.
WE BUILT THIS LITTLE SANCTUARY AS A PLACE TO CONTINUE OUR SCIENCE UNDETECTED. HIDDEN AWAY FROM YOUR VINDICTIVE GAZE.
BIDING OUR TIME UNTIL WE COULD TAKE BACK WHAT WAS RIGHTFULLY OURS.
A.I.M.
AND YOU OF COURSE. A FAULTY PRODUCT...
...THAT NEEDS TO BE RETURNED.
"YOU DIDN'T GET THE GLUTEN-FREE KIND..."

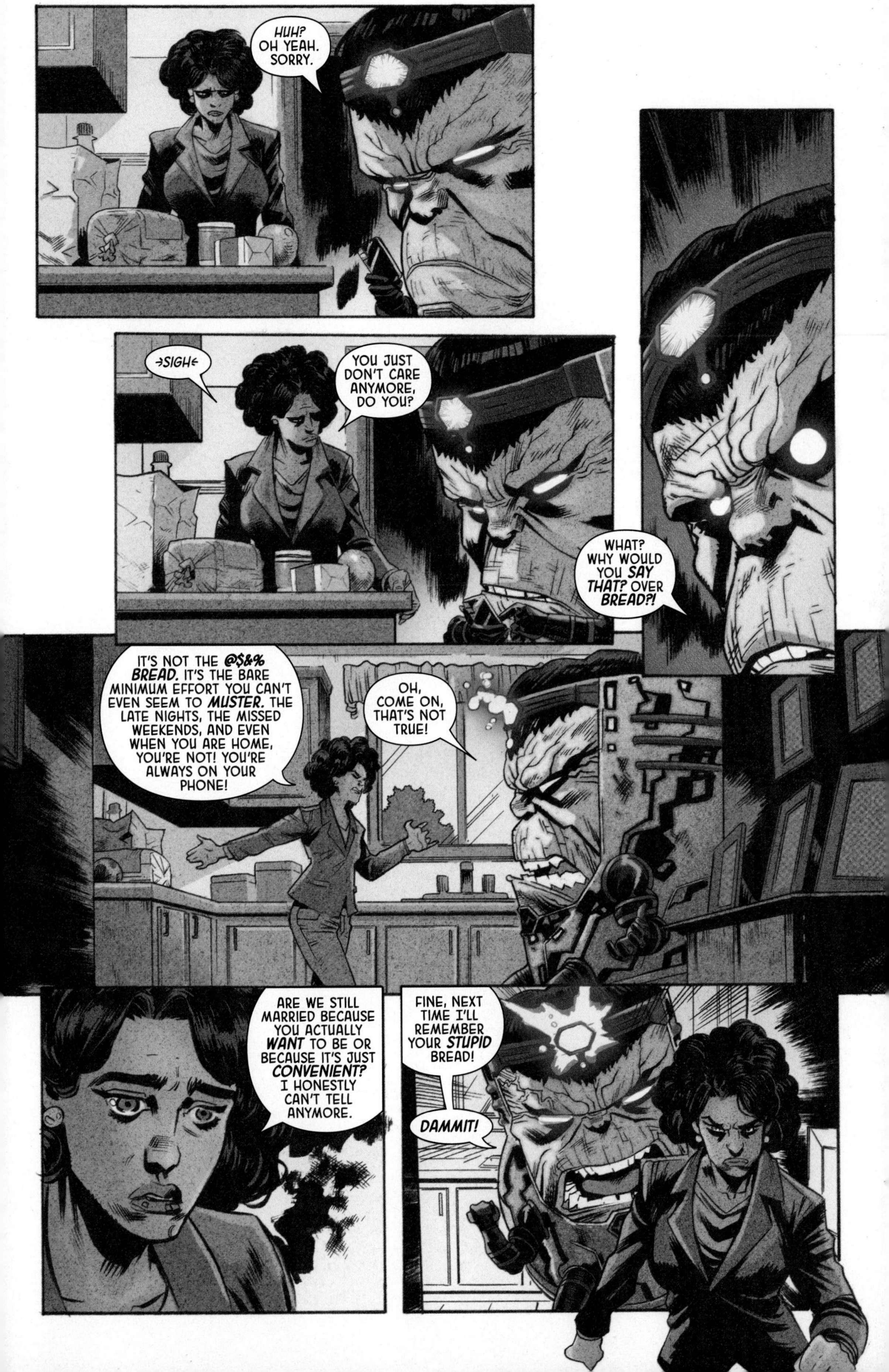
HUH? OH YEAH. SORRY.
→SIGH←
YOU JUST DON'T CARE ANYMORE, DO YOU?
WHAT? WHY WOULD YOU SAY THAT? OVER BREAD?!
IT'S NOT THE @$&% BREAD. IT'S THE BARE MINIMUM EFFORT YOU CAN'T EVEN SEEM TO MUSTER. THE LATE NIGHTS, THE MISSED WEEKENDS, AND EVEN WHEN YOU ARE HOME, YOU'RE NOT! YOU'RE ALWAYS ON YOUR PHONE!
OH, COME ON, THAT'S NOT TRUE!
ARE WE STILL MARRIED BECAUSE YOU ACTUALLY WANT TO BE OR BECAUSE IT'S JUST CONVENIENT? I HONESTLY CAN'T TELL ANYMORE.
FINE, NEXT TIME I'LL REMEMBER YOUR STUPID BREAD!
DAMMIT!

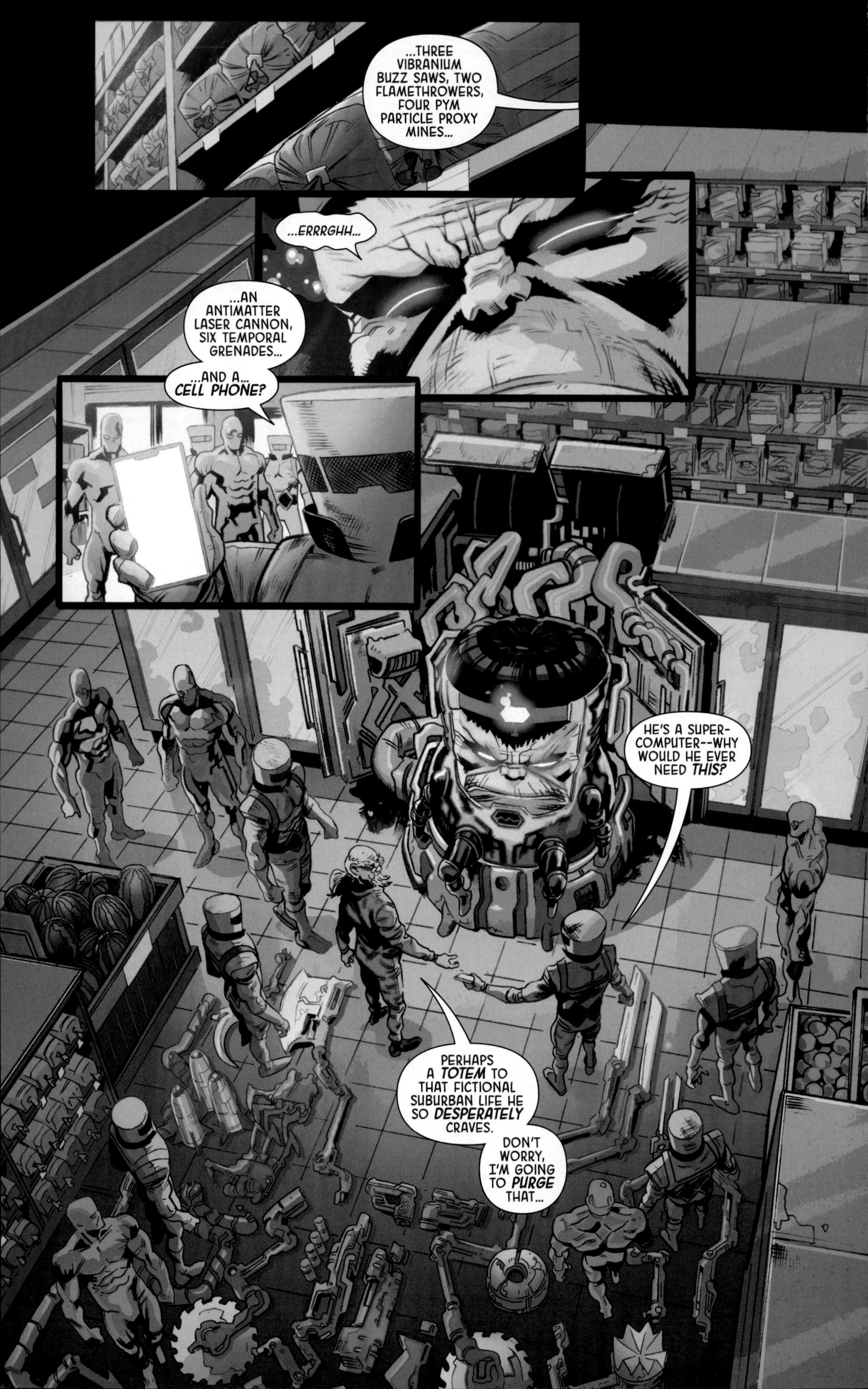
...THREE VIBRANIUM BUZZ SAWS, TWO FLAMETHROWERS, FOUR PYM PARTICLE PROXY MINES...
...ERRRGHH...
...AN ANTIMATTER LASER CANNON, SIX TEMPORAL GRENADES...
...AND A... CELL PHONE?
HE'S A SUPER-COMPUTER--WHY WOULD HE EVER NEED THIS?
PERHAPS A TOTEM TO THAT FICTIONAL SUBURBAN LIFE HE SO DESPERATELY CRAVES.
DON'T WORRY, I'M GOING TO PURGE THAT...

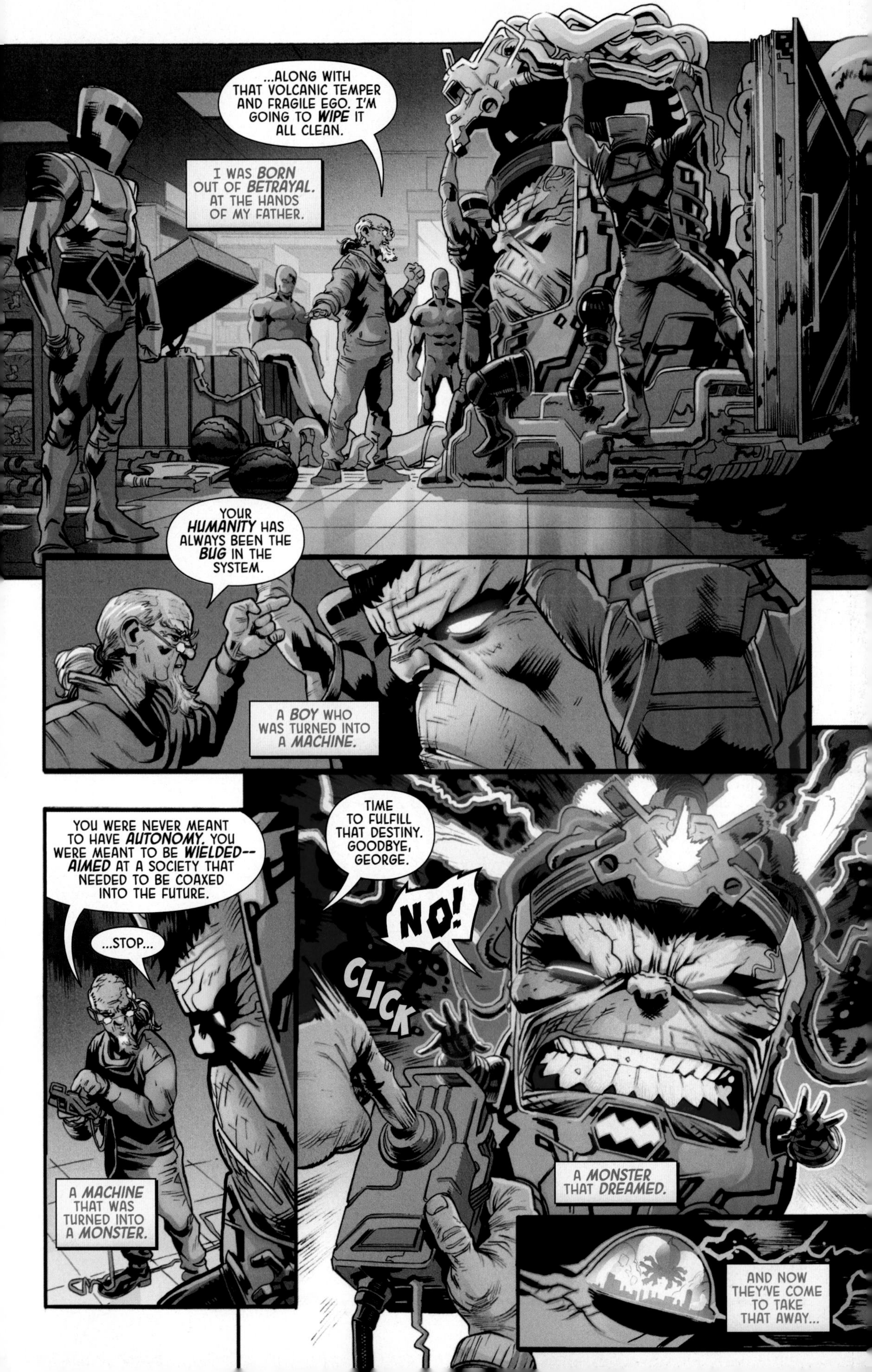
...ALONG WITH THAT VOLCANIC TEMPER AND FRAGILE EGO. I'M GOING TO WIPE IT ALL CLEAN.
I WAS BORN OUT OF BETRAYAL. AT THE HANDS OF MY FATHER.
YOUR HUMANITY HAS ALWAYS BEEN THE BUG IN THE SYSTEM.
A BOY WHO WAS TURNED INTO A MACHINE.
YOU WERE NEVER MEANT TO HAVE AUTONOMY. YOU WERE MEANT TO BE WIELDED-- AIMED AT A SOCIETY THAT NEEDED TO BE COAXED INTO THE FUTURE.
...STOP...
A MACHINE THAT WAS TURNED INTO A MONSTER.
TIME TO FULFILL THAT DESTINY. GOODBYE, GEORGE.
NO!
CLICK
A MONSTER THAT DREAMED.
AND NOW THEY'VE COME TO TAKE THAT AWAY...

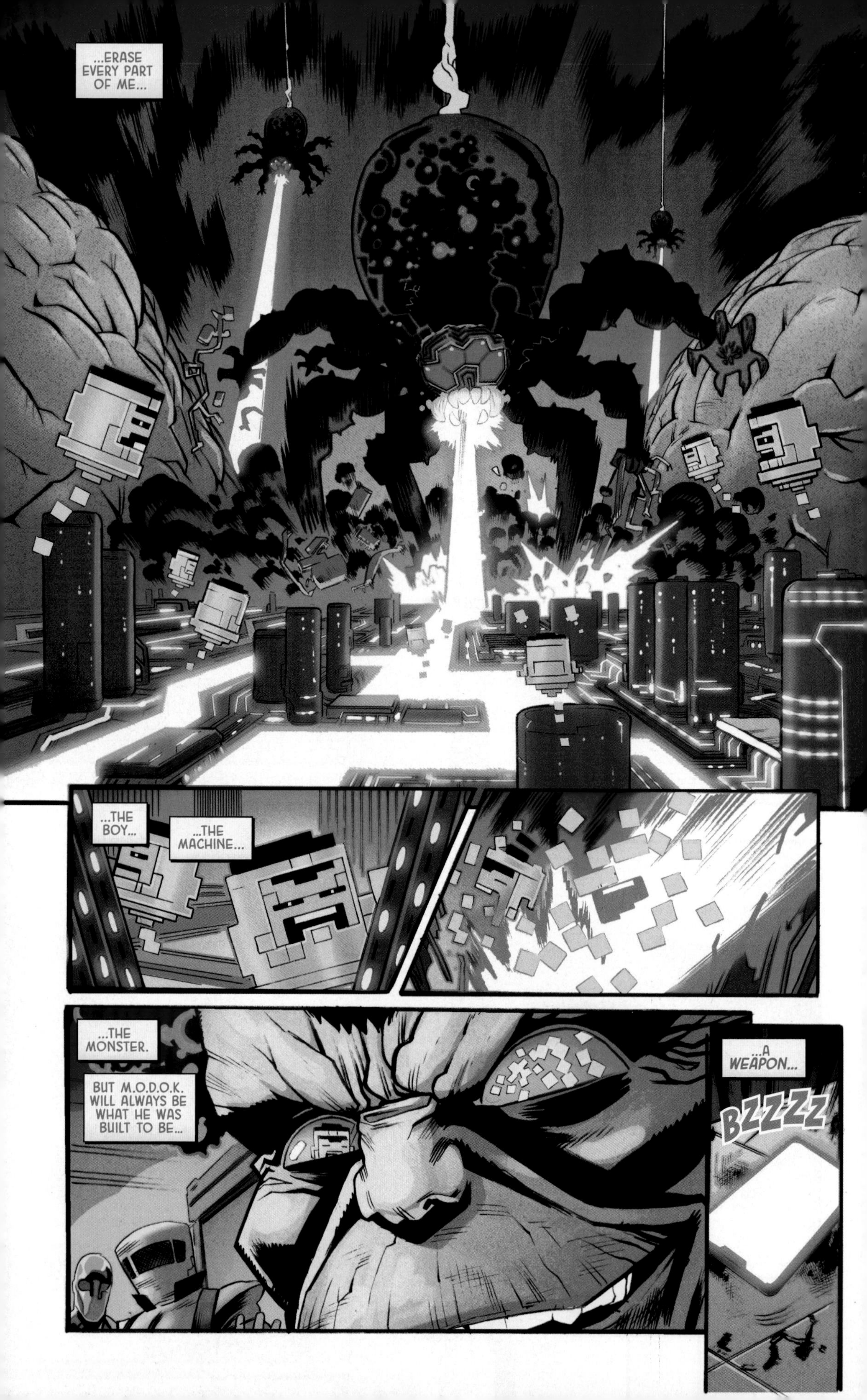

...ERASE EVERY PART OF ME...
...THE BOY...
...THE MACHINE...
...THE MONSTER.
BUT M.O.D.O.K. WILL ALWAYS BE WHAT HE WAS BUILT TO BE...
...A WEAPON...
BZZZZ

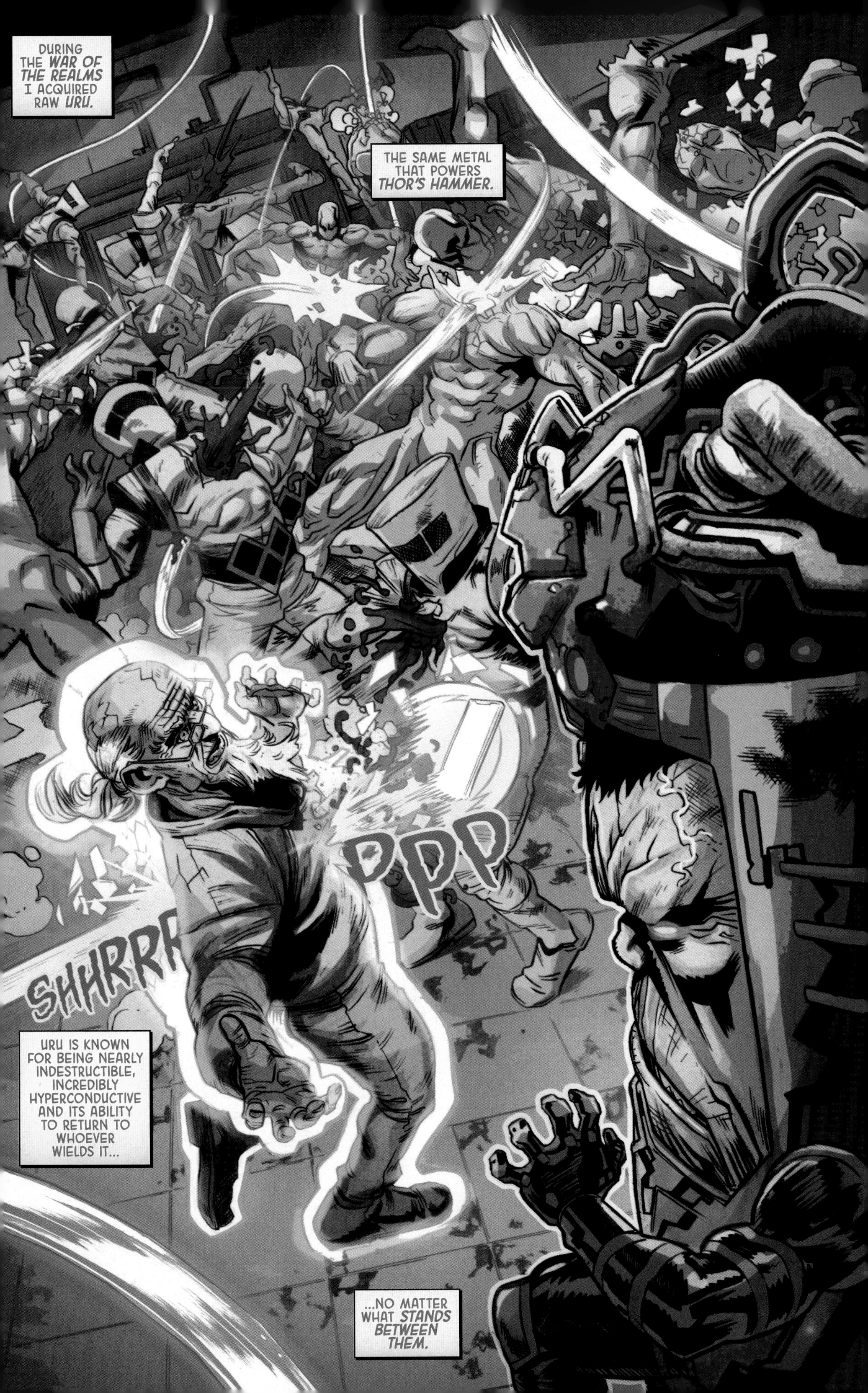

DURING THE WAR OF THE REALMS I ACQUIRED RAW URU.
THE SAME METAL THAT POWERS THOR'S HAMMER.
SHHRRR
PPP
URU IS KNOWN FOR BEING NEARLY INDESTRUCTIBLE, INCREDIBLY HYPERCONDUCTIVE AND ITS ABILITY TO RETURN TO WHOEVER WIELDS IT...
...NO MATTER WHAT STANDS BETWEEN THEM.

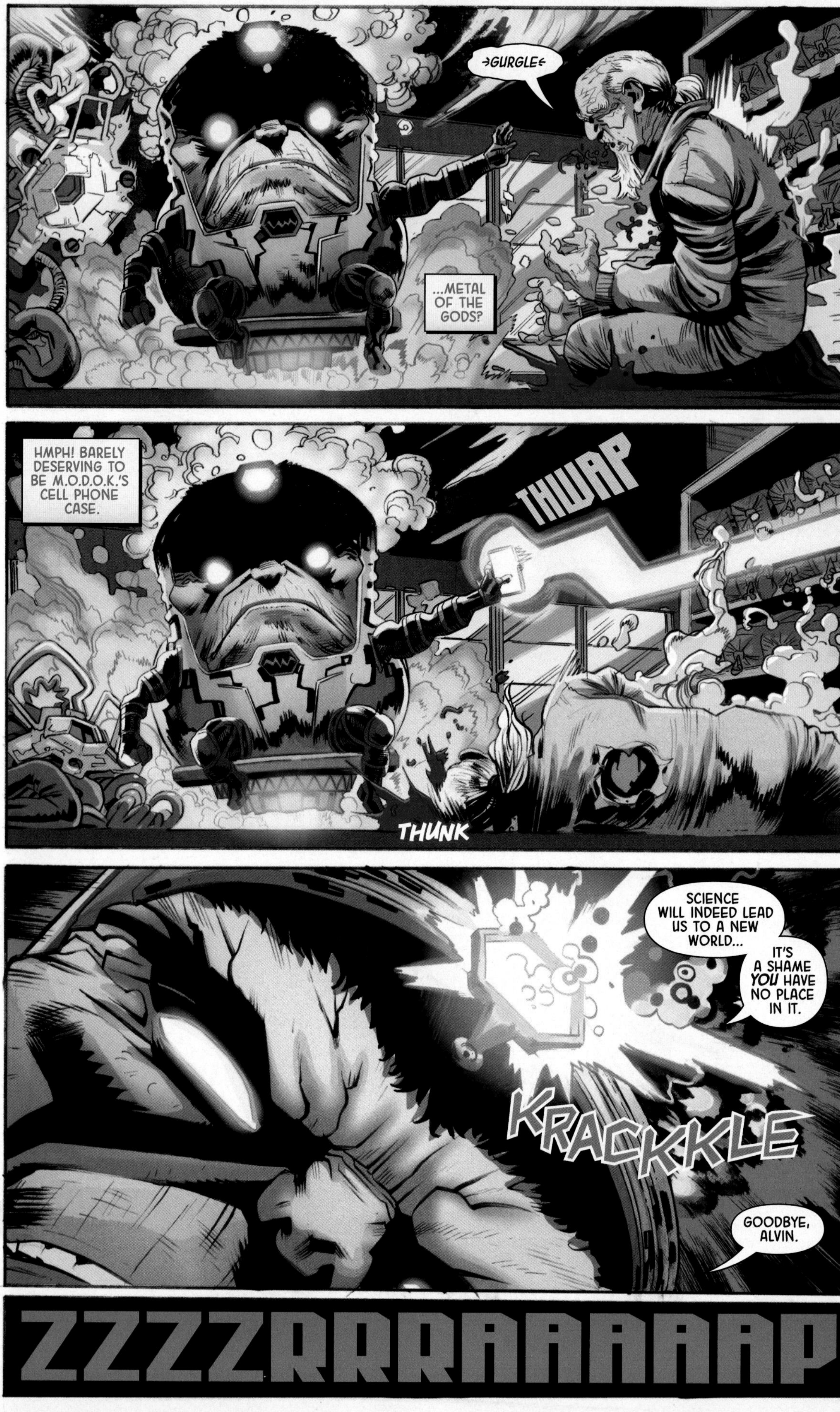

GURGLE
...METAL OF THE GODS?
HMPH! BARELY DESERVING TO BE M.O.D.O.K.'S CELL PHONE CASE.
THWAP
THUNK
SCIENCE WILL INDEED LEAD US TO A NEW WORLD...
IT'S A SHAME YOU HAVE NO PLACE IN IT.
KRACKKLE
GOODBYE, ALVIN.
ZZZZRRRRAAAAAAP

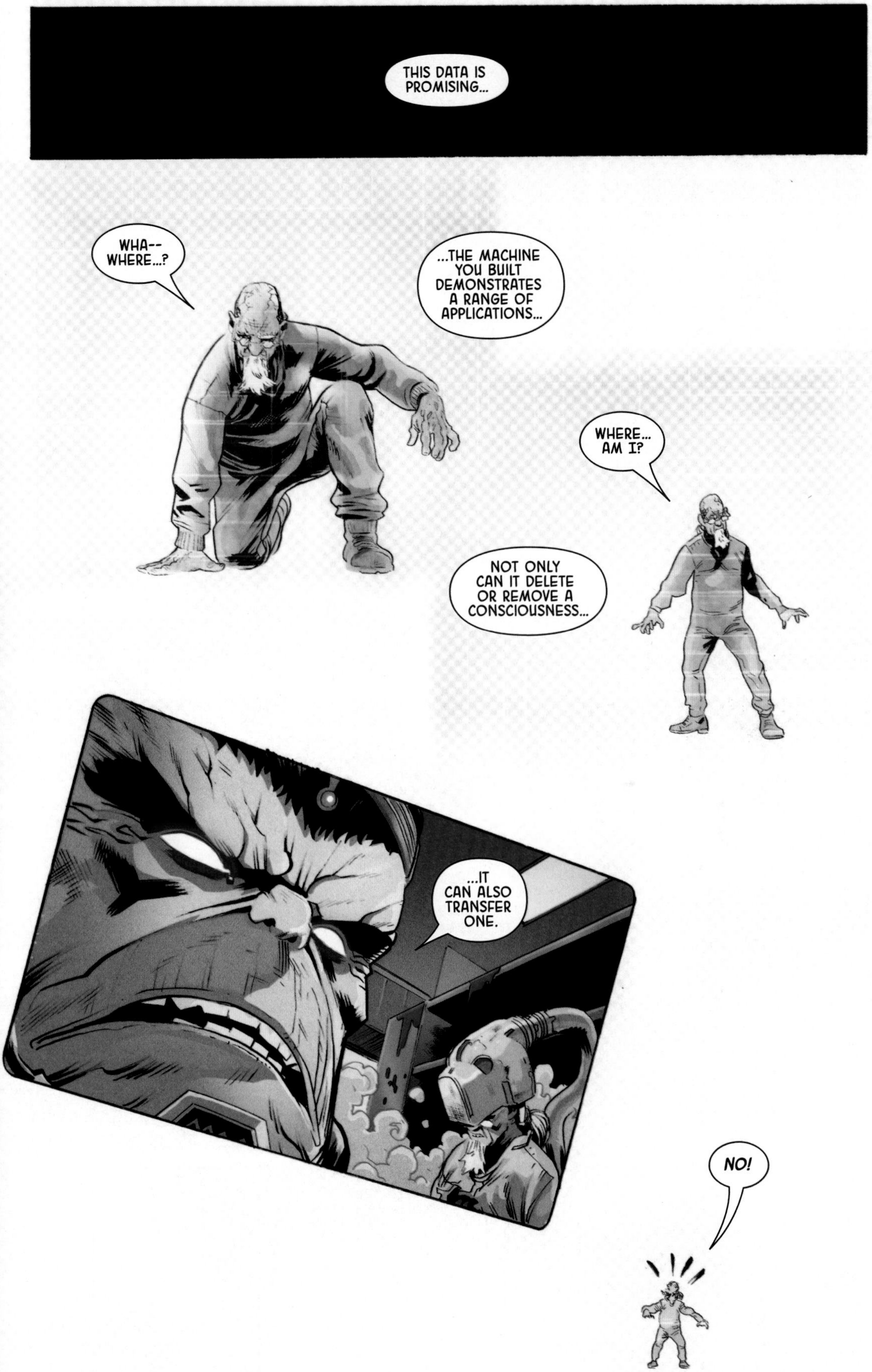
THIS DATA IS PROMISING...
WHA-- WHERE...?
...THE MACHINE YOU BUILT DEMONSTRATES A RANGE OF APPLICATIONS...
WHERE... AM I?
NOT ONLY CAN IT DELETE OR REMOVE A CONSCIOUSNESS...
...IT CAN ALSO TRANSFER ONE.
NO!

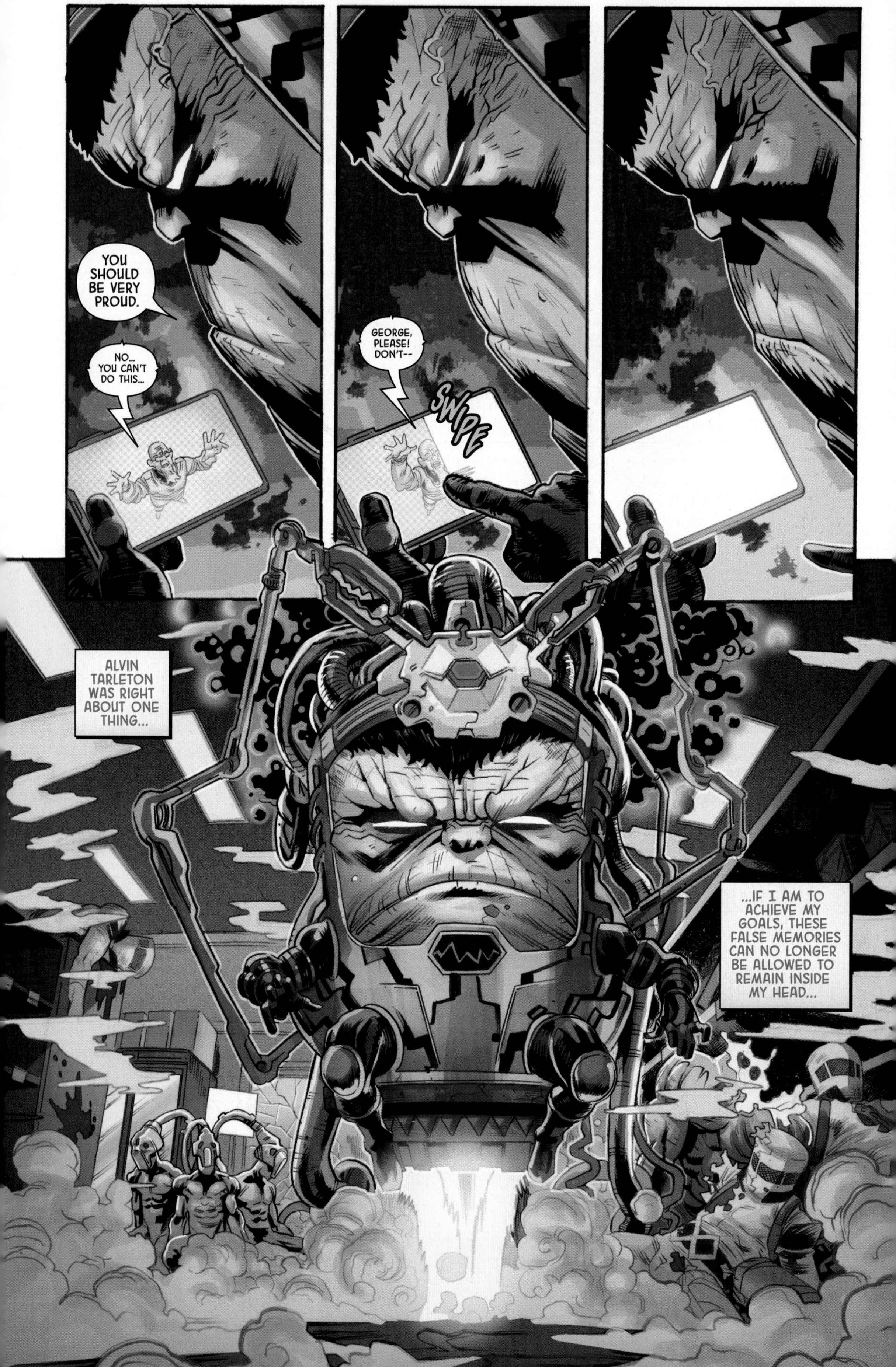
YOU SHOULD BE VERY PROUD.
NO... YOU CAN'T DO THIS...
GEORGE, PLEASE! DON'T--
SWIPE
ALVIN TARLETON WAS RIGHT ABOUT ONE THING...
...IF I AM TO ACHIEVE MY GOALS, THESE FALSE MEMORIES CAN NO LONGER BE ALLOWED TO REMAIN INSIDE MY HEAD...

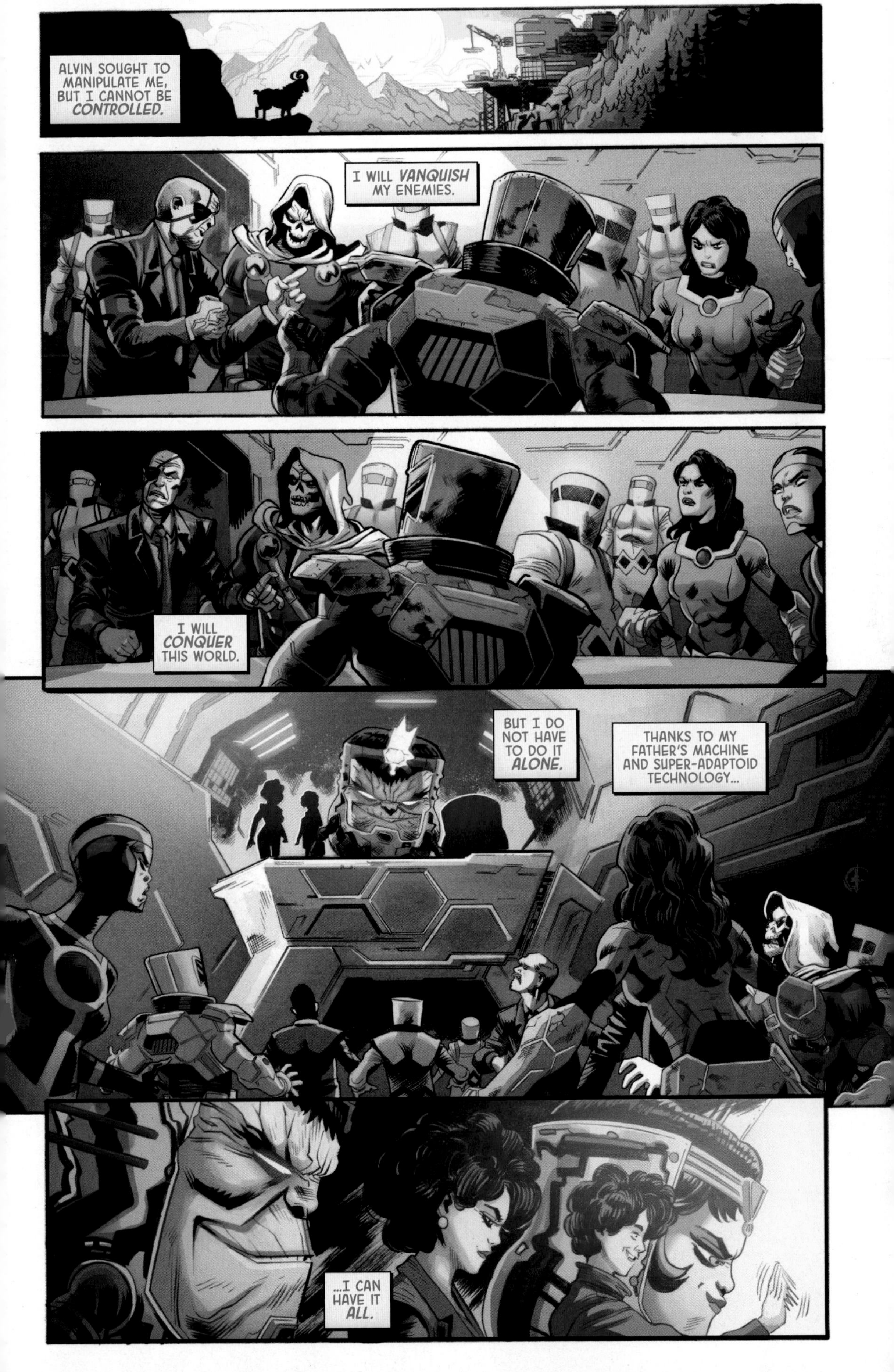
ALVIN SOUGHT TO MANIPULATE ME, BUT I CANNOT BE CONTROLLED.
I WILL VANQUISH MY ENEMIES.
I WILL CONQUER THIS WORLD.
BUT I DO NOT HAVE TO DO IT ALONE.
THANKS TO MY FATHER'S MACHINE AND SUPER-ADAPTOID TECHNOLOGY...
...I CAN HAVE IT ALL.

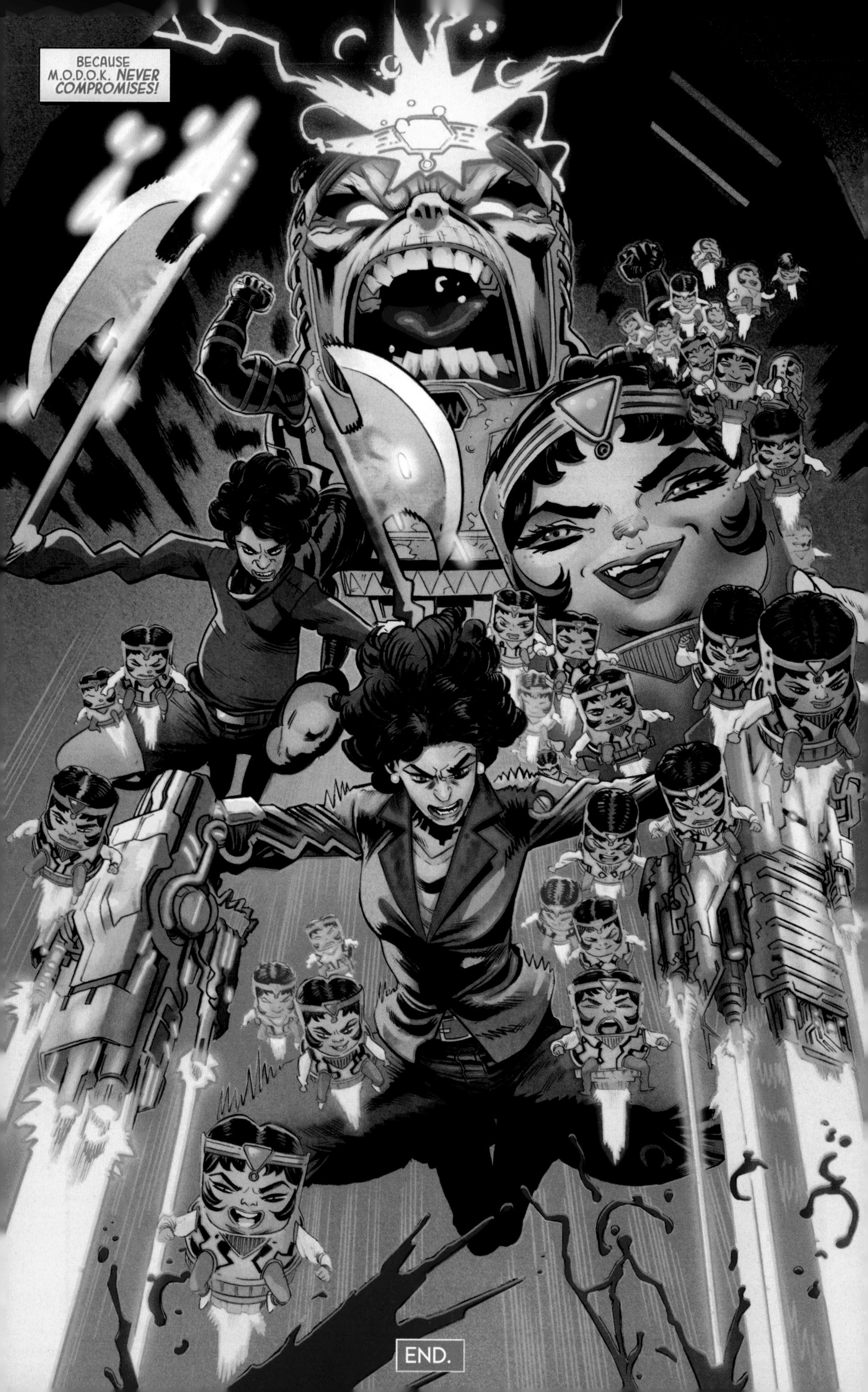
BECAUSE M.O.D.O.K. NEVER COMPROMISES!
END.

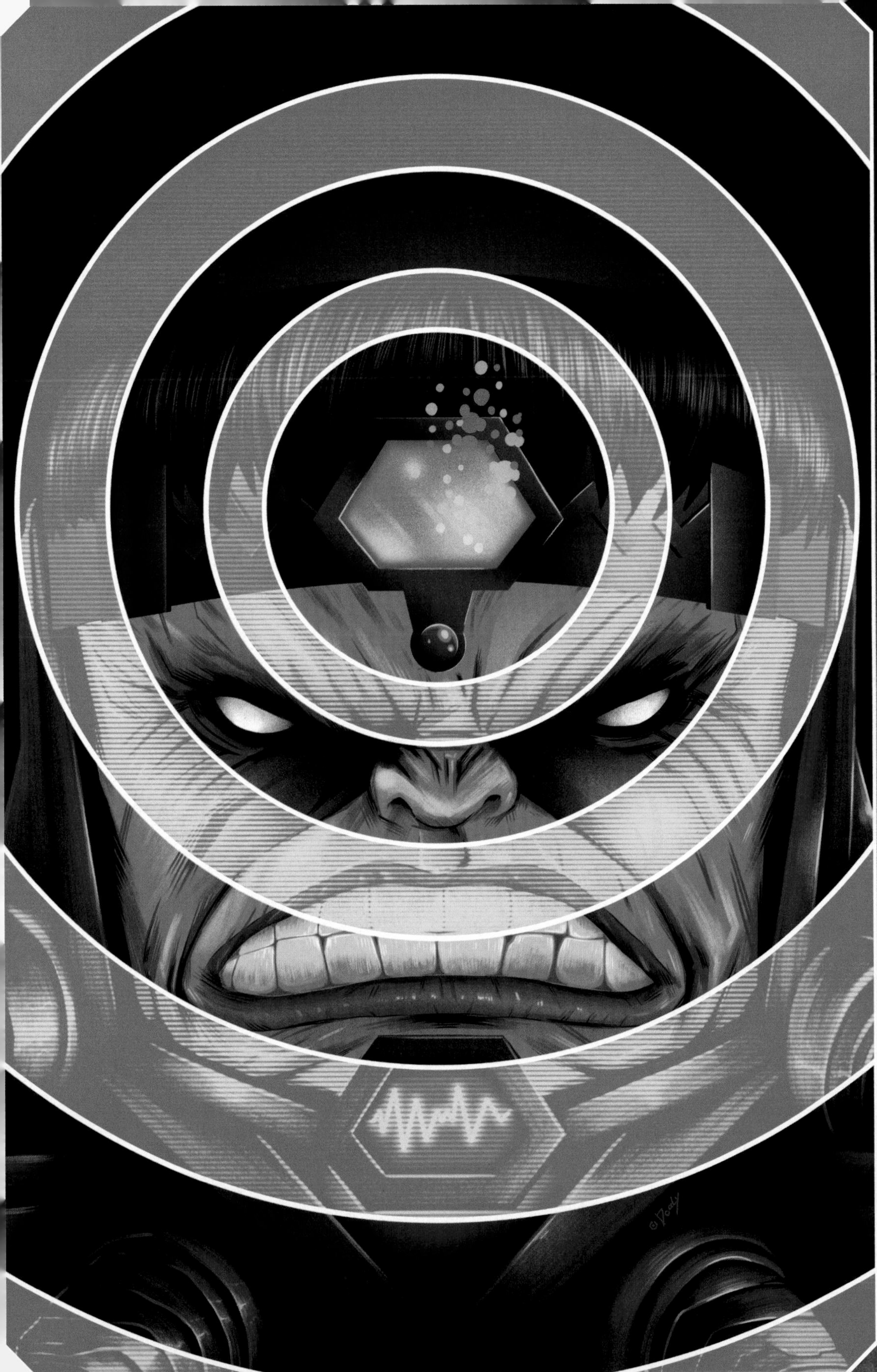

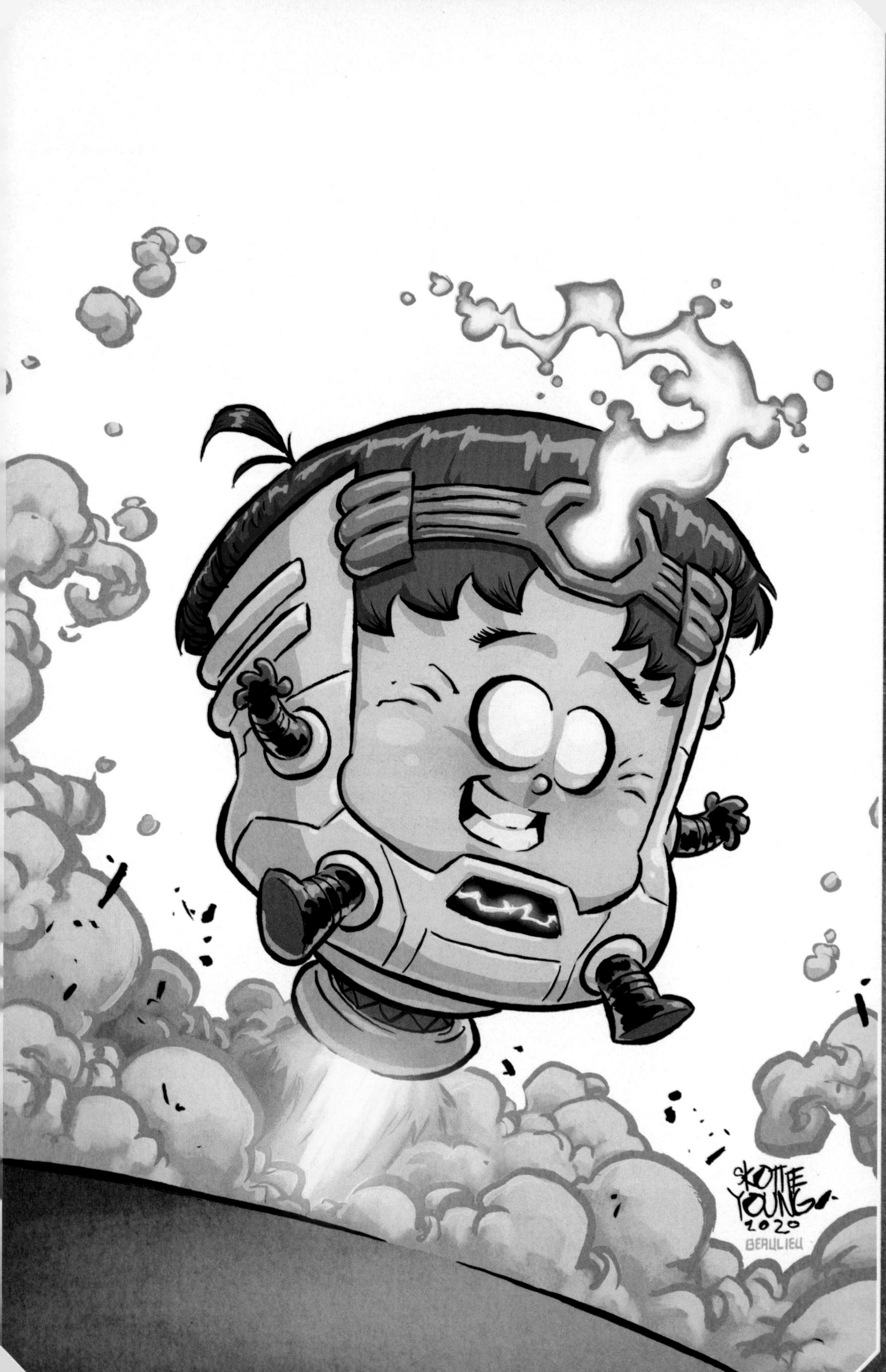
SKOTTIE YOUNG 2020
BEAULIEU

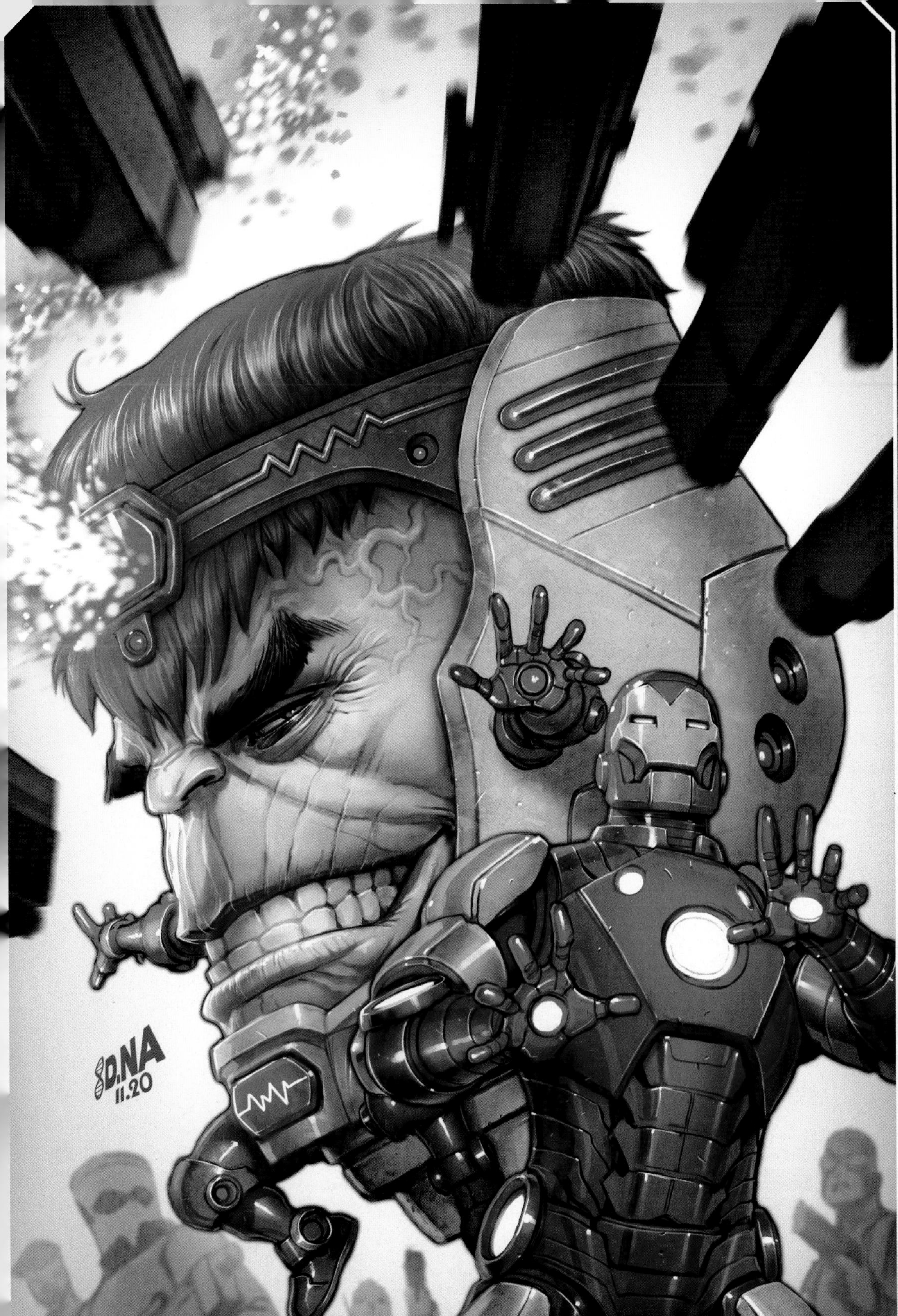
D.NA
11.20

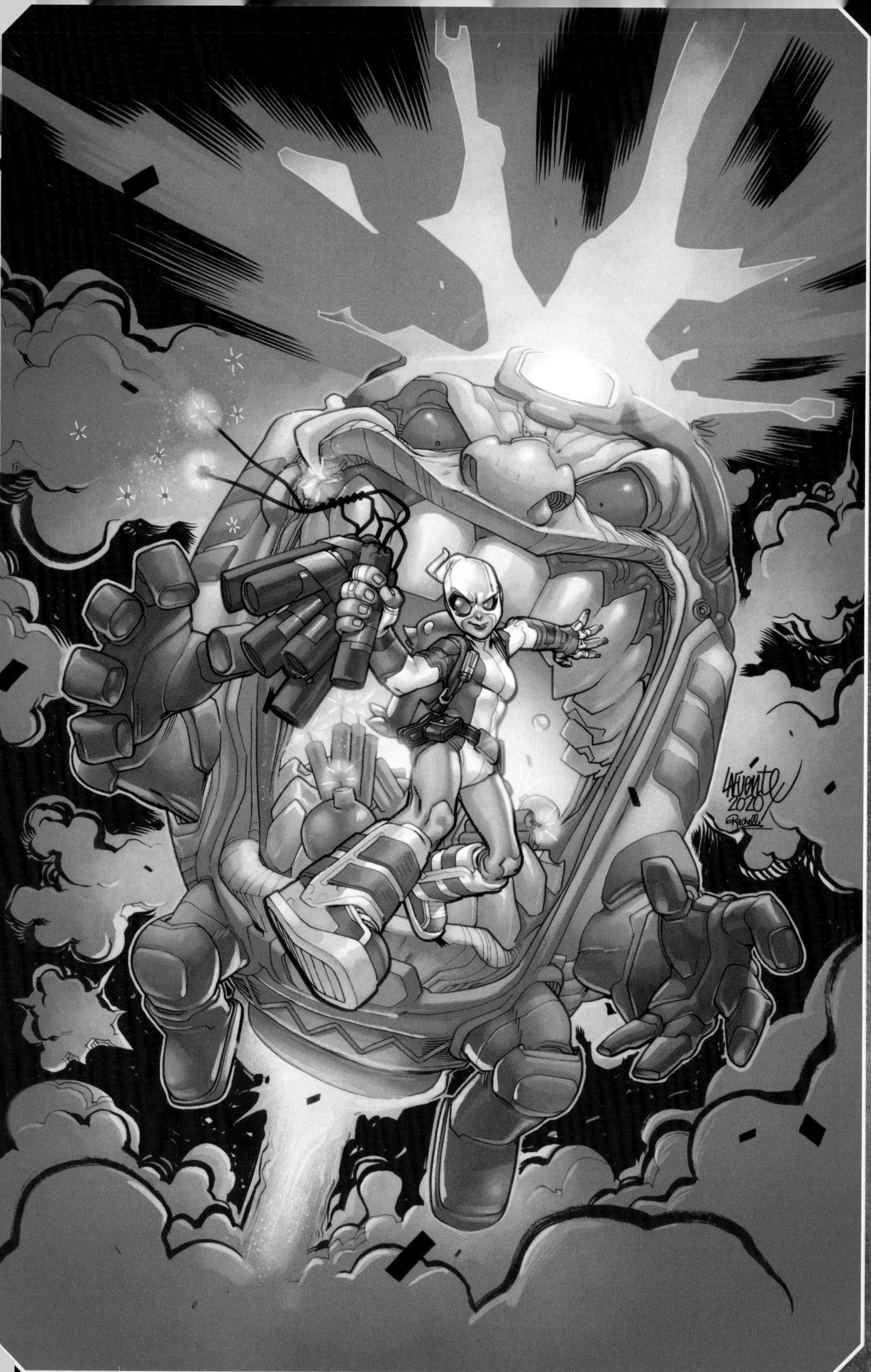

M.O.D.O.K.: REIGN DELAY

M.O.D.O.K.'S PLANS HAVE BEEN THWARTED COUNTLESS TIMES BY SUPER HEROES, BUT HIS FAMILY CAN DO AN EVEN BETTER JOB!

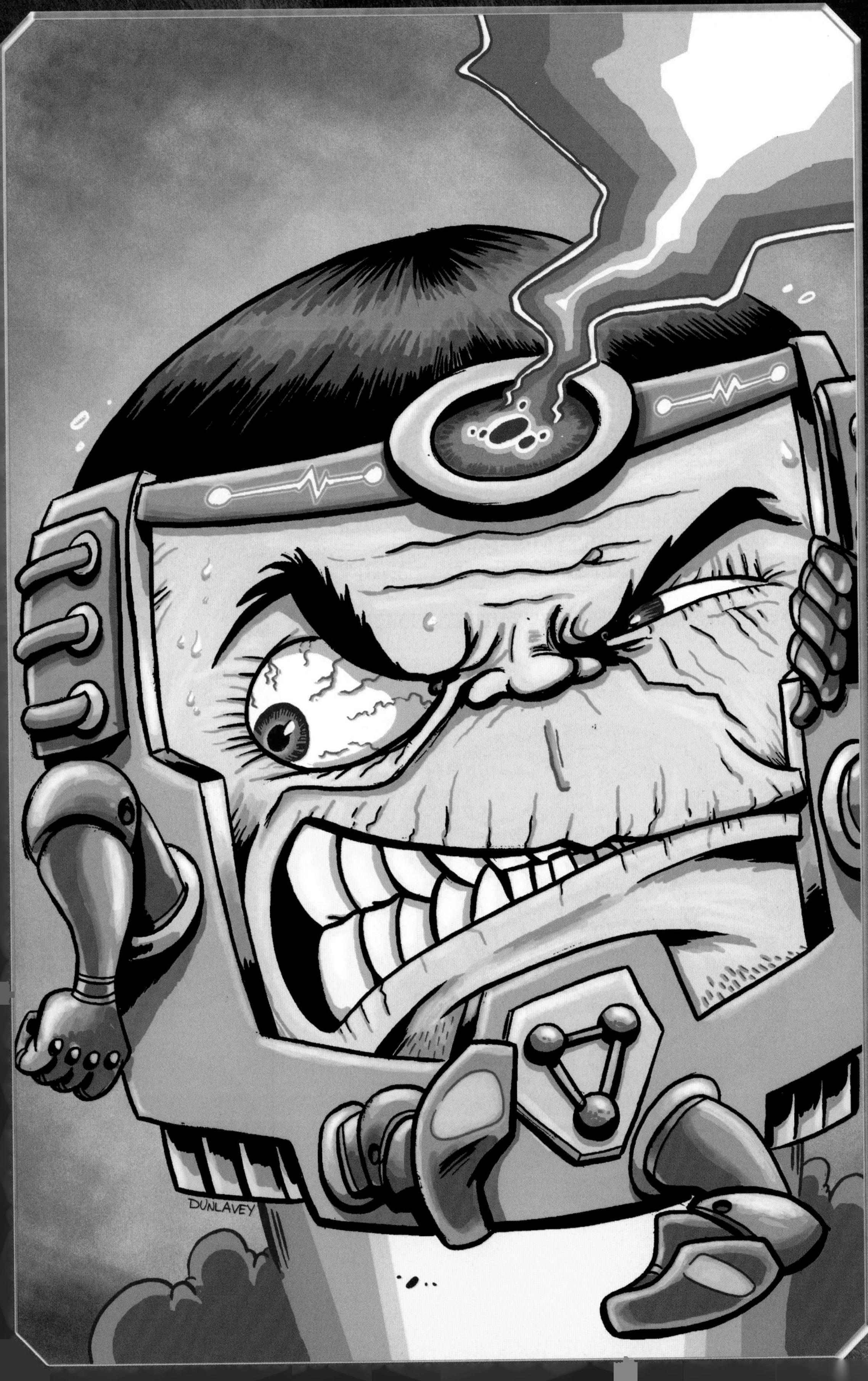
DUNLAVEY

M.O.D.O.K.

REIGN DELAY

WORDS, LINES, COLORS, LETTERS, & COVER BY
RYAN DUNLAVEY

EDITOR: JORDAN D. WHITE
CONSULTING EDITOR: NATHAN COSBY
EDITOR IN CHIEF: JOE QUESADA
PUBLISHER: DAN BUCKLEY
EXEC. PRODUCER: ALAN FINE

DIRECTOR OF DIGITAL CONTENT: JOHN CERILLI
DIGITAL COORDINATOR: HARRY GO
DIGITAL PRODUCTION MANAGER: TIM SMITH 3

ORIGINALLY PRESENTED EXCLUSIVELY ON MARVEL DIGITAL COMICS UNLIMITED.

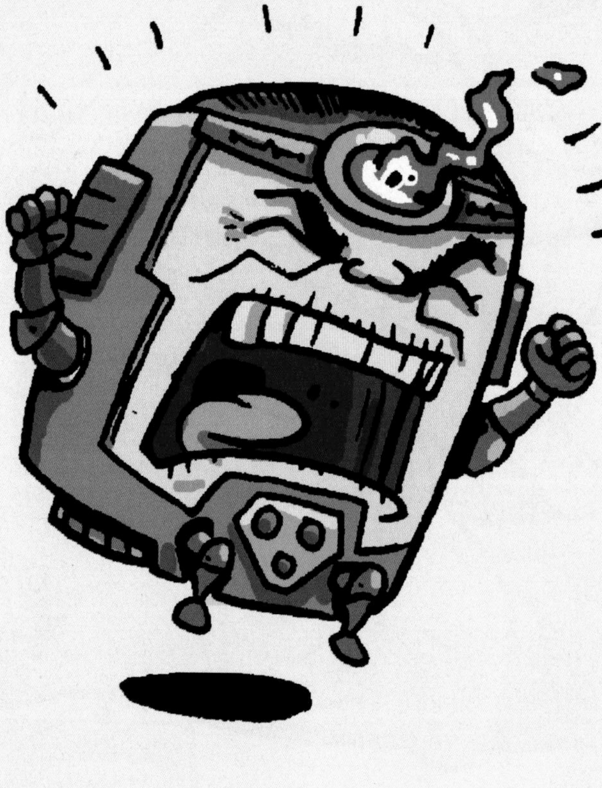

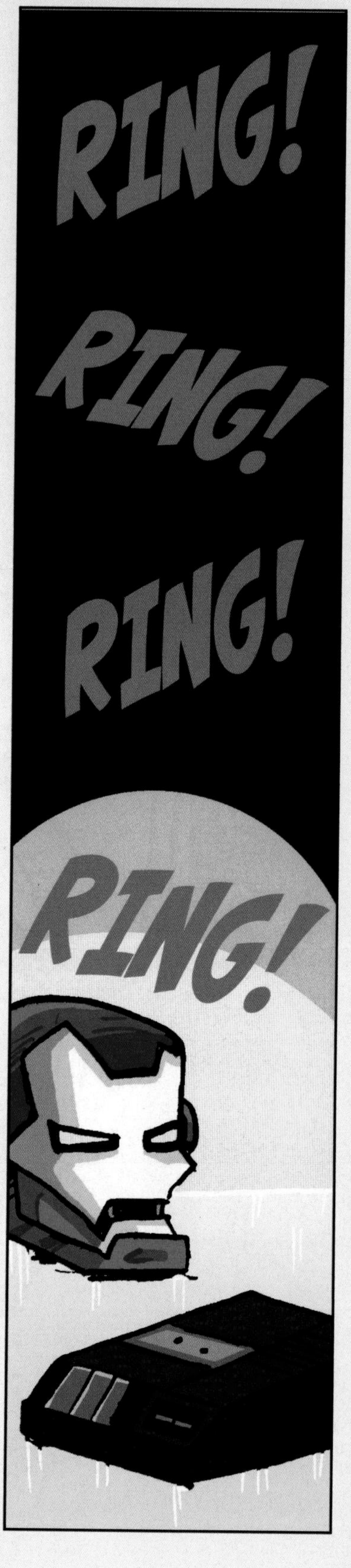
RING!
RING!
RING!
RING!

≥BEEP≤

YOU'VE REACHED THE VOICE MAIL OF *NORMAN OSBORN*. LEAVE A MESSAGE AND *MAKE IT QUICK.*

SERIOUSLY, I HAVE *28 CAMEO APPEARANCES* THIS MONTH, SO *DON'T* ANNOY ME.

ALSO, MY BUDDY JIM NEEDS A ROOMMATE -- PRIVATE BEDROOM, 1000 A MONTH, MUST LIKE PETS, NO FATTIES. LMK.

≥BEEP≤

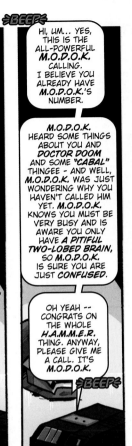

≥BEEP≤

HI, UM... YES, THIS IS THE ALL-POWERFUL *M.O.D.O.K.* CALLING. I BELIEVE YOU ALREADY HAVE *M.O.D.O.K.'S* NUMBER.

M.O.D.O.K. HEARD SOME THINGS ABOUT YOU AND *DOCTOR DOOM* AND SOME *"CABAL"* THINGEE - AND WELL, *M.O.D.O.K.* WAS JUST WONDERING WHY YOU HAVEN'T CALLED HIM YET. *M.O.D.O.K.* KNOWS YOU MUST BE VERY BUSY AND IS AWARE YOU ONLY HAVE *A PITIFUL TWO-LOBED BRAIN,* SO *M.O.D.O.K.* IS SURE YOU ARE JUST *CONFUSED.*

OH YEAH -- CONGRATS ON THE WHOLE *H.A.M.M.E.R.* THING. ANYWAY, PLEASE GIVE ME A CALL. IT'S *M.O.D.O.K.*

≥BEEP≤

≥BEEP≤

718-555-8571. I *KNOW* YOU ALREADY HAVE MY NUMBER, BUT JUST IN CASE. IT'S *M.O.D.O.K.* BY THE WAY.

WE *REALLY* NEED TO MEET TO DISCUSS MY ROLE IN *"THE BIG PLAN"* ASAP. I HEARD YOU PUT *MANDRILL* IN CHARGE OF *NEW ORLEANS,* WHICH SUCKS BECAUSE *M.O.D.O.K.* LOVES A GOOD *GUMBO...*

...

...BUT NEVER-MIND THAT! IT DOES NOT MATTER!

PLEASE CALL BACK SOON - *EMAIL* IS OK WITH ME TOO - IT'S *BIGHED71@ GMAIL.COM.*

OH! YOU CAN ALSO TRY MY CEL IT'S 646-67--

≥BEEP≤

≥BEEP≤

HEY, *ME AGAIN!* CALLED EARLIER BUT MAYBE YOU DELETED MY MESSAGE BY MISTAKE. JUST THOUGHT YOU SHOULD KNOW I HAVE A *WHOLE LOT OF THINGS* HAPPENING *SOON* BUT I WANT TO SETTLE THINGS UP WITH *YOU* FIRST SO I CAN MAKE HELPING YOU OUT MY *NUMBER ONE PRIORITY* BEFORE I MOVE ON TO THIS *OTHER STUFF* I'VE GOT GOING ON, SO...

UM...

CALL ME *BACK.*

IT'S *M.O.D.O.K.*

I... I HAVE MINIONS.

≥BEEP≤

≥BEEP≤

SORRY, *M.O.D.O.K.* WAS JUST CALLING TO SEE IF MAYBE YOU TRIED TO CALL *M.O.D.O.K.* WHEN *M.O.D.O.K.* WAS LEAVING THAT LAST MESSAGE.

SORRY, SORRY, WHATEVER. JUST *CALL ME BACK.*

IT'S *M.O.D.O.K.*

≥BEEP≤

≥BEEP≤

OSBORN! I WILL NOT TOLERATE ANY MORE DELAYS! RETURN MY CALLS IMMEDIATELY OR SUFFER M.O.D.O.K.'S MIND BLASTS!!!

EMAIL IS FINE TOO.

≥BEEP≤

≥BEEP≤

OKAY, I APOLOGIZE, THAT LAST CALL WAS A LITTLE OVER THE EDGE. IT'S JUST BEEN A BAD WEEK FOR ME...

-: SIGH :-

ANYWAY, I SHOULDN'T HAVE TAKEN IT OUT ON *YOU.* SORRY. CAN WE START OVER? IT'S *M.O.D.O.K.* 646-678-2--

≥BEEP≤

≥BEEP≤

SEVEN! ONE! EIGHT! FIVE! FIVE! FIVE!

EIGHTFIVE SEVENONE !!!

CALL OR BE *ANNIHILATED !!!*

≥BEEP≤

≥BEEP≤

OKAY, THE THING IS, I'VE GOT *NOTHING* GOING ON. I HAD TO LET SOME OF MY MINIONS GO TODAY, *REALLY* NOT GOOD FOR MORALE. LET ME KNOW *WHAT'S* GOING ON, *WHAT* YOU WANT ME TO DO AND *WHEN* I CAN *GET STARTED.*

IT'S *M.O.D.O.K.*

≥BEEP≤

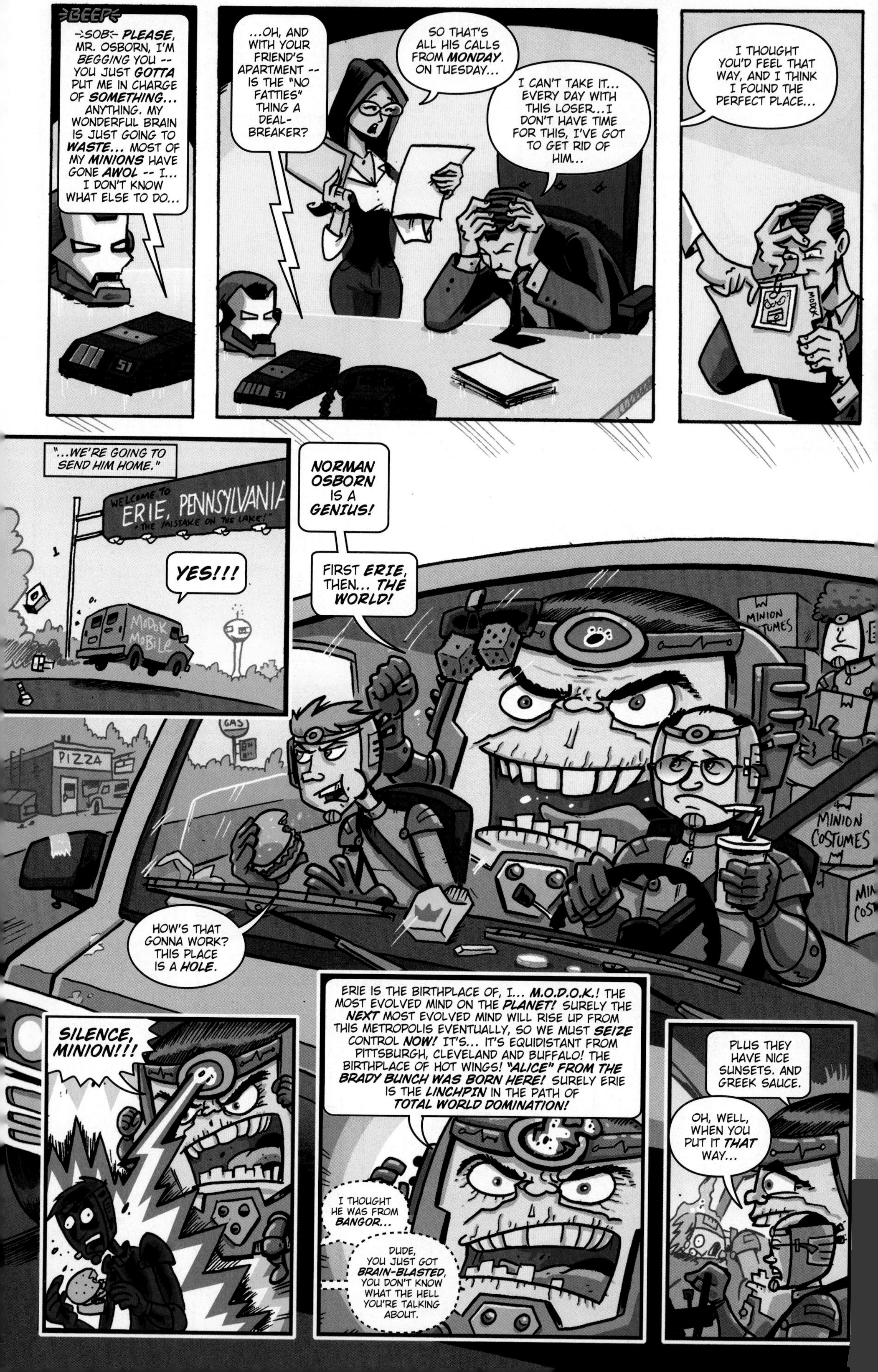
BEEP
-SOB- PLEASE, MR. OSBORN, I'M BEGGING YOU -- YOU JUST GOTTA PUT ME IN CHARGE OF SOMETHING... ANYTHING. MY WONDERFUL BRAIN IS JUST GOING TO WASTE... MOST OF MY MINIONS HAVE GONE AWOL -- I... I DON'T KNOW WHAT ELSE TO DO...
51
SO THAT'S ALL HIS CALLS FROM MONDAY. ON TUESDAY...
...OH, AND WITH YOUR FRIEND'S APARTMENT -- IS THE "NO FATTIES" THING A DEAL-BREAKER?
I CAN'T TAKE IT... EVERY DAY WITH THIS LOSER...I DON'T HAVE TIME FOR THIS, I'VE GOT TO GET RID OF HIM...
51
I THOUGHT YOU'D FEEL THAT WAY, AND I THINK I FOUND THE PERFECT PLACE...
MODOK
"...WE'RE GOING TO SEND HIM HOME."
WELCOME TO ERIE, PENNSYLVANIA "THE MISTAKE ON THE LAKE!"
YES!!!
MODOK MOBILE
NORMAN OSBORN IS A GENIUS!
FIRST ERIE, THEN... THE WORLD!
MINION COSTUMES
GAS
PIZZA
MINION COSTUMES
HOW'S THAT GONNA WORK? THIS PLACE IS A HOLE.
SILENCE, MINION!!!
ERIE IS THE BIRTHPLACE OF, I... M.O.D.O.K.! THE MOST EVOLVED MIND ON THE PLANET! SURELY THE NEXT MOST EVOLVED MIND WILL RISE UP FROM THIS METROPOLIS EVENTUALLY, SO WE MUST SEIZE CONTROL NOW! IT'S... IT'S EQUIDISTANT FROM PITTSBURGH, CLEVELAND AND BUFFALO! THE BIRTHPLACE OF HOT WINGS! "ALICE" FROM THE BRADY BUNCH WAS BORN HERE! SURELY ERIE IS THE LINCHPIN IN THE PATH OF TOTAL WORLD DOMINATION!
I THOUGHT HE WAS FROM BANGOR...
DUDE, YOU JUST GOT BRAIN-BLASTED, YOU DON'T KNOW WHAT THE HELL YOU'RE TALKING ABOUT.
PLUS THEY HAVE NICE SUNSETS. AND GREEK SAUCE.
OH, WELL, WHEN YOU PUT IT THAT WAY...

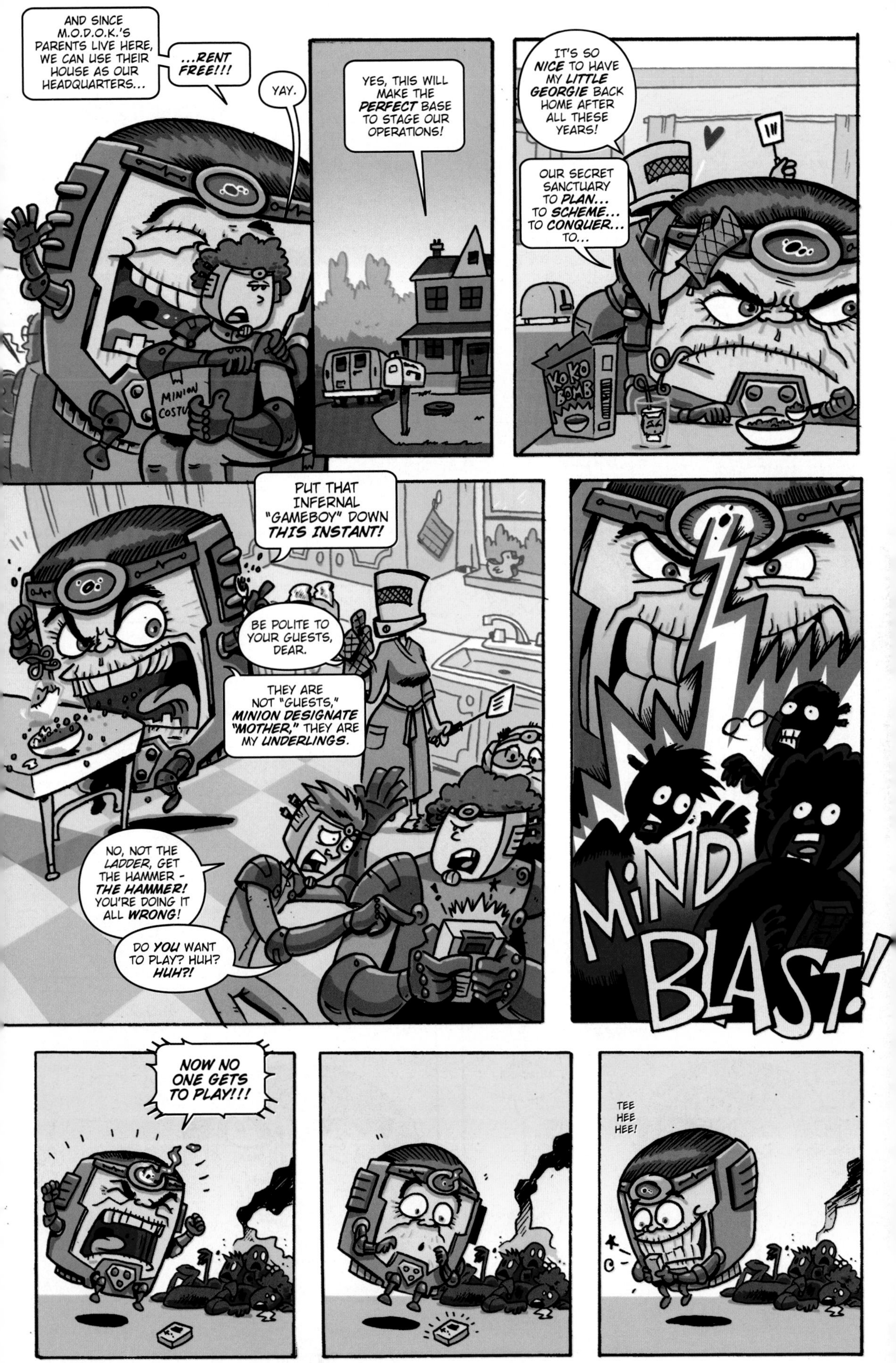
AND SINCE M.O.D.O.K.'S PARENTS LIVE HERE, WE CAN USE THEIR HOUSE AS OUR HEADQUARTERS...
...RENT FREE!!!
YAY.
MINION COSTU
YES, THIS WILL MAKE THE PERFECT BASE TO STAGE OUR OPERATIONS!
IT'S SO NICE TO HAVE MY LITTLE GEORGIE BACK HOME AFTER ALL THESE YEARS!
OUR SECRET SANCTUARY TO PLAN... TO SCHEME... TO CONQUER... TO...
KOKO BOMB
PUT THAT INFERNAL "GAMEBOY" DOWN THIS INSTANT!
BE POLITE TO YOUR GUESTS, DEAR.
THEY ARE NOT "GUESTS," MINION DESIGNATE "MOTHER," THEY ARE MY UNDERLINGS.
NO, NOT THE LADDER, GET THE HAMMER - THE HAMMER! YOU'RE DOING IT ALL WRONG!
DO YOU WANT TO PLAY? HUH? HUH?!
MIND BLAST!
NOW NO ONE GETS TO PLAY!!!
TEE HEE HEE!

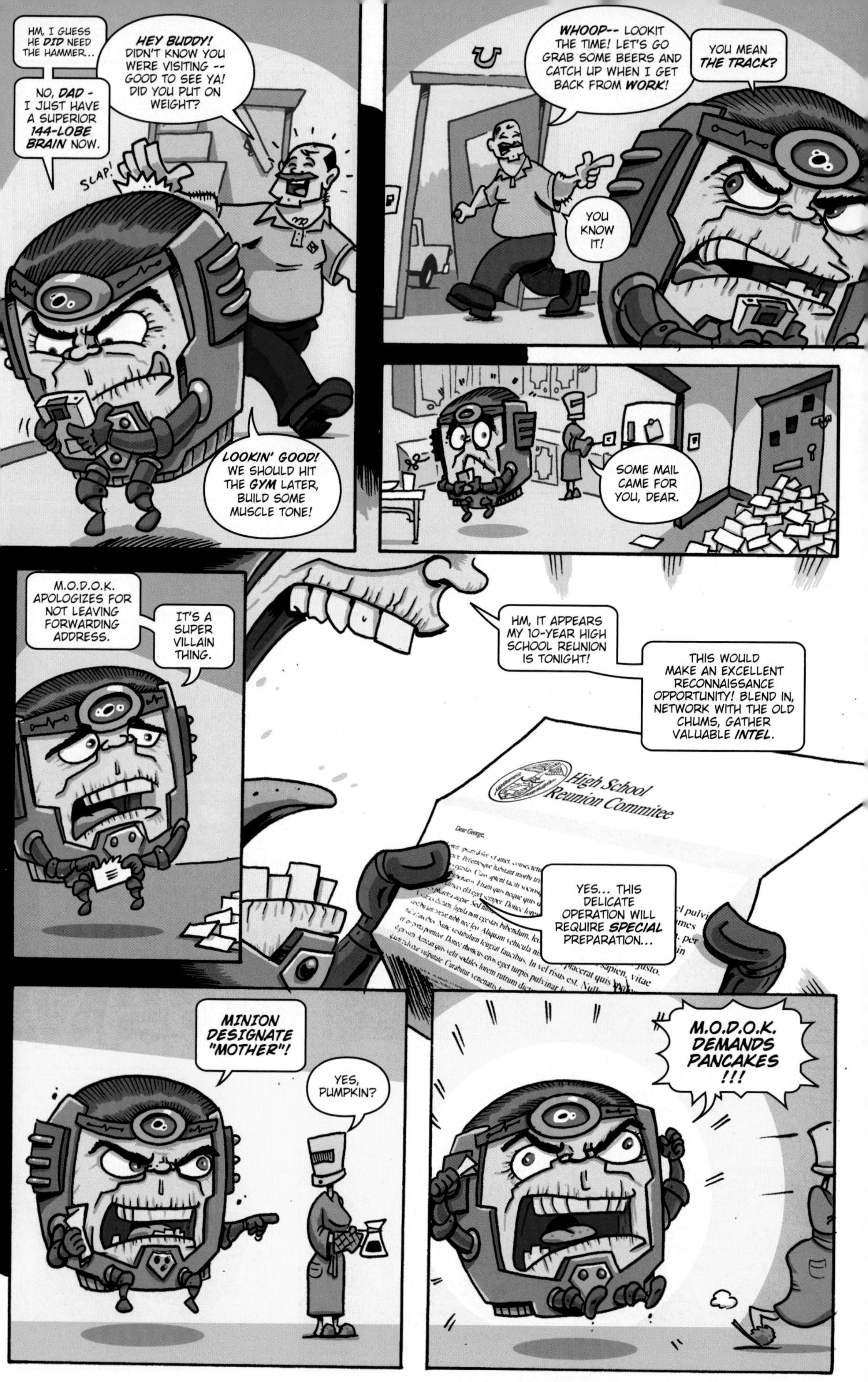
HM, I GUESS HE DID NEED THE HAMMER...
NO, DAD - I JUST HAVE A SUPERIOR 144-LOBE BRAIN NOW.
HEY BUDDY! DIDN'T KNOW YOU WERE VISITING -- GOOD TO SEE YA! DID YOU PUT ON WEIGHT?
SCAP!
LOOKIN' GOOD! WE SHOULD HIT THE GYM LATER, BUILD SOME MUSCLE TONE!
WHOOP-- LOOKIT THE TIME! LET'S GO GRAB SOME BEERS AND CATCH UP WHEN I GET BACK FROM WORK!
YOU MEAN THE TRACK?
YOU KNOW IT!
SOME MAIL CAME FOR YOU, DEAR.
M.O.D.O.K. APOLOGIZES FOR NOT LEAVING FORWARDING ADDRESS.
IT'S A SUPER VILLAIN THING.
HM, IT APPEARS MY 10-YEAR HIGH SCHOOL REUNION IS TONIGHT!
THIS WOULD MAKE AN EXCELLENT RECONNAISSANCE OPPORTUNITY! BLEND IN, NETWORK WITH THE OLD CHUMS, GATHER VALUABLE INTEL.
High School Reunion Commitee
Dear George,
YES... THIS DELICATE OPERATION WILL REQUIRE SPECIAL PREPARATION...
MINION DESIGNATE "MOTHER"!
YES, PUMPKIN?
M.O.D.O.K. DEMANDS PANCAKES !!!

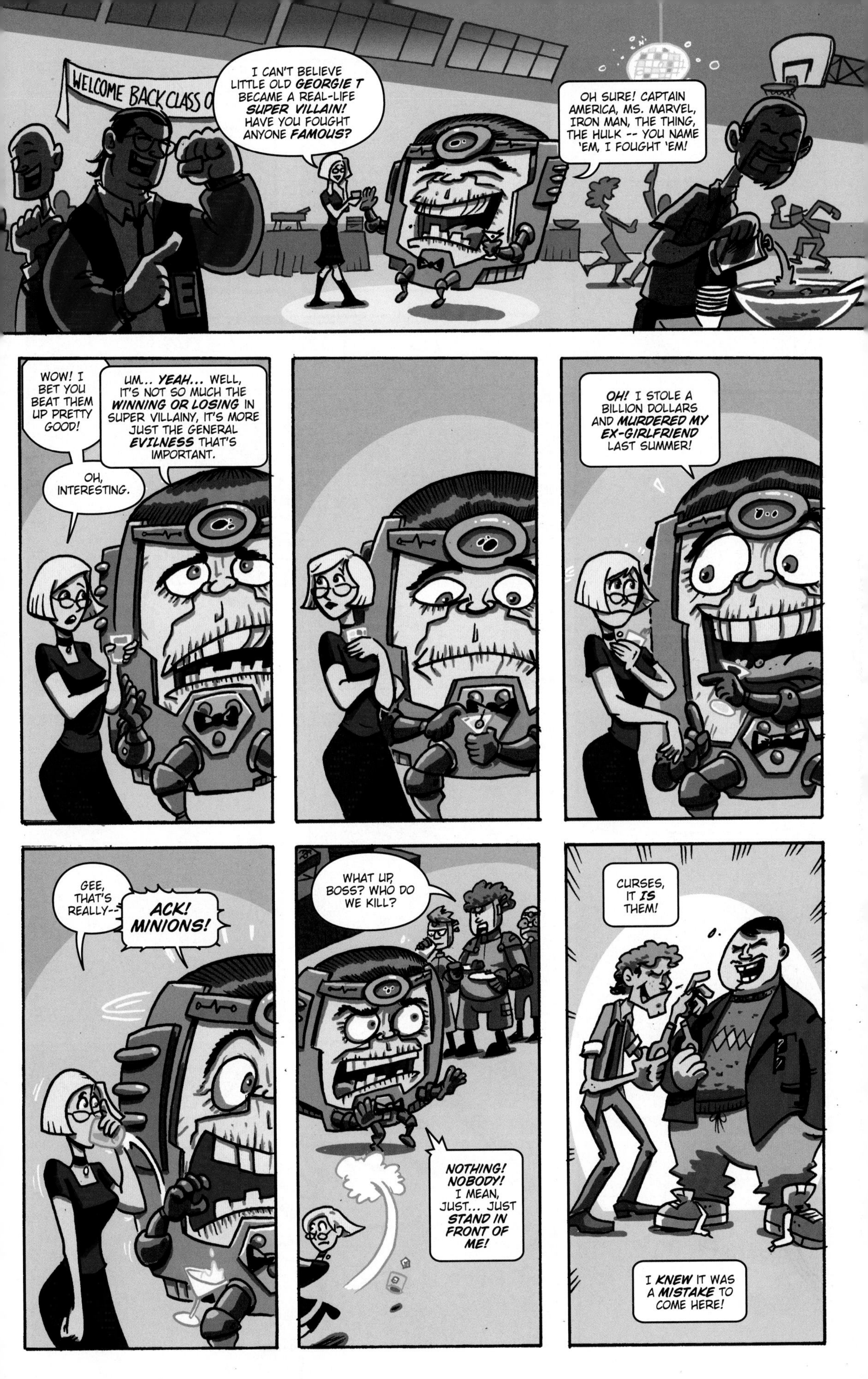
WELCOME BACK CLASS O
I CAN'T BELIEVE LITTLE OLD GEORGIE T BECAME A REAL-LIFE SUPER VILLAIN! HAVE YOU FOUGHT ANYONE FAMOUS?
OH SURE! CAPTAIN AMERICA, MS. MARVEL, IRON MAN, THE THING, THE HULK -- YOU NAME 'EM, I FOUGHT 'EM!
WOW! I BET YOU BEAT THEM UP PRETTY GOOD!
UM... YEAH... WELL, IT'S NOT SO MUCH THE WINNING OR LOSING IN SUPER VILLAINY, IT'S MORE JUST THE GENERAL EVILNESS THAT'S IMPORTANT.
OH, INTERESTING.
OH! I STOLE A BILLION DOLLARS AND MURDERED MY EX-GIRLFRIEND LAST SUMMER!
GEE, THAT'S REALLY--
ACK! MINIONS!
WHAT UP, BOSS? WHO DO WE KILL?
NOTHING! NOBODY! I MEAN, JUST... JUST STAND IN FRONT OF ME!
CURSES, IT IS THEM!
I KNEW IT WAS A MISTAKE TO COME HERE!

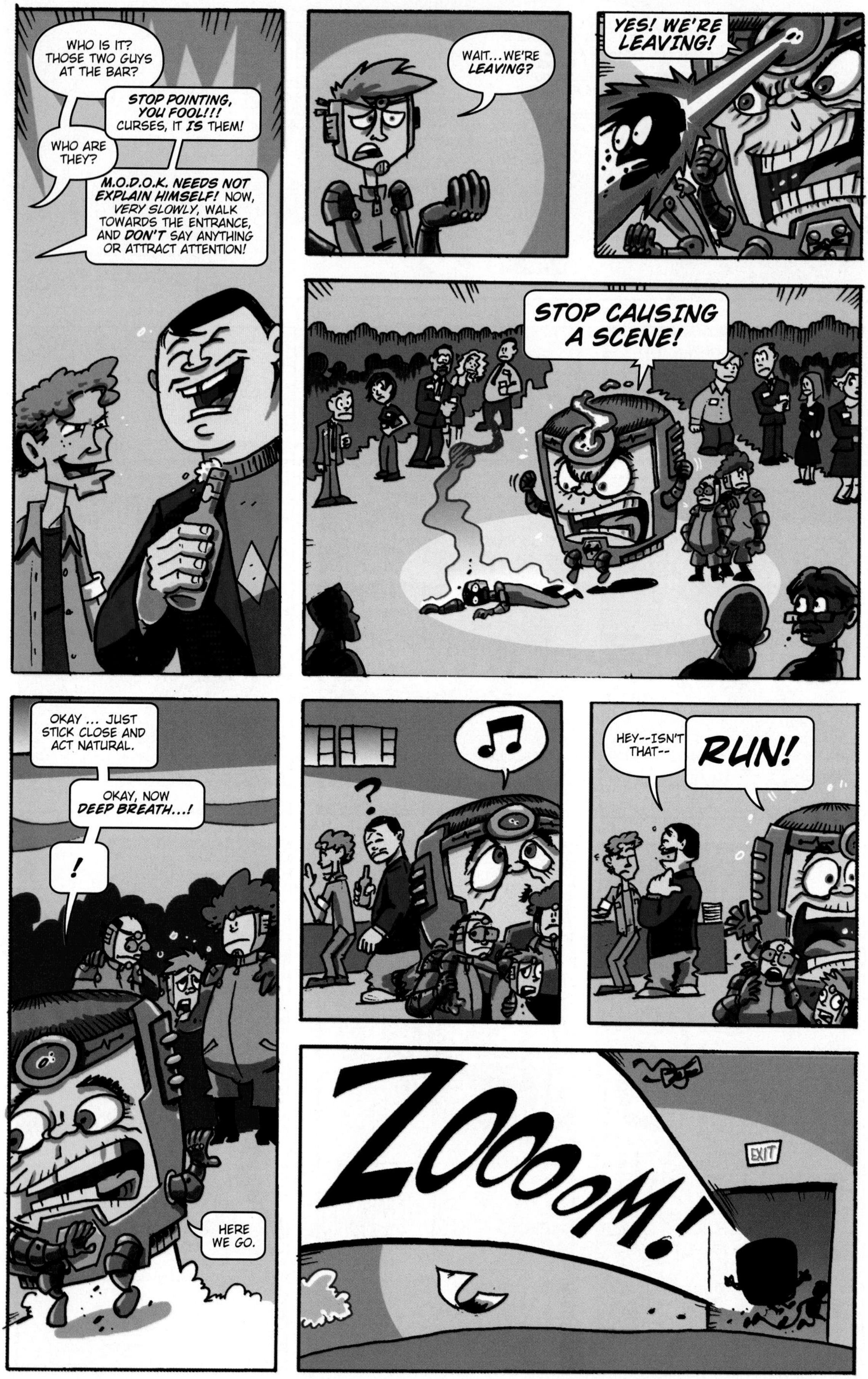
WHO IS IT? THOSE TWO GUYS AT THE BAR?
STOP POINTING, YOU FOOL!!! CURSES, IT IS THEM!
WHO ARE THEY?
M.O.D.O.K. NEEDS NOT EXPLAIN HIMSELF! NOW, VERY SLOWLY, WALK TOWARDS THE ENTRANCE, AND DON'T SAY ANYTHING OR ATTRACT ATTENTION!
WAIT...WE'RE LEAVING?
YES! WE'RE LEAVING!
STOP CAUSING A SCENE!
OKAY ... JUST STICK CLOSE AND ACT NATURAL.
OKAY, NOW DEEP BREATH...!
!
HERE WE GO.
♫
?
HEY--ISN'T THAT--
RUN!
ZOOOOOM!
EXIT

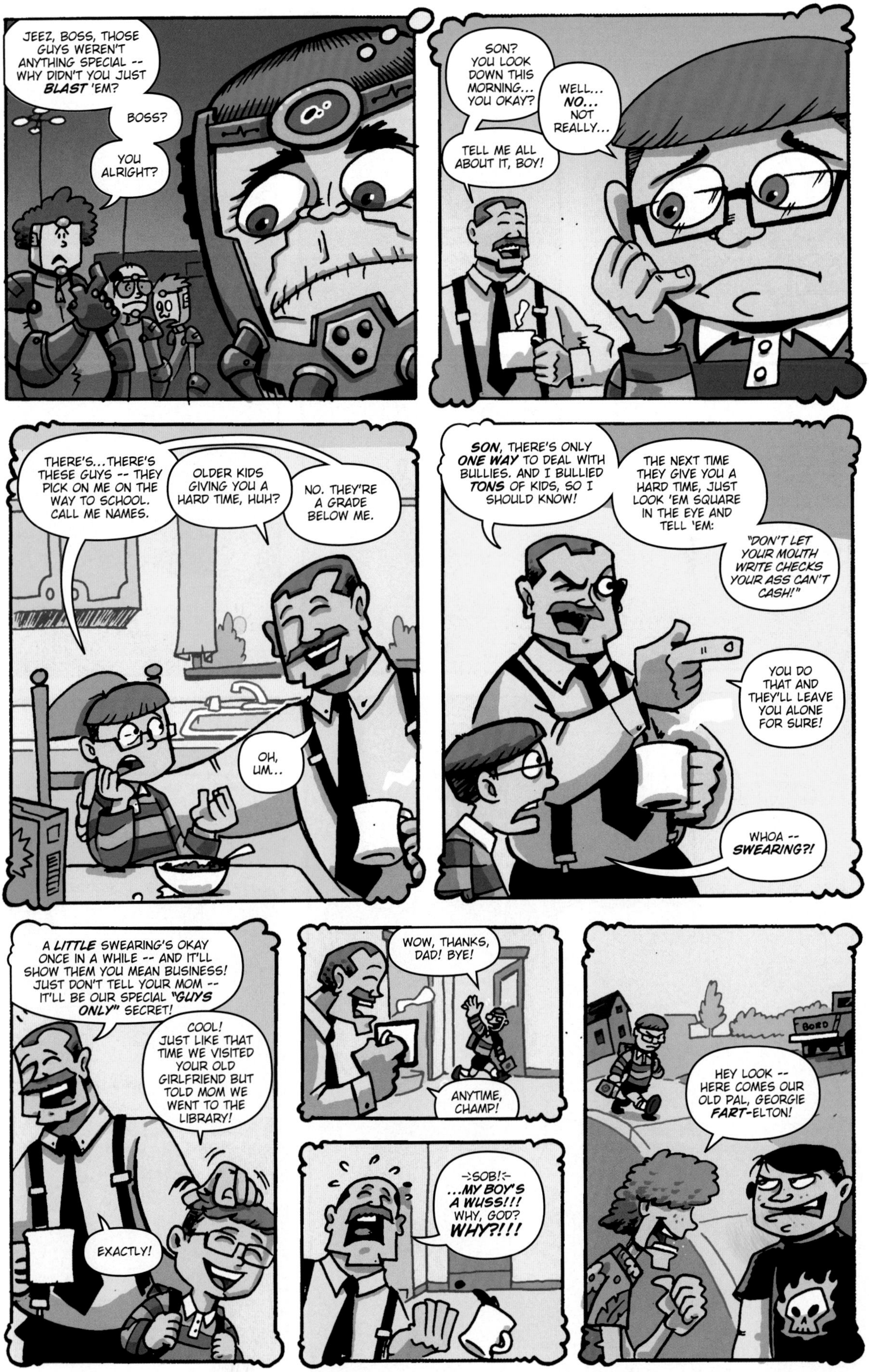
JEEZ, BOSS, THOSE GUYS WEREN'T ANYTHING SPECIAL -- WHY DIDN'T YOU JUST BLAST 'EM?
BOSS?
YOU ALRIGHT?
SON? YOU LOOK DOWN THIS MORNING... YOU OKAY?
WELL... NO... NOT REALLY...
TELL ME ALL ABOUT IT, BOY!
THERE'S...THERE'S THESE GUYS -- THEY PICK ON ME ON THE WAY TO SCHOOL. CALL ME NAMES.
OLDER KIDS GIVING YOU A HARD TIME, HUH?
NO. THEY'RE A GRADE BELOW ME.
OH, UM...
SON, THERE'S ONLY ONE WAY TO DEAL WITH BULLIES. AND I BULLIED TONS OF KIDS, SO I SHOULD KNOW!
THE NEXT TIME THEY GIVE YOU A HARD TIME, JUST LOOK 'EM SQUARE IN THE EYE AND TELL 'EM:
"DON'T LET YOUR MOUTH WRITE CHECKS YOUR ASS CAN'T CASH!"
YOU DO THAT AND THEY'LL LEAVE YOU ALONE FOR SURE!
WHOA -- SWEARING?!
A LITTLE SWEARING'S OKAY ONCE IN A WHILE -- AND IT'LL SHOW THEM YOU MEAN BUSINESS! JUST DON'T TELL YOUR MOM -- IT'LL BE OUR SPECIAL "GUYS ONLY" SECRET!
COOL! JUST LIKE THAT TIME WE VISITED YOUR OLD GIRLFRIEND BUT TOLD MOM WE WENT TO THE LIBRARY!
EXACTLY!
WOW, THANKS, DAD! BYE!
ANYTIME, CHAMP!
-SOB!- ...MY BOY'S A WUSS!!! WHY, GOD? WHY?!!!
BORD
HEY LOOK -- HERE COMES OUR OLD PAL, GEORGIE FART-ELTON!

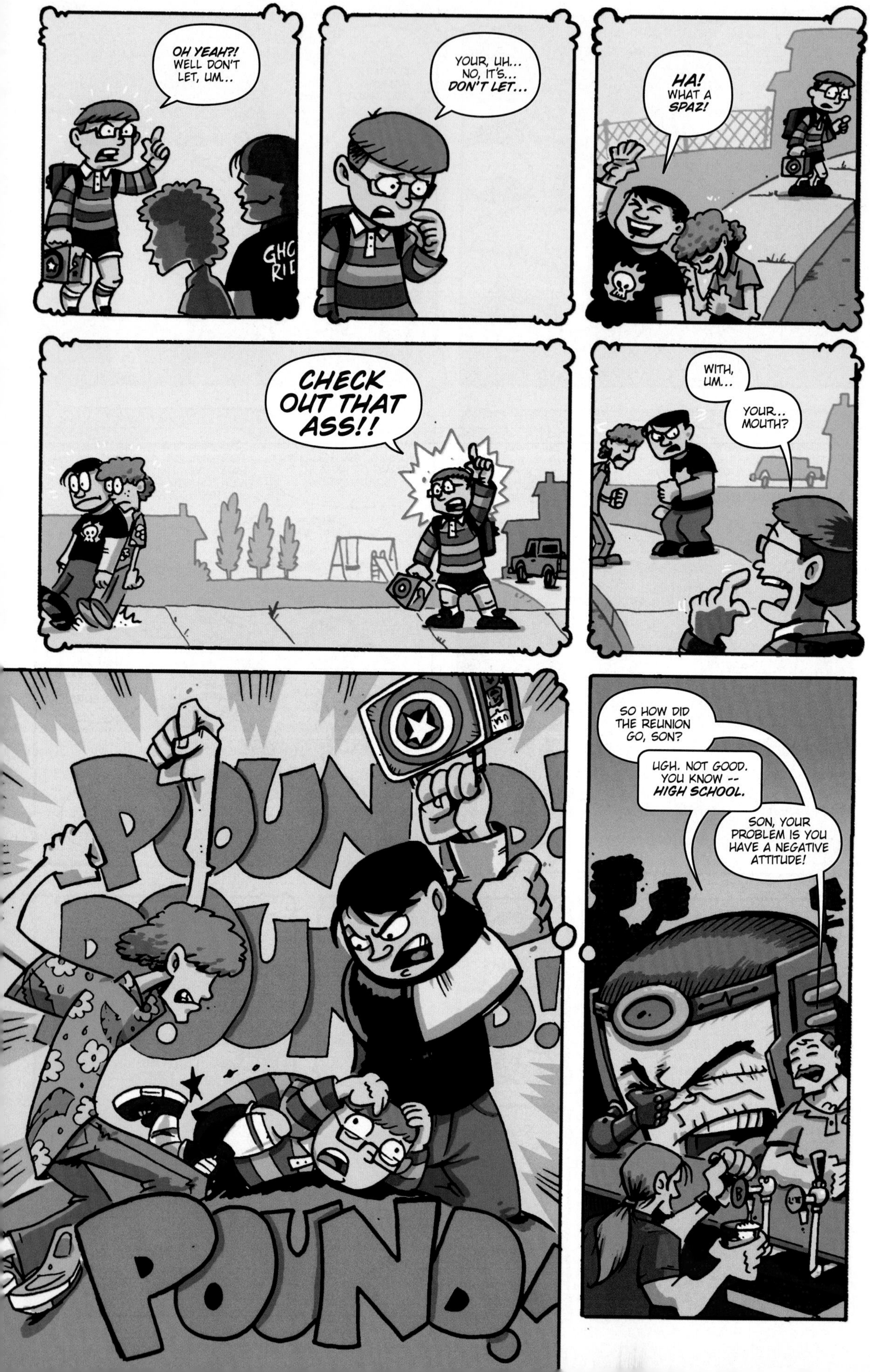
OH YEAH?! WELL DON'T LET, UM...
GHO RID
YOUR, UH... NO, IT'S... DON'T LET...
HA! WHAT A SPAZ!
CHECK OUT THAT ASS!!
WITH, UM...
YOUR... MOUTH?
POUND!
POUND!
POUND!
SO HOW DID THE REUNION GO, SON?
UGH. NOT GOOD. YOU KNOW -- HIGH SCHOOL.
SON, YOUR PROBLEM IS YOU HAVE A NEGATIVE ATTITUDE!

NOW FOR ME, HIGH SCHOOL WAS *GREAT!* I WAS ALWAYS REALLY POPULAR -- LOTS OF FRIENDS, LOTS OF GIRLS -- GOOD TIMES!

OF COURSE, IT'S EASY TO BE POPULAR WHEN YOU'RE THE *SECOND PLACE ALL-STATE HIGH SCHOOL RUSHING YARDS LEADER* FOR TWO NON-CONSECUTIVE SEASONS!

HAVE YOU MET MY SON, GEORGE? HE'S A BIG-TIME SUPER VILLAIN IN *MANHATTAN* -- JUST LIKE *TRUMP!*

BROOKLYN, DAD. AND THAT GUY IS *WAY* MORE EVIL THAN M.O.D.O.K.

~:PFFT:~ ...YOU WERE ONLY RUSHING LEADER FOR *ONE* YEAR, TARTLETON -- *PEE-WEE* BALL DON'T COUNT...

...AND AS FOR SONNY BOY THERE -- I HEAR MISTER BIG-SHOT BAD-GUY GOT BEAT BY *SQUIRREL GIRL.*

DON'T BE RUDE! M.O.D.O.K.'S FATHER WAS TALKING!!!

MINIONS, ORDER US ANOTHER ROUND. M.O.D.O.K. NEEDS TO GO TAKE CARE OF LITTLE M.O.D.O.K.

CURSE MY PATHETIC UNEVOLVED ARMS!

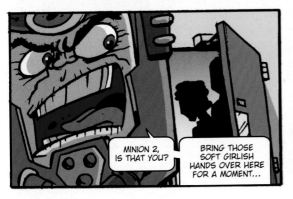

MINION 2, IS THAT YOU?

BRING THOSE SOFT GIRLISH HANDS OVER HERE FOR A MOMENT...

GEORGIE...

...*FART*-ELTON.

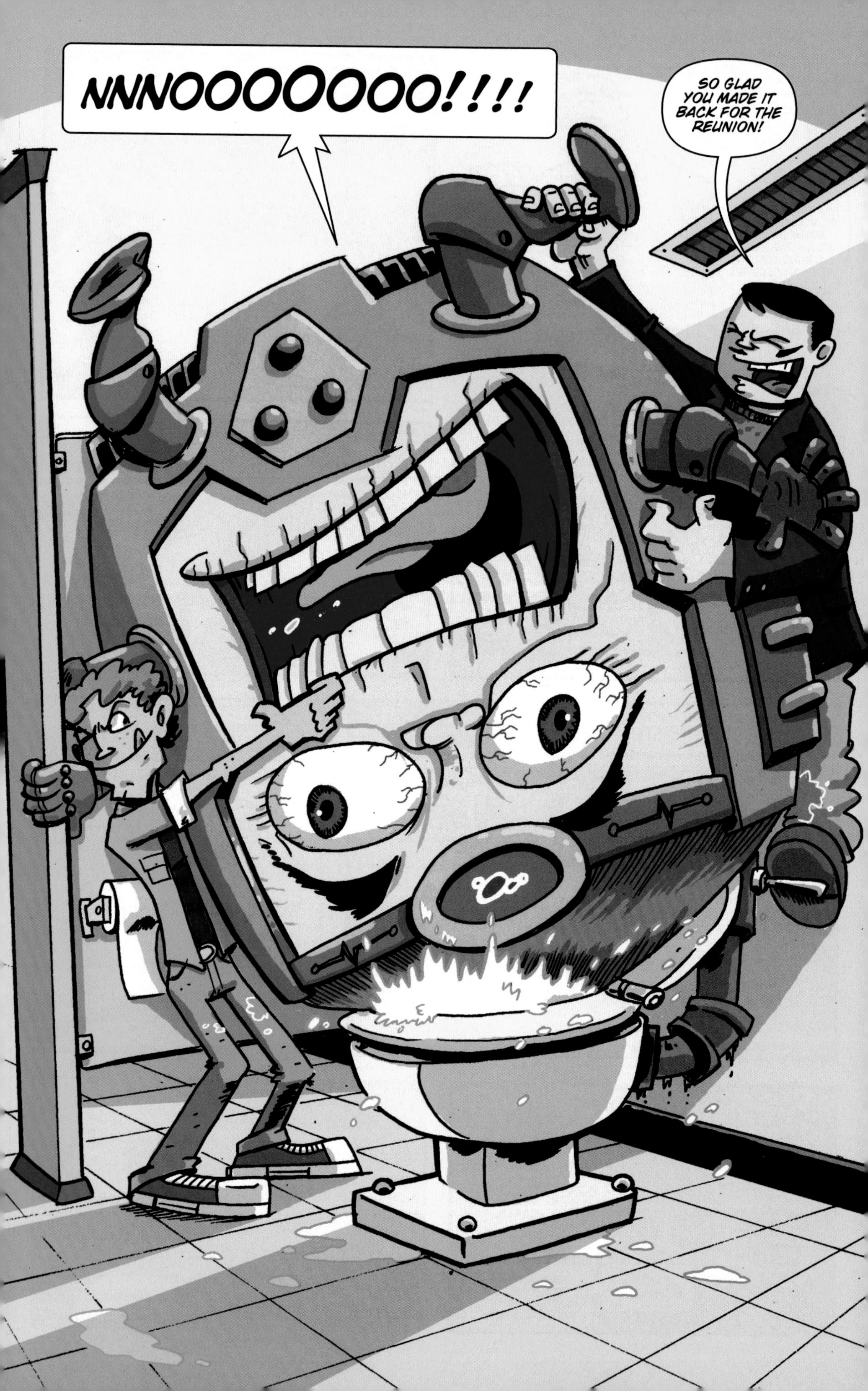
NNNOOOOOOOO!!!!
SO GLAD YOU MADE IT BACK FOR THE REUNION!

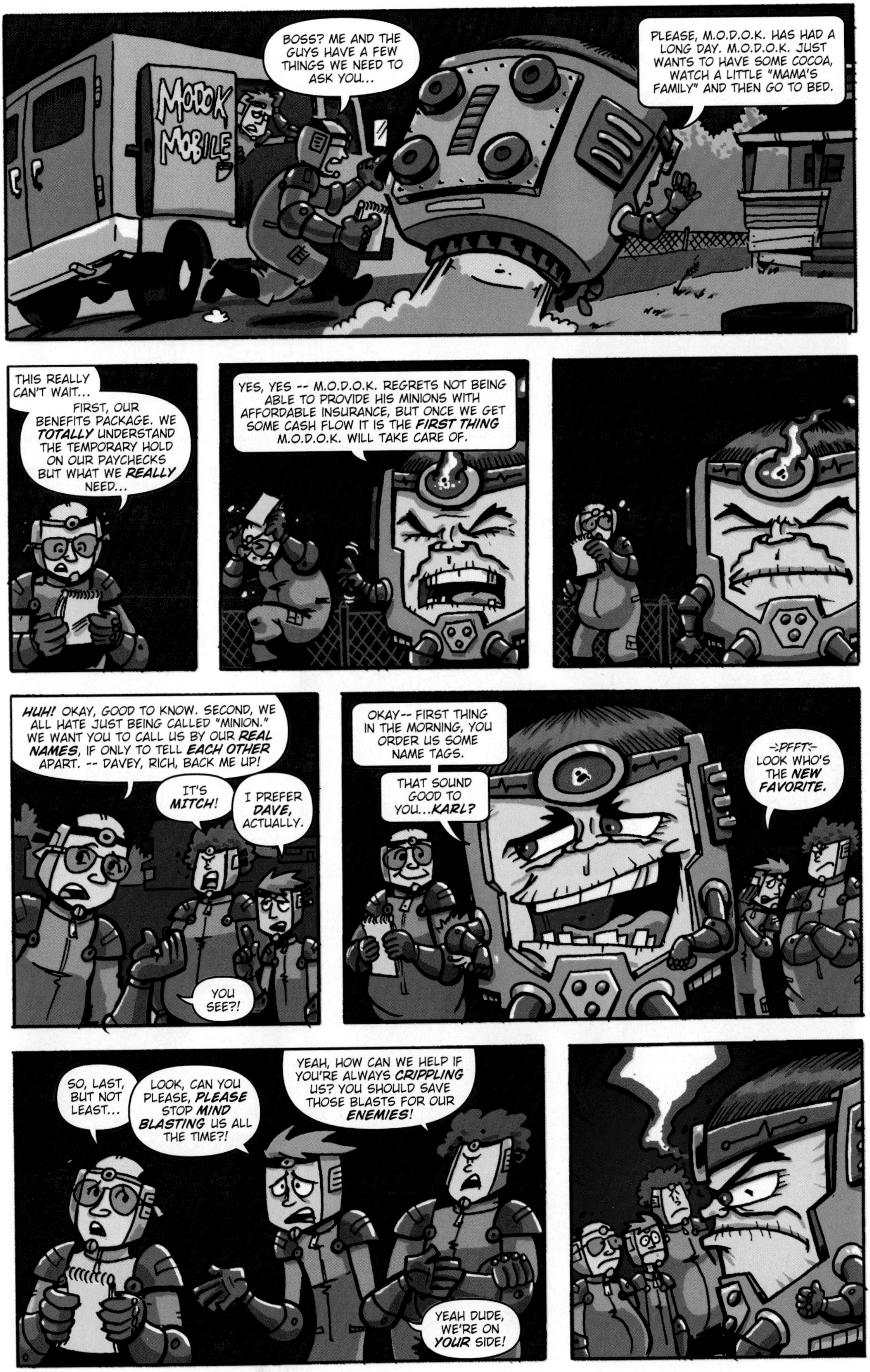
BOSS? ME AND THE GUYS HAVE A FEW THINGS WE NEED TO ASK YOU...
MODOK MOBILE
PLEASE, M.O.D.O.K. HAS HAD A LONG DAY. M.O.D.O.K. JUST WANTS TO HAVE SOME COCOA, WATCH A LITTLE "MAMA'S FAMILY" AND THEN GO TO BED.
THIS REALLY CAN'T WAIT... FIRST, OUR BENEFITS PACKAGE. WE TOTALLY UNDERSTAND THE TEMPORARY HOLD ON OUR PAYCHECKS BUT WHAT WE REALLY NEED...
YES, YES -- M.O.D.O.K. REGRETS NOT BEING ABLE TO PROVIDE HIS MINIONS WITH AFFORDABLE INSURANCE, BUT ONCE WE GET SOME CASH FLOW IT IS THE FIRST THING M.O.D.O.K. WILL TAKE CARE OF.
HUH! OKAY, GOOD TO KNOW. SECOND, WE ALL HATE JUST BEING CALLED "MINION." WE WANT YOU TO CALL US BY OUR REAL NAMES, IF ONLY TO TELL EACH OTHER APART. -- DAVEY, RICH, BACK ME UP!
IT'S MITCH!
I PREFER DAVE, ACTUALLY.
YOU SEE?!
OKAY-- FIRST THING IN THE MORNING, YOU ORDER US SOME NAME TAGS.
THAT SOUND GOOD TO YOU...KARL?
PFFT LOOK WHO'S THE NEW FAVORITE.
SO, LAST, BUT NOT LEAST...
LOOK, CAN YOU PLEASE, PLEASE STOP MIND BLASTING US ALL THE TIME?!
YEAH, HOW CAN WE HELP IF YOU'RE ALWAYS CRIPPLING US? YOU SHOULD SAVE THOSE BLASTS FOR OUR ENEMIES!
YEAH DUDE, WE'RE ON YOUR SIDE!

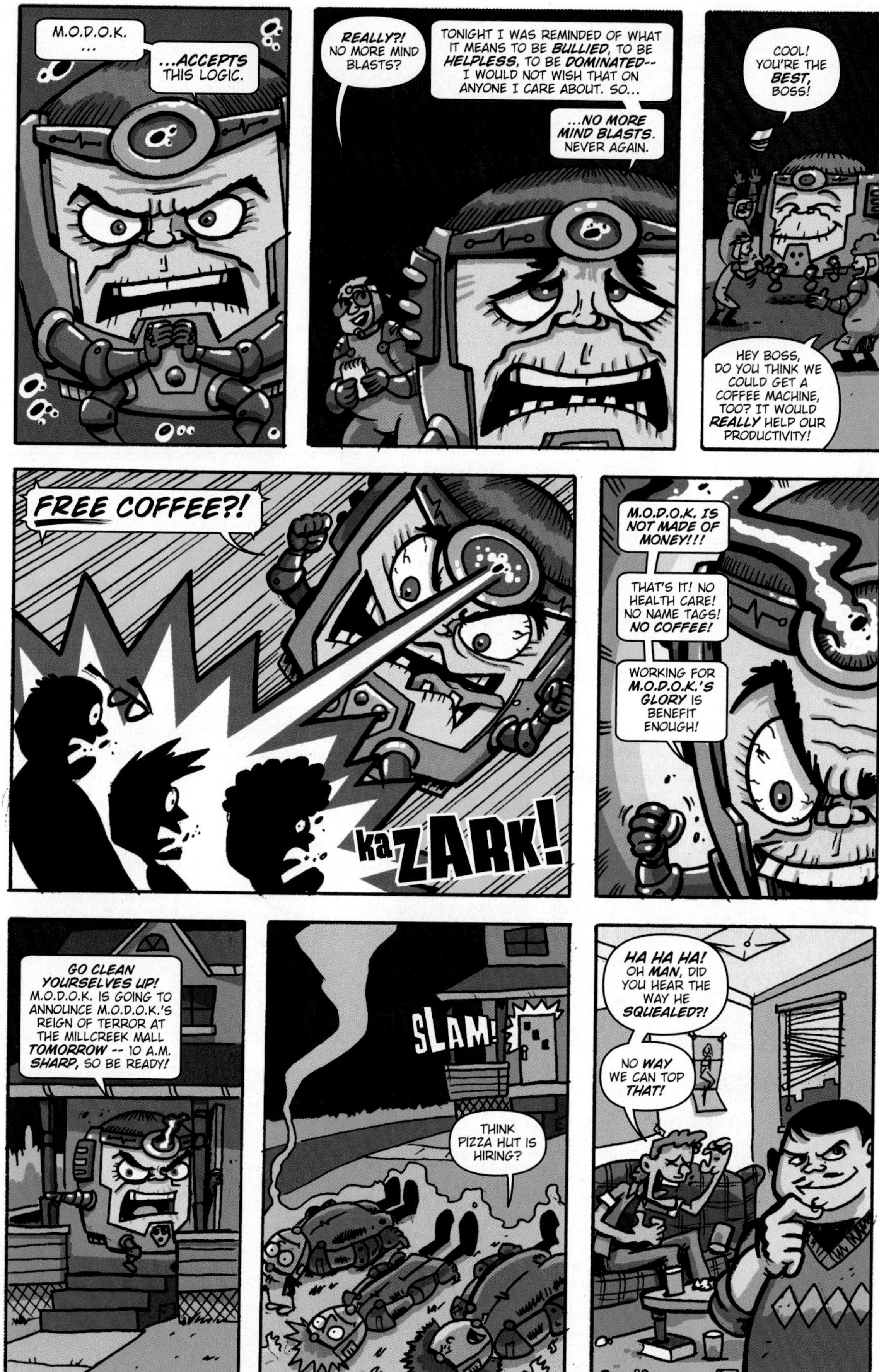
M.O.D.O.K. ...
...ACCEPTS THIS LOGIC.
REALLY?! NO MORE MIND BLASTS?
TONIGHT I WAS REMINDED OF WHAT IT MEANS TO BE BULLIED, TO BE HELPLESS, TO BE DOMINATED-- I WOULD NOT WISH THAT ON ANYONE I CARE ABOUT. SO...
...NO MORE MIND BLASTS. NEVER AGAIN.
COOL! YOU'RE THE BEST, BOSS!
HEY BOSS, DO YOU THINK WE COULD GET A COFFEE MACHINE, TOO? IT WOULD REALLY HELP OUR PRODUCTIVITY!
FREE COFFEE?!
kaZARK!
M.O.D.O.K. IS NOT MADE OF MONEY!!!
THAT'S IT! NO HEALTH CARE! NO NAME TAGS! NO COFFEE!
WORKING FOR M.O.D.O.K.'S GLORY IS BENEFIT ENOUGH!
GO CLEAN YOURSELVES UP! M.O.D.O.K. IS GOING TO ANNOUNCE M.O.D.O.K.'S REIGN OF TERROR AT THE MILLCREEK MALL TOMORROW -- 10 A.M. SHARP, SO BE READY!
SLAM!
THINK PIZZA HUT IS HIRING?
HA HA HA! OH MAN, DID YOU HEAR THE WAY HE SQUEALED?!
NO WAY WE CAN TOP THAT!

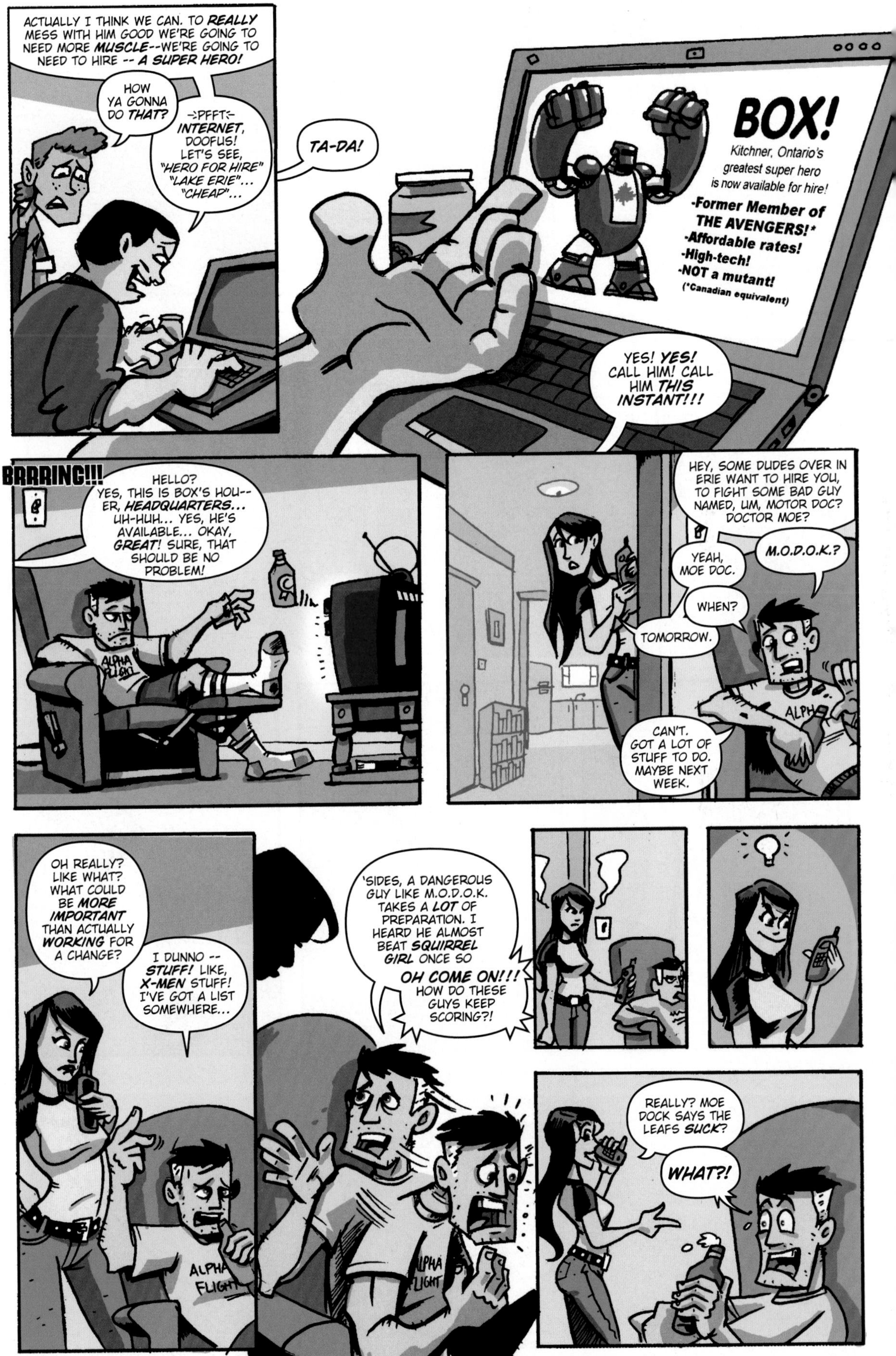

ACTUALLY I THINK WE CAN. TO REALLY MESS WITH HIM GOOD WE'RE GOING TO NEED MORE MUSCLE--WE'RE GOING TO NEED TO HIRE -- A SUPER HERO!
HOW YA GONNA DO THAT?
PFFT. INTERNET, DOOFUS! LET'S SEE, "HERO FOR HIRE" "LAKE ERIE"... "CHEAP"...
TA-DA!
BOX!
Kitchner, Ontario's greatest super hero is now available for hire!
-Former Member of THE AVENGERS!*
-Affordable rates!
-High-tech!
-NOT a mutant!
(*Canadian equivalent)
YES! YES! CALL HIM! CALL HIM THIS INSTANT!!!
BRRRING!!!
HELLO? YES, THIS IS BOX'S HOU-- ER, HEADQUARTERS... UH-HUH... YES, HE'S AVAILABLE... OKAY, GREAT! SURE, THAT SHOULD BE NO PROBLEM!
HEY, SOME DUDES OVER IN ERIE WANT TO HIRE YOU, TO FIGHT SOME BAD GUY NAMED, UM, MOTOR DOC? DOCTOR MOE?
M.O.D.O.K.?
YEAH, MOE DOC.
WHEN?
TOMORROW.
CAN'T. GOT A LOT OF STUFF TO DO. MAYBE NEXT WEEK.
OH REALLY? LIKE WHAT? WHAT COULD BE MORE IMPORTANT THAN ACTUALLY WORKING FOR A CHANGE?
I DUNNO -- STUFF! LIKE, X-MEN STUFF! I'VE GOT A LIST SOMEWHERE...
'SIDES, A DANGEROUS GUY LIKE M.O.D.O.K. TAKES A LOT OF PREPARATION. I HEARD HE ALMOST BEAT SQUIRREL GIRL ONCE SO
OH COME ON!!! HOW DO THESE GUYS KEEP SCORING?!
REALLY? MOE DOCK SAYS THE LEAFS SUCK?
WHAT?!

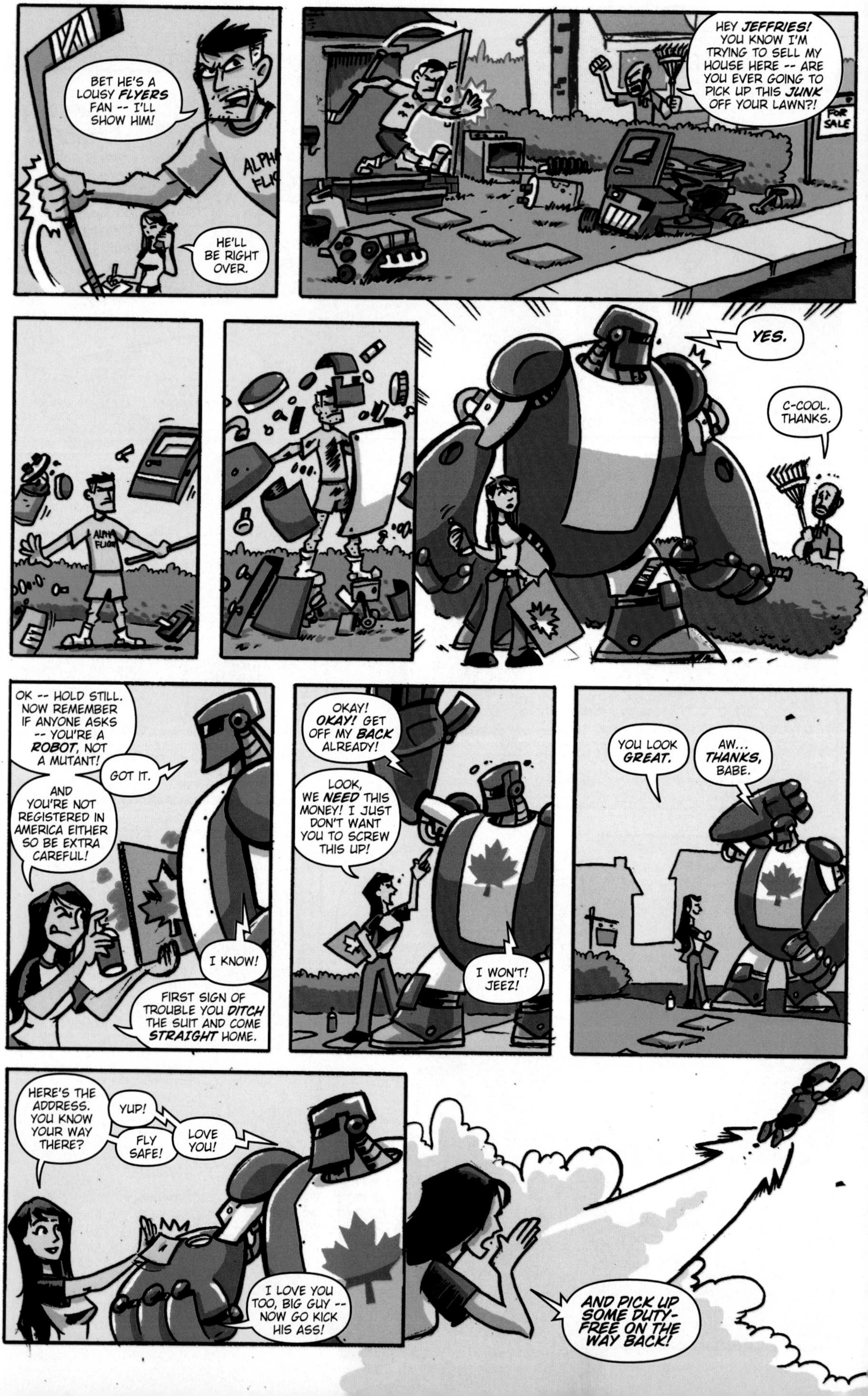
BET HE'S A LOUSY FLYERS FAN -- I'LL SHOW HIM!
HE'LL BE RIGHT OVER.
HEY JEFFRIES! YOU KNOW I'M TRYING TO SELL MY HOUSE HERE -- ARE YOU EVER GOING TO PICK UP THIS JUNK OFF YOUR LAWN?!
FOR SALE
YES.
C-COOL. THANKS.
OK -- HOLD STILL. NOW REMEMBER IF ANYONE ASKS -- YOU'RE A ROBOT, NOT A MUTANT!
GOT IT.
AND YOU'RE NOT REGISTERED IN AMERICA EITHER SO BE EXTRA CAREFUL!
I KNOW!
FIRST SIGN OF TROUBLE YOU DITCH THE SUIT AND COME STRAIGHT HOME.
OKAY! OKAY! GET OFF MY BACK ALREADY!
LOOK, WE NEED THIS MONEY! I JUST DON'T WANT YOU TO SCREW THIS UP!
I WON'T! JEEZ!
YOU LOOK GREAT.
AW... THANKS, BABE.
HERE'S THE ADDRESS. YOU KNOW YOUR WAY THERE?
YUP!
FLY SAFE!
LOVE YOU!
I LOVE YOU TOO, BIG GUY -- NOW GO KICK HIS ASS!
AND PICK UP SOME DUTY-FREE ON THE WAY BACK!

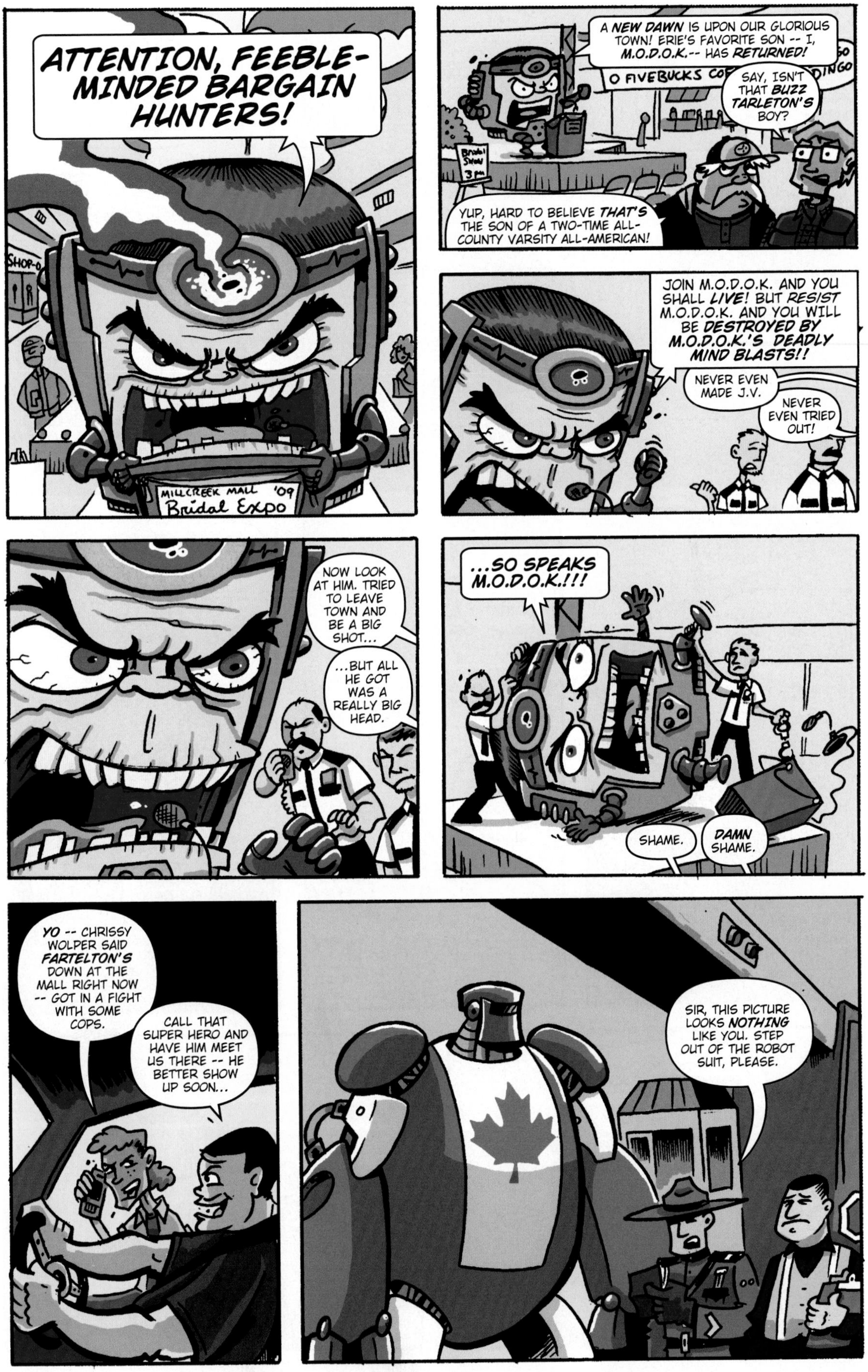
ATTENTION, FEEBLE-MINDED BARGAIN HUNTERS!
SHOP-O
MILLCREEK MALL '09 Bridal Expo
A NEW DAWN IS UPON OUR GLORIOUS TOWN! ERIE'S FAVORITE SON -- I, M.O.D.O.K.-- HAS RETURNED!
FIVEBUCKS CO
SAY, ISN'T THAT BUZZ TARLETON'S BOY?
Bridal Show 3 pm
YUP, HARD TO BELIEVE THAT'S THE SON OF A TWO-TIME ALL-COUNTY VARSITY ALL-AMERICAN!
JOIN M.O.D.O.K. AND YOU SHALL LIVE! BUT RESIST M.O.D.O.K. AND YOU WILL BE DESTROYED BY M.O.D.O.K.'S DEADLY MIND BLASTS!!
NEVER EVEN MADE J.V.
NEVER EVEN TRIED OUT!
NOW LOOK AT HIM. TRIED TO LEAVE TOWN AND BE A BIG SHOT...
...BUT ALL HE GOT WAS A REALLY BIG HEAD.
...SO SPEAKS M.O.D.O.K.!!!
SHAME.
DAMN SHAME.
YO -- CHRISSY WOLPER SAID FARTELTON'S DOWN AT THE MALL RIGHT NOW -- GOT IN A FIGHT WITH SOME COPS.
CALL THAT SUPER HERO AND HAVE HIM MEET US THERE -- HE BETTER SHOW UP SOON...
SIR, THIS PICTURE LOOKS NOTHING LIKE YOU. STEP OUT OF THE ROBOT SUIT, PLEASE.

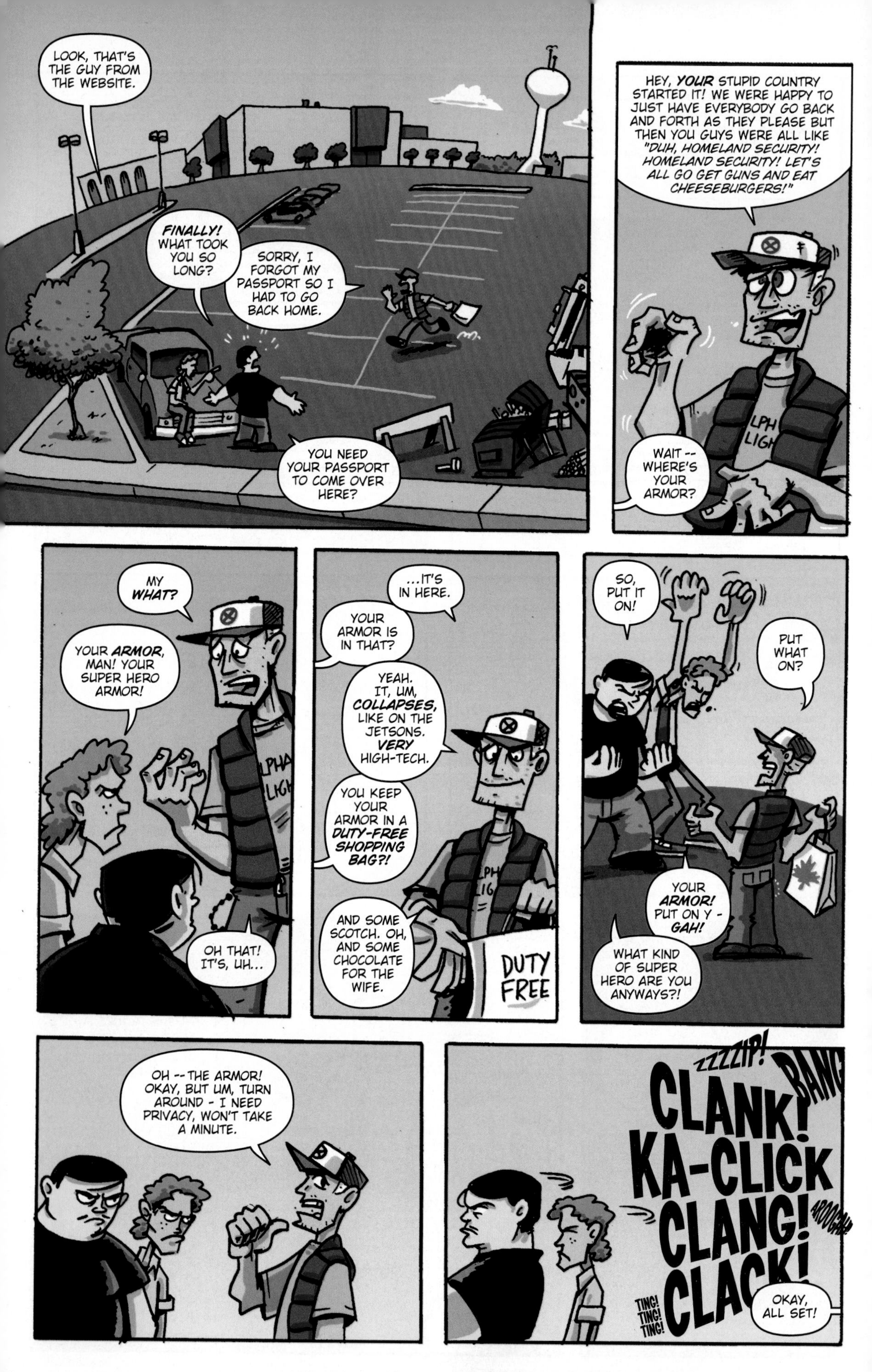
LOOK, THAT'S THE GUY FROM THE WEBSITE.
FINALLY! WHAT TOOK YOU SO LONG?
SORRY, I FORGOT MY PASSPORT SO I HAD TO GO BACK HOME.
YOU NEED YOUR PASSPORT TO COME OVER HERE?
HEY, YOUR STUPID COUNTRY STARTED IT! WE WERE HAPPY TO JUST HAVE EVERYBODY GO BACK AND FORTH AS THEY PLEASE BUT THEN YOU GUYS WERE ALL LIKE "DUH, HOMELAND SECURITY! HOMELAND SECURITY! LET'S ALL GO GET GUNS AND EAT CHEESEBURGERS!"
WAIT -- WHERE'S YOUR ARMOR?
MY WHAT?
YOUR ARMOR, MAN! YOUR SUPER HERO ARMOR!
OH THAT! IT'S, UH...
...IT'S IN HERE.
YOUR ARMOR IS IN THAT?
YEAH. IT, UM, COLLAPSES, LIKE ON THE JETSONS. VERY HIGH-TECH.
YOU KEEP YOUR ARMOR IN A DUTY-FREE SHOPPING BAG?!
AND SOME SCOTCH. OH, AND SOME CHOCOLATE FOR THE WIFE.
DUTY FREE
SO, PUT IT ON!
PUT WHAT ON?
YOUR ARMOR! PUT ON Y - GAH!
WHAT KIND OF SUPER HERO ARE YOU ANYWAYS?!
OH -- THE ARMOR! OKAY, BUT UM, TURN AROUND - I NEED PRIVACY, WON'T TAKE A MINUTE.
ZZZZIP!
BANG
CLANK!
KA-CLICK
CLANG!
CLACK!
TING! TING! TING!
OKAY, ALL SET!

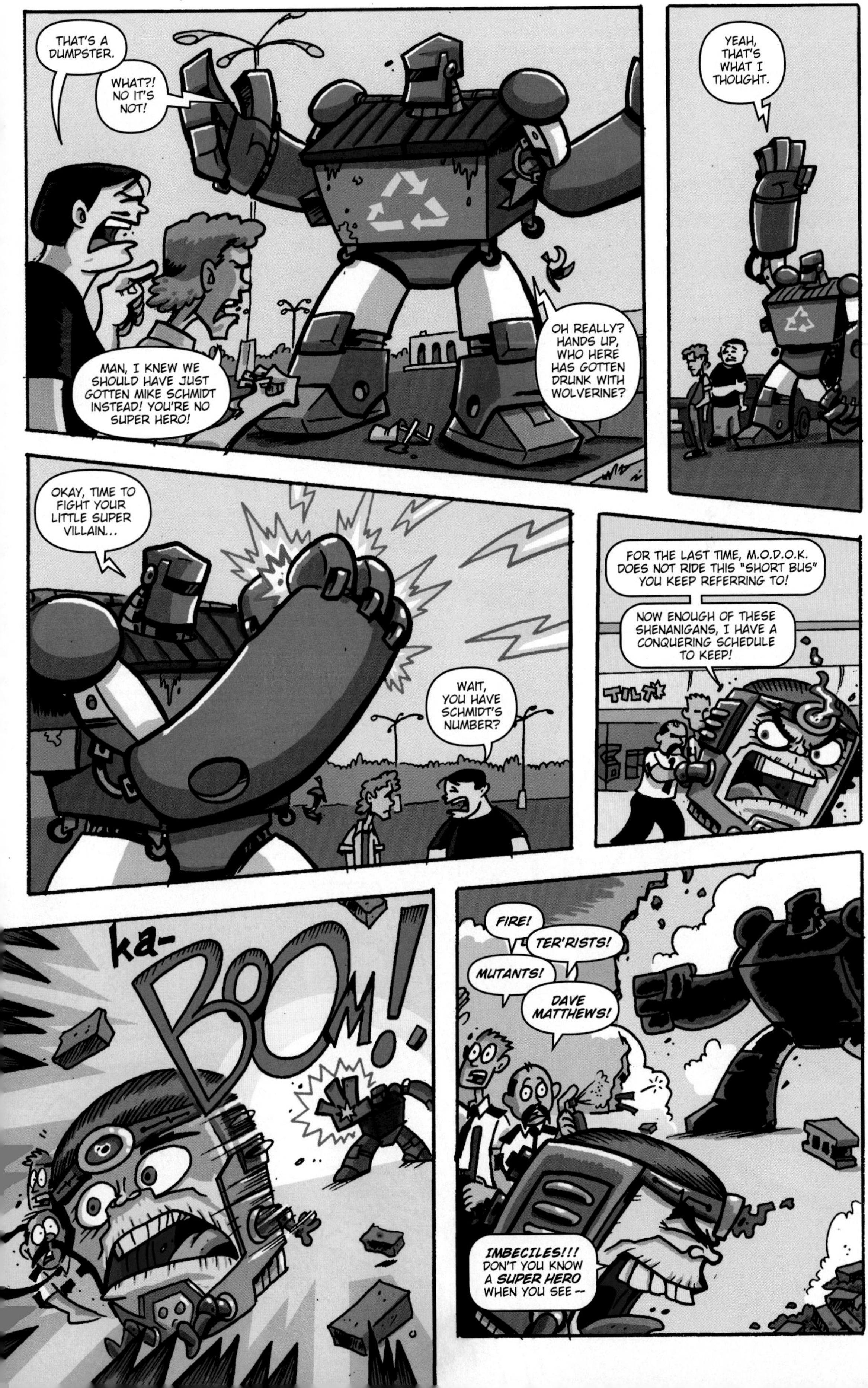
THAT'S A DUMPSTER.
WHAT?! NO IT'S NOT!
MAN, I KNEW WE SHOULD HAVE JUST GOTTEN MIKE SCHMIDT INSTEAD! YOU'RE NO SUPER HERO!
OH REALLY? HANDS UP, WHO HERE HAS GOTTEN DRUNK WITH WOLVERINE?
YEAH, THAT'S WHAT I THOUGHT.
OKAY, TIME TO FIGHT YOUR LITTLE SUPER VILLAIN...
WAIT, YOU HAVE SCHMIDT'S NUMBER?
FOR THE LAST TIME, M.O.D.O.K. DOES NOT RIDE THIS "SHORT BUS" YOU KEEP REFERRING TO!
NOW ENOUGH OF THESE SHENANIGANS, I HAVE A CONQUERING SCHEDULE TO KEEP!
TILT
ka-BOOM!
FIRE!
TER'RISTS!
MUTANTS!
DAVE MATTHEWS!
IMBECILES!!! DON'T YOU KNOW A SUPER HERO WHEN YOU SEE --

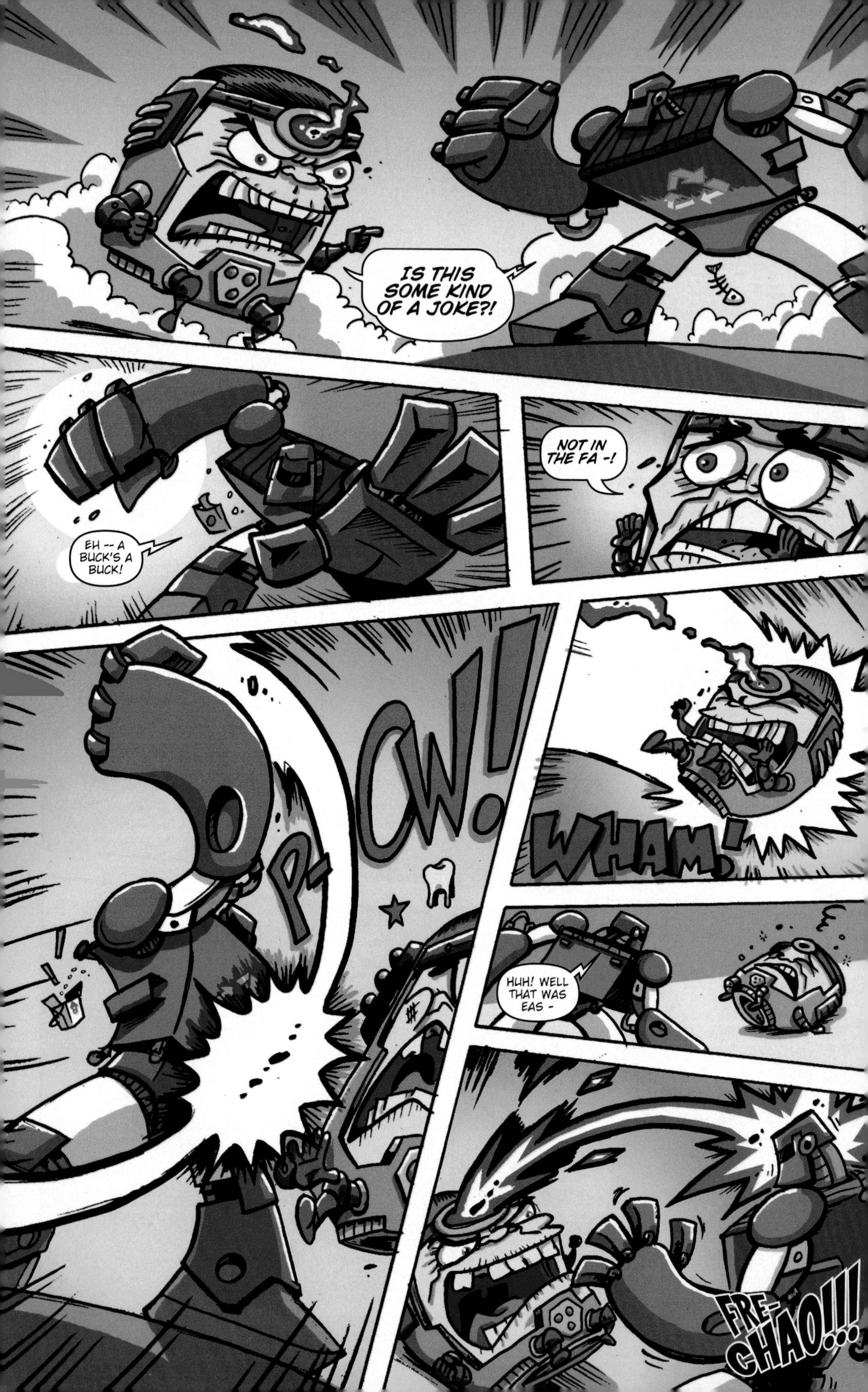
IS THIS SOME KIND OF A JOKE?!
EH -- A BUCK'S A BUCK!
NOT IN THE FA -!
POW!!
WHAM!
HUH! WELL THAT WAS EAS -
FRE-CHAO!!!

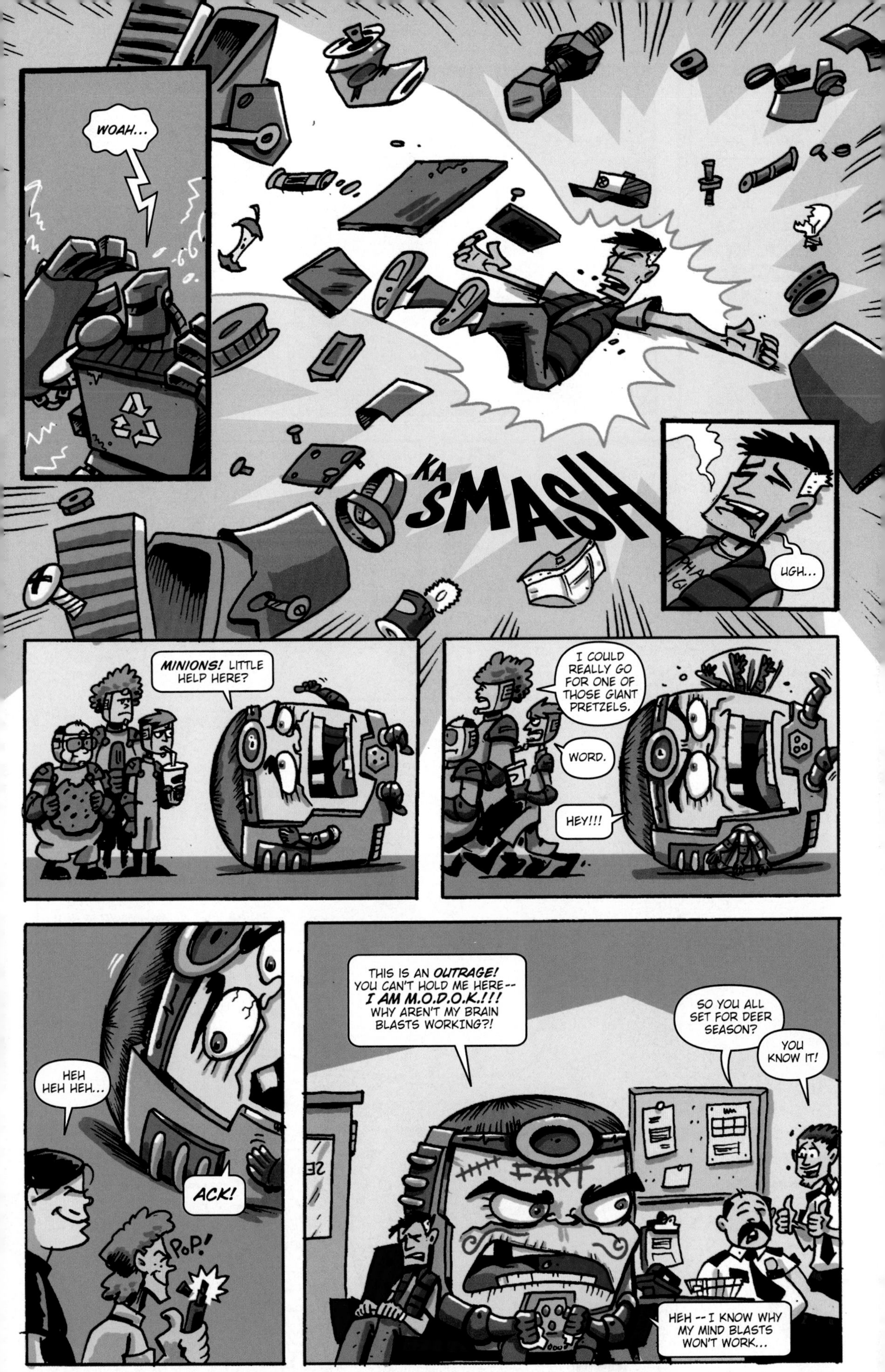
WOAH...
KA SMASH
UGH...
MINIONS! LITTLE HELP HERE?
I COULD REALLY GO FOR ONE OF THOSE GIANT PRETZELS.
WORD.
HEY!!!
HEH HEH HEH...
ACK!
POP!
THIS IS AN OUTRAGE! YOU CAN'T HOLD ME HERE-- I AM M.O.D.O.K.!!! WHY AREN'T MY BRAIN BLASTS WORKING?!
SO YOU ALL SET FOR DEER SEASON?
YOU KNOW IT!
FART
HEH -- I KNOW WHY MY MIND BLASTS WON'T WORK...

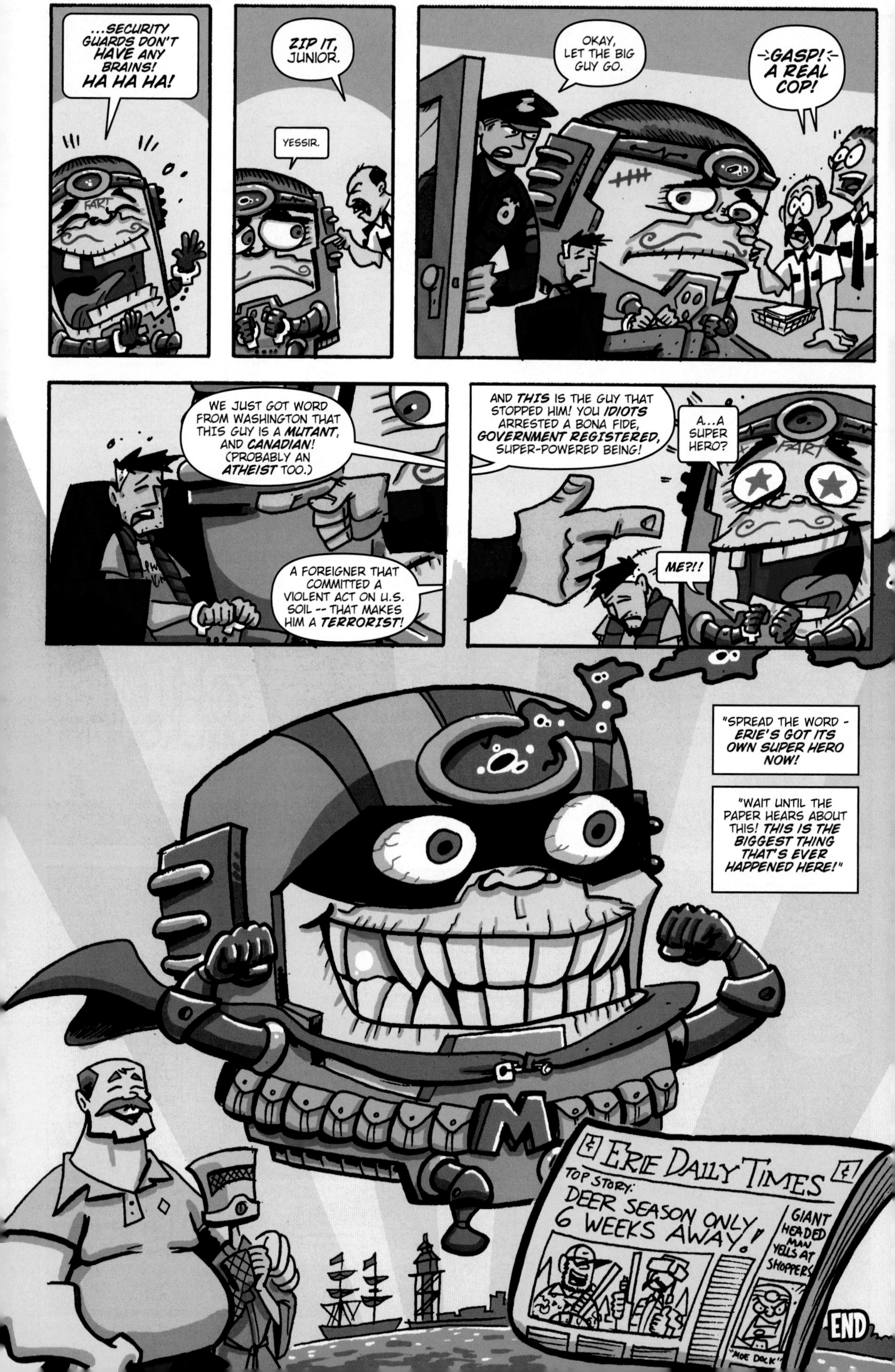
...SECURITY GUARDS DON'T HAVE ANY BRAINS! HA HA HA!
FART
ZIP IT, JUNIOR.
YESSIR.
OKAY, LET THE BIG GUY GO.
-GASP!- A REAL COP!
WE JUST GOT WORD FROM WASHINGTON THAT THIS GUY IS A MUTANT, AND CANADIAN! (PROBABLY AN ATHEIST TOO.)
A FOREIGNER THAT COMMITTED A VIOLENT ACT ON U.S. SOIL -- THAT MAKES HIM A TERRORIST!
AND THIS IS THE GUY THAT STOPPED HIM! YOU IDIOTS ARRESTED A BONA FIDE, GOVERNMENT REGISTERED, SUPER-POWERED BEING!
A...A SUPER HERO?
ME?!!
"SPREAD THE WORD - ERIE'S GOT ITS OWN SUPER HERO NOW!
"WAIT UNTIL THE PAPER HEARS ABOUT THIS! THIS IS THE BIGGEST THING THAT'S EVER HAPPENED HERE!"
M
ERIE DAILY TIMES
TOP STORY:
DEER SEASON ONLY 6 WEEKS AWAY!
GIANT HEADED MAN YELLS AT SHOPPERS
"MOE DOCK"
END

FALL OF THE HULKS: M.O.D.O.K.

THE "BIG BRAIN" VILLAINS OF THE MARVEL UNIVERSE HAVE JOINED FORCES! NOW IF ONLY THESE EVIL NERDS COULD BE FREE OF LAME-BRAIN JOCKS!

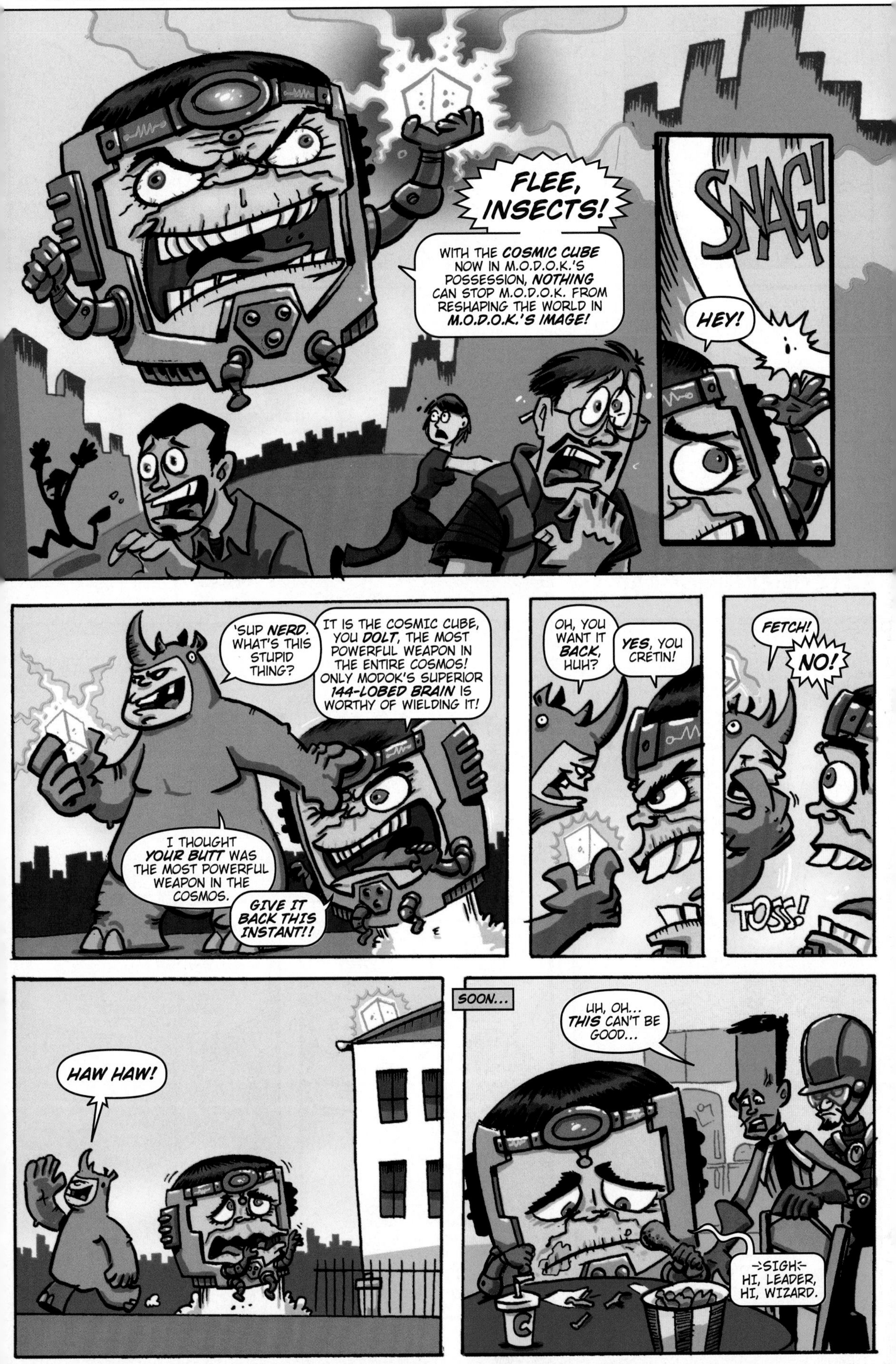

FLEE, INSECTS!
WITH THE COSMIC CUBE NOW IN M.O.D.O.K.'S POSSESSION, NOTHING CAN STOP M.O.D.O.K. FROM RESHAPING THE WORLD IN M.O.D.O.K.'S IMAGE!
SNAG!
HEY!
'SUP NERD. WHAT'S THIS STUPID THING?
IT IS THE COSMIC CUBE, YOU DOLT, THE MOST POWERFUL WEAPON IN THE ENTIRE COSMOS! ONLY MODOK'S SUPERIOR 144-LOBED BRAIN IS WORTHY OF WIELDING IT!
I THOUGHT YOUR BUTT WAS THE MOST POWERFUL WEAPON IN THE COSMOS.
GIVE IT BACK THIS INSTANT!!
OH, YOU WANT IT BACK, HUH?
YES, YOU CRETIN!
FETCH!
NO!
TOSS!
HAW HAW!
SOON...
UH, OH... THIS CAN'T BE GOOD...
-SIGH- HI, LEADER, HI, WIZARD.

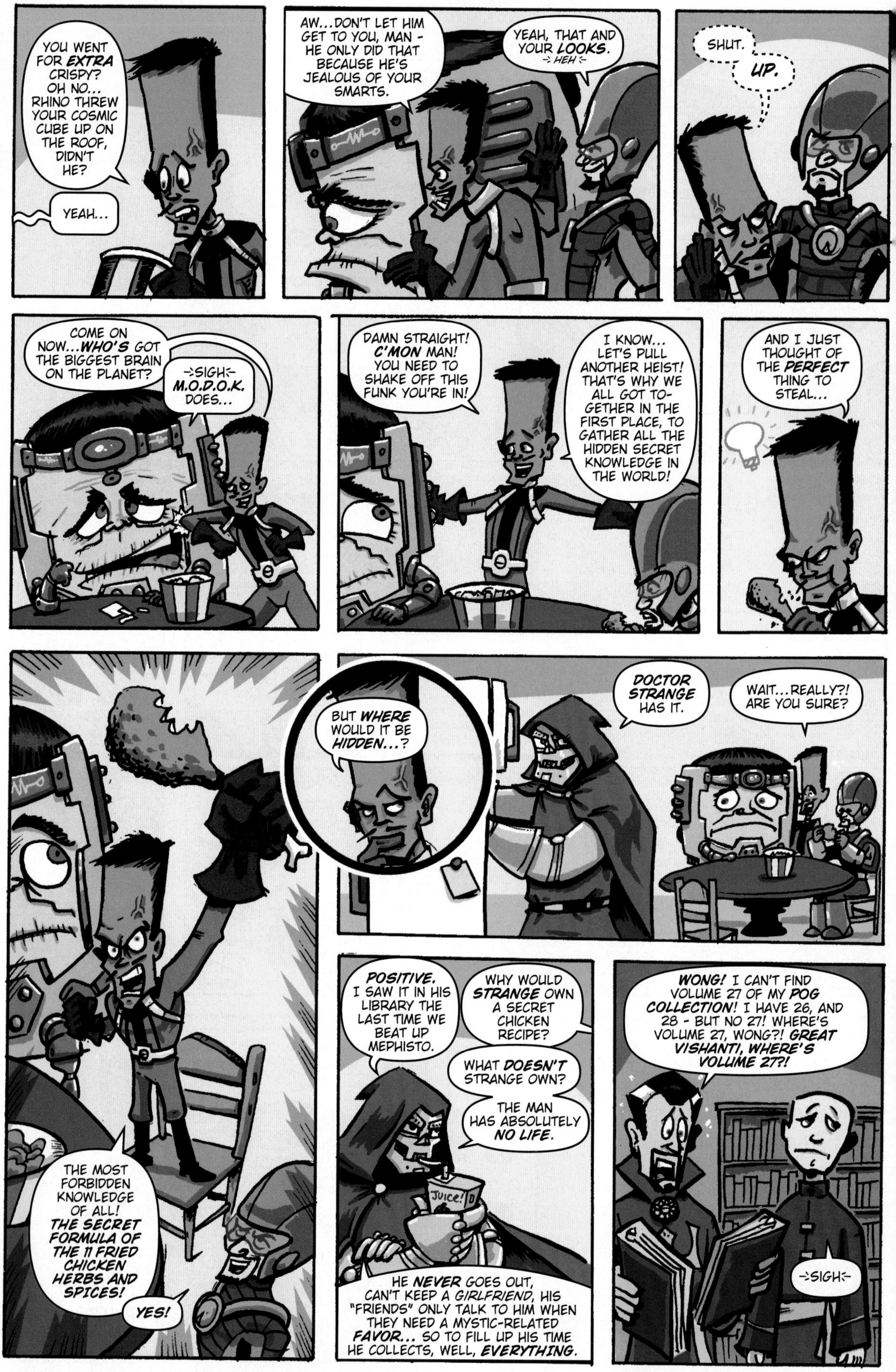

YOU WENT FOR EXTRA CRISPY? OH NO... RHINO THREW YOUR COSMIC CUBE UP ON THE ROOF, DIDN'T HE?
YEAH...
AW...DON'T LET HIM GET TO YOU, MAN - HE ONLY DID THAT BECAUSE HE'S JEALOUS OF YOUR SMARTS.
YEAH, THAT AND YOUR LOOKS. HEH
SHUT. UP.
COME ON NOW...WHO'S GOT THE BIGGEST BRAIN ON THE PLANET?
SIGH M.O.D.O.K. DOES...
DAMN STRAIGHT! C'MON MAN! YOU NEED TO SHAKE OFF THIS FUNK YOU'RE IN!
I KNOW... LET'S PULL ANOTHER HEIST! THAT'S WHY WE ALL GOT TOGETHER IN THE FIRST PLACE, TO GATHER ALL THE HIDDEN SECRET KNOWLEDGE IN THE WORLD!
AND I JUST THOUGHT OF THE PERFECT THING TO STEAL...
THE MOST FORBIDDEN KNOWLEDGE OF ALL! THE SECRET FORMULA OF THE 11 FRIED CHICKEN HERBS AND SPICES!
YES!
BUT WHERE WOULD IT BE HIDDEN...?
DOCTOR STRANGE HAS IT.
WAIT...REALLY?! ARE YOU SURE?
POSITIVE. I SAW IT IN HIS LIBRARY THE LAST TIME WE BEAT UP MEPHISTO.
WHY WOULD STRANGE OWN A SECRET CHICKEN RECIPE?
WHAT DOESN'T STRANGE OWN?
THE MAN HAS ABSOLUTELY NO LIFE.
JUICE!
HE NEVER GOES OUT, CAN'T KEEP A GIRLFRIEND, HIS "FRIENDS" ONLY TALK TO HIM WHEN THEY NEED A MYSTIC-RELATED FAVOR... SO TO FILL UP HIS TIME HE COLLECTS, WELL, EVERYTHING.
WONG! I CAN'T FIND VOLUME 27 OF MY POG COLLECTION! I HAVE 26, AND 28 - BUT NO 27! WHERE'S VOLUME 27, WONG?! GREAT VISHANTI, WHERE'S VOLUME 27?!
SIGH

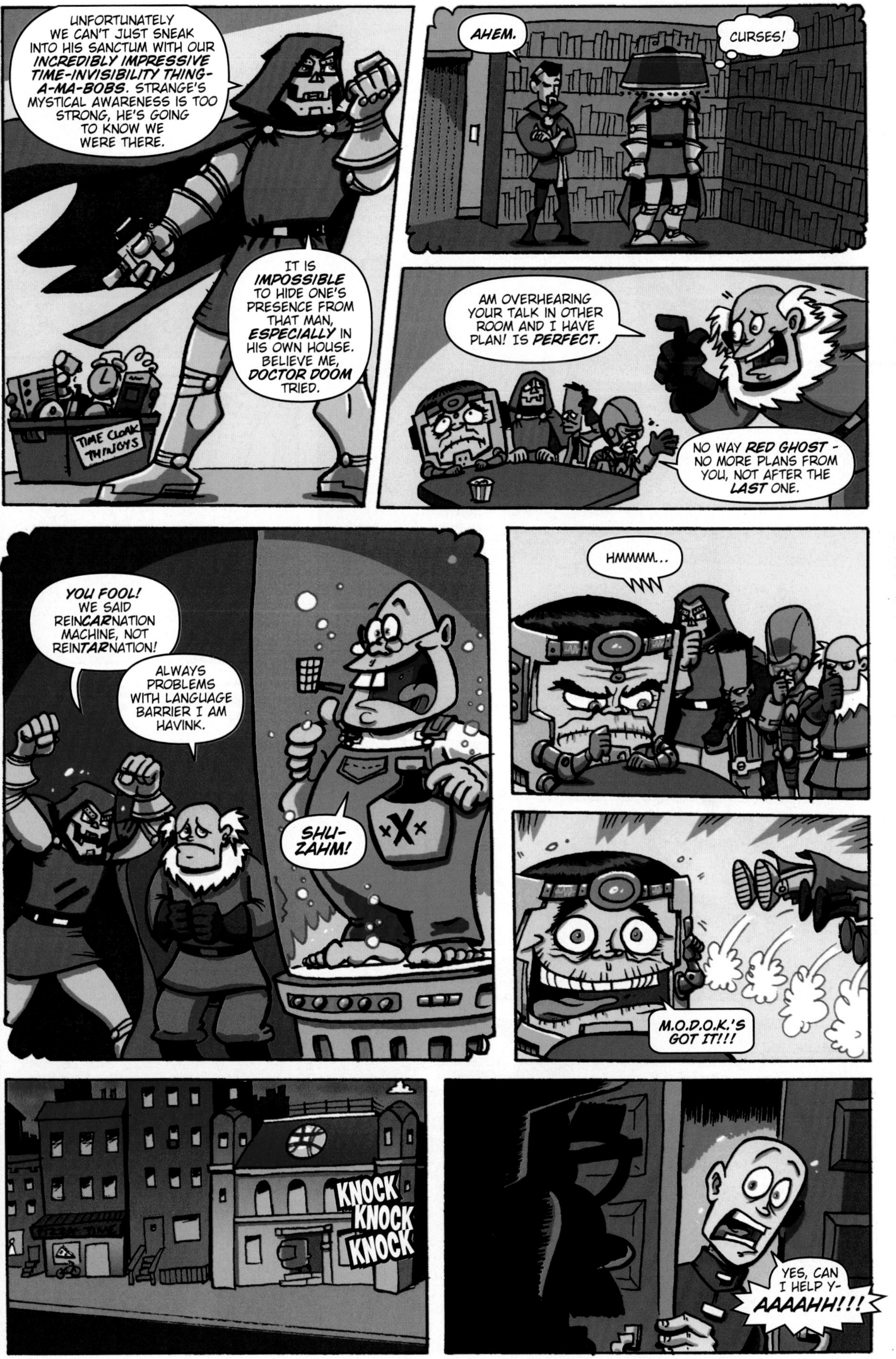
UNFORTUNATELY WE CAN'T JUST SNEAK INTO HIS SANCTUM WITH OUR INCREDIBLY IMPRESSIVE TIME-INVISIBILITY THING-A-MA-BOBS. STRANGE'S MYSTICAL AWARENESS IS TOO STRONG, HE'S GOING TO KNOW WE WERE THERE.
TIME CLOAK THINGYS
IT IS IMPOSSIBLE TO HIDE ONE'S PRESENCE FROM THAT MAN, ESPECIALLY IN HIS OWN HOUSE. BELIEVE ME, DOCTOR DOOM TRIED.
AHEM.
CURSES!
AM OVERHEARING YOUR TALK IN OTHER ROOM AND I HAVE PLAN! IS PERFECT.
NO WAY RED GHOST - NO MORE PLANS FROM YOU, NOT AFTER THE LAST ONE.
YOU FOOL! WE SAID REINCARNATION MACHINE, NOT REINTARNATION!
ALWAYS PROBLEMS WITH LANGUAGE BARRIER I AM HAVINK.
SHU-ZAHM!
HMMMM...
M.O.D.O.K.'S GOT IT!!!
KNOCK KNOCK KNOCK
YES, CAN I HELP Y-AAAAHH!!!

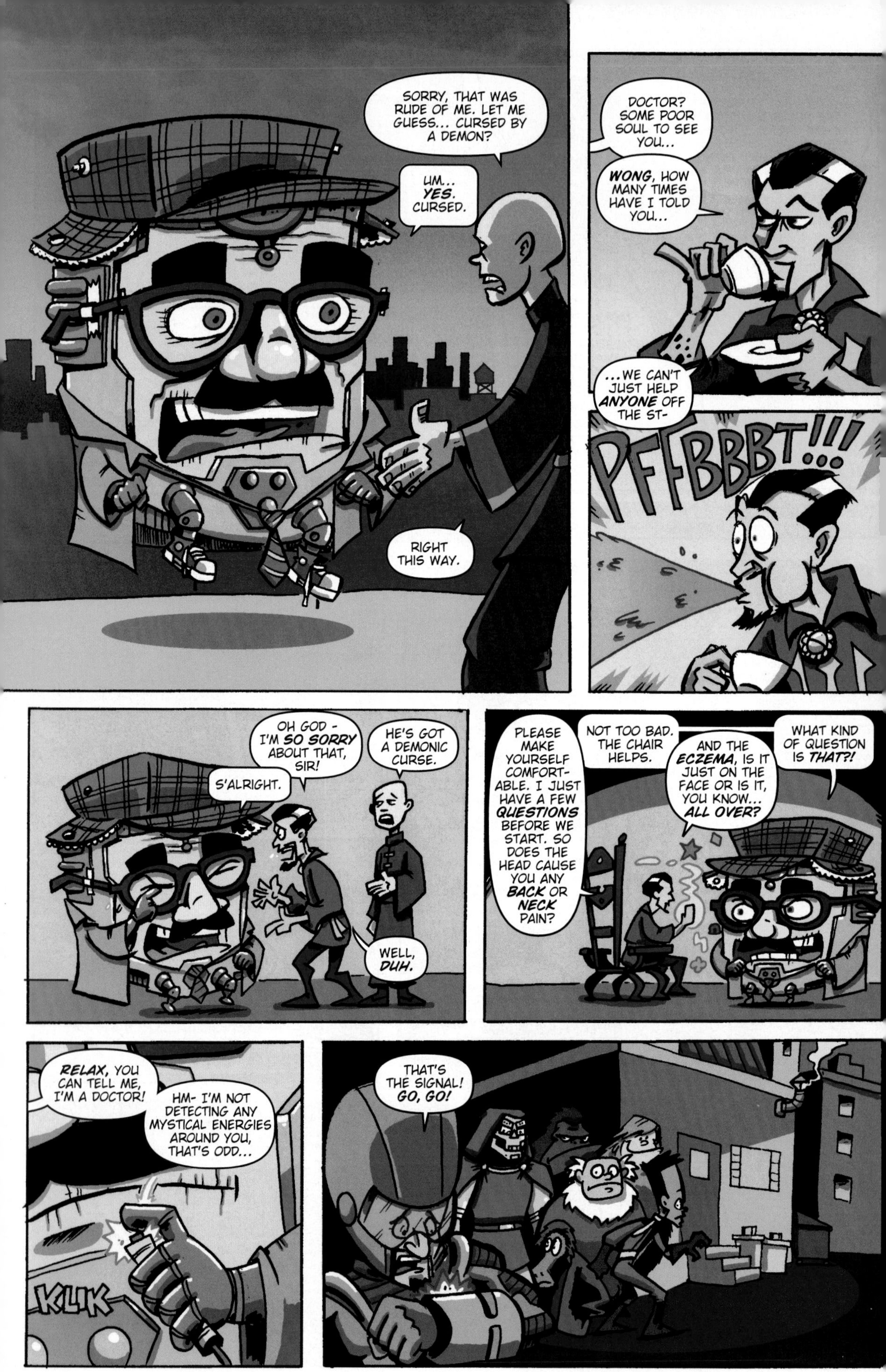
SORRY, THAT WAS RUDE OF ME. LET ME GUESS... CURSED BY A DEMON?
UM... YES. CURSED.
RIGHT THIS WAY.
DOCTOR? SOME POOR SOUL TO SEE YOU...
WONG, HOW MANY TIMES HAVE I TOLD YOU...
...WE CAN'T JUST HELP ANYONE OFF THE ST-
PFFBBBT!!!
OH GOD - I'M SO SORRY ABOUT THAT, SIR!
S'ALRIGHT.
HE'S GOT A DEMONIC CURSE.
WELL, DUH.
PLEASE MAKE YOURSELF COMFORT-ABLE. I JUST HAVE A FEW QUESTIONS BEFORE WE START. SO DOES THE HEAD CAUSE YOU ANY BACK OR NECK PAIN?
NOT TOO BAD. THE CHAIR HELPS.
AND THE ECZEMA, IS IT JUST ON THE FACE OR IS IT, YOU KNOW... ALL OVER?
WHAT KIND OF QUESTION IS THAT?!
RELAX, YOU CAN TELL ME, I'M A DOCTOR!
HM- I'M NOT DETECTING ANY MYSTICAL ENERGIES AROUND YOU, THAT'S ODD...
KLIK
THAT'S THE SIGNAL! GO, GO!

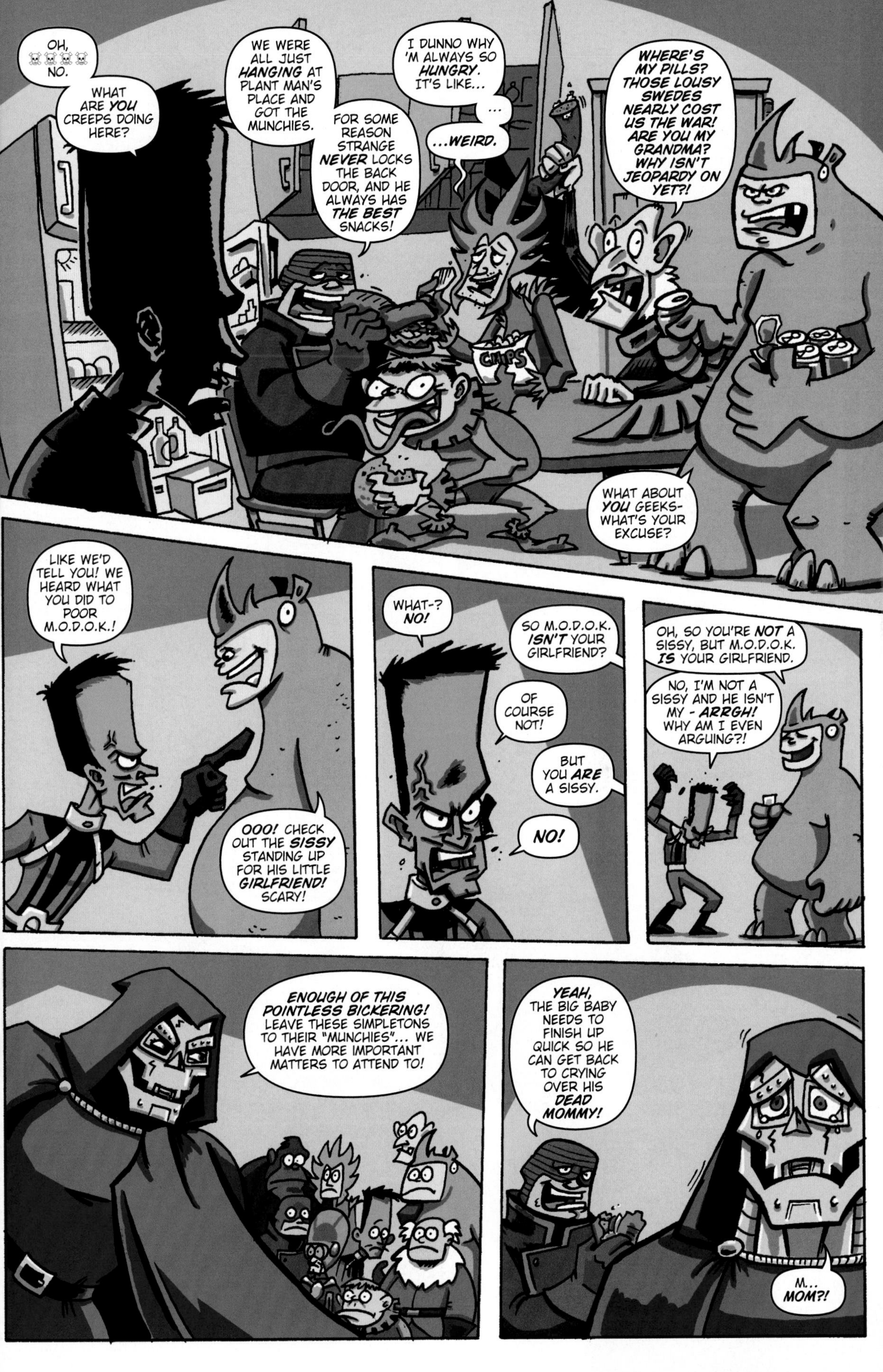
OH, ☠☠☠☠ NO.
WHAT ARE *YOU* CREEPS DOING HERE?
WE WERE ALL JUST *HANGING* AT PLANT MAN'S PLACE AND GOT THE MUNCHIES.
FOR SOME REASON STRANGE *NEVER* LOCKS THE BACK DOOR, AND HE ALWAYS HAS *THE BEST* SNACKS!
I DUNNO WHY 'M ALWAYS SO *HUNGRY*. IT'S LIKE...
...
...WEIRD.
WHERE'S MY PILLS? THOSE LOUSY SWEDES NEARLY COST US THE WAR! ARE YOU MY GRANDMA? WHY ISN'T JEOPARDY ON YET?!
CHIPS
WHAT ABOUT *YOU* GEEKS-WHAT'S YOUR EXCUSE?
LIKE WE'D TELL YOU! WE HEARD WHAT YOU DID TO POOR M.O.D.O.K.!
OOO! CHECK OUT THE *SISSY* STANDING UP FOR HIS LITTLE *GIRLFRIEND!* SCARY!
WHAT-? *NO!*
SO M.O.D.O.K. *ISN'T* YOUR GIRLFRIEND?
OF COURSE NOT!
BUT YOU *ARE* A SISSY.
NO!
OH, SO YOU'RE *NOT* A SISSY, BUT M.O.D.O.K. *IS* YOUR GIRLFRIEND.
NO, I'M NOT A SISSY AND HE ISN'T MY *- ARRGH!* WHY AM I EVEN ARGUING?!
ENOUGH OF THIS POINTLESS BICKERING! LEAVE THESE SIMPLETONS TO THEIR "MUNCHIES"... WE HAVE MORE IMPORTANT MATTERS TO ATTEND TO!
YEAH, THE BIG BABY NEEDS TO FINISH UP QUICK SO HE CAN GET BACK TO CRYING OVER HIS *DEAD MOMMY!*
M... *MOM?!*

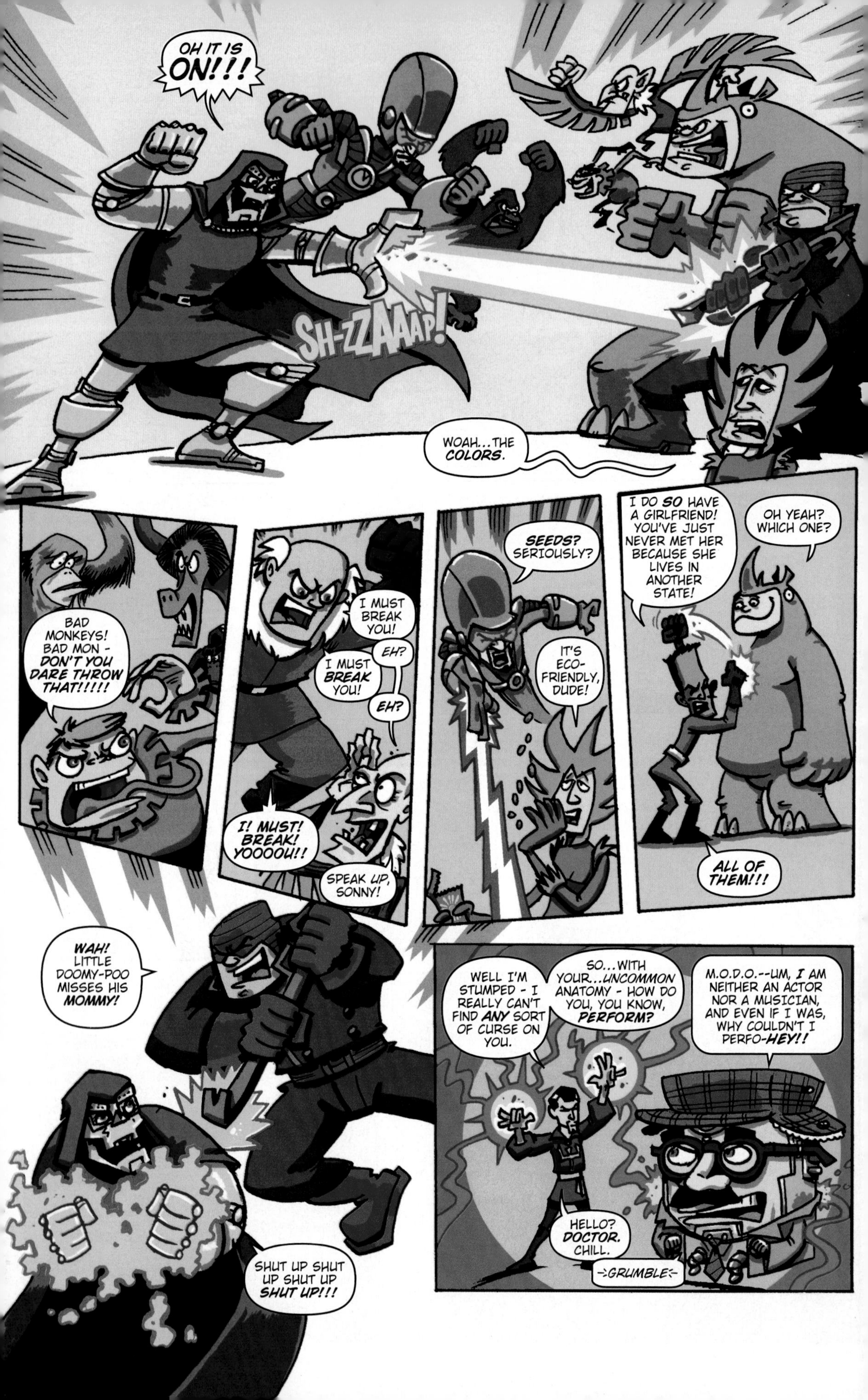
OH IT IS ON!!!
SH-ZZAAAP!
WOAH...THE COLORS.
BAD MONKEYS! BAD MON - DON'T YOU DARE THROW THAT!!!!!
I MUST BREAK YOU!
EH?
I MUST BREAK YOU!
EH?
I! MUST! BREAK! YOOOOU!!
SPEAK UP, SONNY!
SEEDS? SERIOUSLY?
IT'S ECO-FRIENDLY, DUDE!
I DO SO HAVE A GIRLFRIEND! YOU'VE JUST NEVER MET HER BECAUSE SHE LIVES IN ANOTHER STATE!
OH YEAH? WHICH ONE?
ALL OF THEM!!!
WAH! LITTLE DOOMY-POO MISSES HIS MOMMY!
SHUT UP SHUT UP SHUT UP SHUT UP!!!
WELL I'M STUMPED - I REALLY CAN'T FIND ANY SORT OF CURSE ON YOU.
SO...WITH YOUR...UNCOMMON ANATOMY - HOW DO YOU, YOU KNOW, PERFORM?
M.O.D.O.--UM, I AM NEITHER AN ACTOR NOR A MUSICIAN, AND EVEN IF I WAS, WHY COULDN'T I PERFO-HEY!!
HELLO? DOCTOR. CHILL.
GRUMBLE

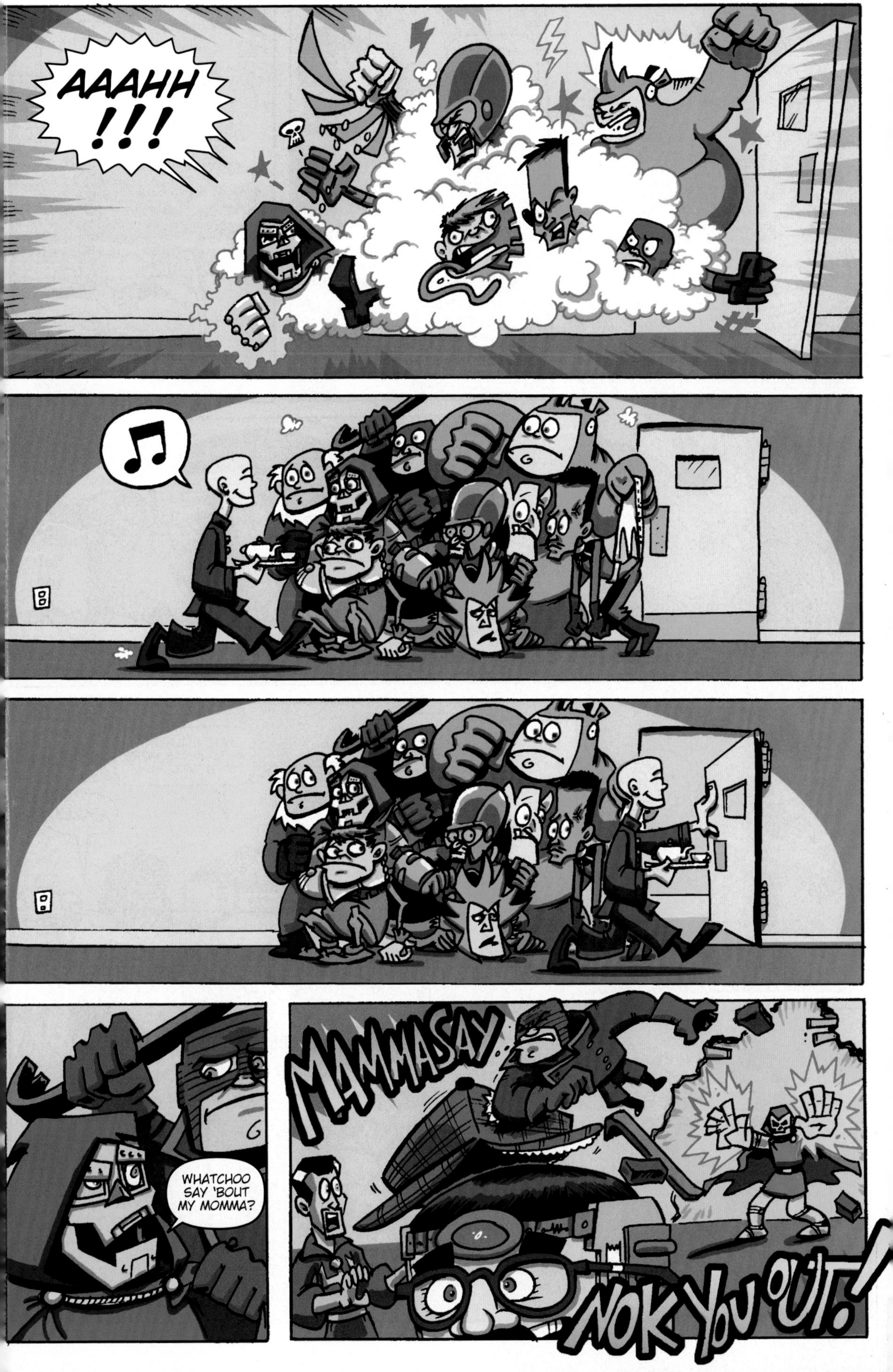
AAAHH!!!
WHATCHOO SAY 'BOUT MY MOMMA?
MAMMASAY
NOK YOU OUT!

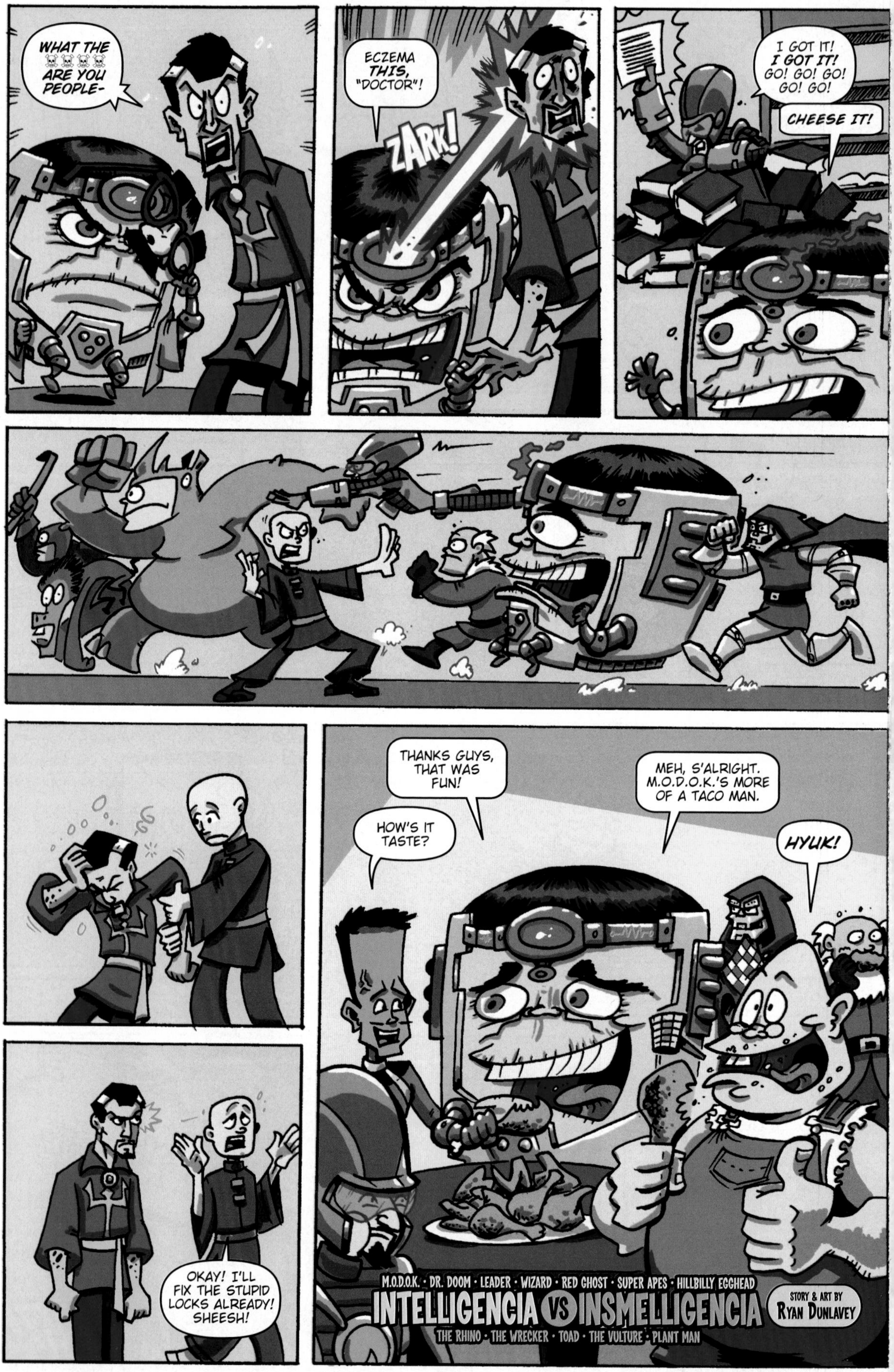
WHAT THE ☠☠☠☠ ARE YOU PEOPLE-
ECZEMA THIS, "DOCTOR"!
ZARK!
I GOT IT! I GOT IT! GO! GO! GO! GO! GO!
CHEESE IT!
THANKS GUYS, THAT WAS FUN!
HOW'S IT TASTE?
MEH, S'ALRIGHT. M.O.D.O.K.'S MORE OF A TACO MAN.
HYUK!
OKAY! I'LL FIX THE STUPID LOCKS ALREADY! SHEESH!
M.O.D.O.K. • DR. DOOM • LEADER • WIZARD • RED GHOST • SUPER APES • HILLBILLY EGGHEAD
INTELLIGENCIA VS INSMELLIGENCIA
THE RHINO • THE WRECKER • TOAD • THE VULTURE • PLANT MAN
STORY & ART BY RYAN DUNLAVEY